Creating a Portfolio Like Warren Buffett

Creating a Portfolio Like Warren Buffett

A High-Return Investment Strategy

Jeeva Ramaswamy

WILEY

John Wiley & Sons, Inc.

Published by John Wiley & Sons, Inc., Hoboken, New Jersey.

Published simultaneously in Canada.

For general information on our other products and services or for technical support, please contact our Customer Care Department within the United States at (800) 762-2974, outside the United States at (317) 572-3993, or fax (317) 572-4002.

Wiley also publishes its books in a variety of electronic formats. Some content that appears in print may not be available in electronic books. For more information about Wiley products, visit our web site at www.wiley.com.

Library of Congress Cataloging-in-Publication Data
Ramaswamy, Jeeva, 1972–
   Creating a portfolio like Warren Buffett : a high return investment strategy / Jeeva Ramaswamy.
     pages cm
  Includes index.
    ISBN 978-1-118-18252-9 (cloth); ISBN 978-1-118-22742-8 (ebk);
    ISBN 978-1-118-24036-6 (ebk); ISBN 978-1-118-26501-7 (ebk)
  1. Investments. 2. Portfolio management. 3. Buffett, Warren. I. Title.
HG4521.R276 2012
332.6–dc23

                         2011045521

Printed in the United States of America

10 9 8 7 6 5 4 3 2 1

To my mentors:
Warren Buffett and Peter Lynch

Contents

Acknowledgments

I get numerous e-mails and phone calls asking "How was the GJ investment fund able to beat the best market index with a wide margin from its inception?" and "What is the secret behind stock market success?" I wrote this book to answer those questions, and more. By simply applying well-known Warren Buffett investment techniques I have learned how to pick stocks and manage a portfolio. All of my ideas are learned from Warren Buffett's teachings.

When I became interested in investing, I was interested in learning from the masters. I started reading Warren Buffett's partnership letters and Berkshire Hathaway's annual reports to uncover investment principles. After reading most of the books written about Warren Buffett, I reverse engineered his initial investment decision and learned about investing and practiced thoroughly. That knowledge gave me great returns, and that confidence led me to start investment funds similar to his partnership. Over the last two years I have been able to beat market indexes by the largest of margins and I performed in the top 5 percent of the hedge fund and mutual fund universe. Whenever I make a buy-and-sell decision, I try to think about what Warren Buffett would do and try to use his previous investment decisions as reference points.

I have to thank, specifically, Warren Buffett and his gracious teaching mentality and willingness to spread great investment principles to the investment community through annual reports, TV appearances, interviews, and annual meetings. He has truly given other investors a lot to write about and expand upon. Apart from being a great investor, he is also a great human being in terms of philanthropy and living a simple lifestyle. That makes him my mentor and hero.

Next I would like to thank Peter Lynch and his investment books, for he elaborated thoroughly on his investment experience and his research methods, and that was very useful for me.

I would like to thank John Wiley & Sons Inc. team members Debra Englander (Editorial Director), Kimberly Bernard (Development Editor), and Tula Batanchiev (Editorial Assistant).

I would like to thank my freelance book editor, Bill M. West.

I would like to thank my mom and dad, who taught me the necessity of working hard for success.

I would like to thank my wife, Girija Jothi Arumugam, for supporting all my endeavors. I am still amazed by her financial acumen, the way she handles the home finances, and her clear thinking about planning the future. My life totally changed when I held my baby Harshini. She calls Warren Buffett a "Thatha," which means Grandpa in Tamil. She was able to pronounce Peter Lynch's name correctly and identify stock charts correctly at the age of 18 months. It makes me happy to realize that she will one day read this book and learn successful stock market investment techniques.

I

WARREN BUFFETT
INVESTMENT PRINCIPLES

Before you start investing in the stock market, you should have a clear understanding of investment principles so that you can profit from the stock market's cycles. A simple investing principle is "Buy low and sell high," but most of the investing public does the opposite.

When good news about a particular company appears in the press, the stock goes up. When that happens, people get greedy and buy at the high price thinking that stock will keep going up, and they can profit by selling at an even higher price than they already paid. After a couple of weeks or months, some bad news comes out about the particular company or a bad economic report or political event happens, and the stock starts coming down in price. When the price goes to less than the price they paid, stockholders get fearful and want to limit their loss or protect their capital and sell at a loss. Unfortunately after they sold, the stock starts to come up in price. Now they are kicking themselves, feeling that they sold too early.

So how do you behave in this market environment? How do you profit from this kind of market behavior? The answer is that you should have a clear understanding of investment principles. The following chapters explain investing principles written by Ben Graham and practiced and improved upon by Warren Buffett. Warren Buffett experienced many boom and bust cycles in his investing career. Those basic principles are guided him during those market cycles and made him one of the greatest stock market investors in the world. Let the journey begin.

Key Points

- Investors should have sound investing principles, patience, and confidence in their own research and belief in themselves.
- Stock investing is part ownership in the company. A business-like investing approach will help you to make intelligent buying and selling decisions.
- Long-term investing includes buying stock at attractive prices, which are less than the intrinsic value of the business, and holding that stock as long as the company's fundamentals are improving.
- Avoid permanent loss of capital. Never react to short-term price variations because of market gyrations. Analyze the underlying company fundamentals and make a rational decision.

CHAPTER 1

Replicating Warren Buffett's Investment Success

Warren Buffett learned investing from Ben Graham. Initially he practiced Ben Graham's teachings, then his principles evolved and he finally beat his mentor's investment successes. When Graham died, he left an estimated $3 million dollars. As I write this book, Warren Buffett's net worth is around $45 billion dollars. Graham once told California investor Charles Brandes, *"Warren has done very well."*[1]

Buffett started with Graham's *cigar-butt* approach, buying the stocks that are trading for less than net current asset value regardless of the company. He started reading Phil Fisher and was influenced by his partner Charlie Munger. He then slowly started to recognize the successes of growth companies. So, he started buying sustainable, competitive, growing companies with fair prices and holding them for the long term.

In this way Buffett learned investing from his mentor and eventually beat his mentor's investment success. We can learn from Warren Buffett and replicate his investment success. The returns from when he ran Buffett Partnership from 1956 to 1969 are shown in Figure 1.1.[2]

As you can see, Buffett generated a gross return of 31.6 percent compound annual return, which excludes the general partner allocation. He generated 25.3 percent compound annual net return after expenses and general partner allocation. After Berkshire Hathaway, apart from investing in the stock market, he started buying whole companies and leaving the existing managers to run the companies. Warren Buffett allocated the money generated by the

On a cumulative or compounded basis, the results are:

Year	Overall Results From Dow	Partnership Results	Limited Partners' Results
1957	− 8.4%	+ 10.4%	+ 8.3 %
1957–1958	+ 26.9	+ 55.6	+ 44.5
1957–1959	+ 52.3	+ 85.8	+ 74.7
1957–1960	+ 42.8	+ 110.8	+ 107.2
1957–1961	+ 74.8	+ 251.0	+ 81.6
1957–1962	+ 61.6	+ 299.8	+ 216.1
1957–1963	+ 94.9	+ 454.5	+ 311.2
1957–1964	+131.3	+ 608.7	+ 402.8
1957–1965	+164.1	+ 843.2	+ 566.5
1957–1966	+122.9	+1166.0	+ 704.2
1957–1967	+165.3	+1606.9	+ 832.5
1957–1968	+185.7	+2610.6	+1409.5
Annual Compounded Rate	+ 0.1	+ 31.6	+ 25.3

Figure 1.1   Buffett Partnership Return

companies. Berkshire Hathaway's book value increased 20.3 percent compounded annual return for 45 years from 1965 to 2009. Achieving such a great return for such a long time made Buffett the most successful investor of this twenty-first century.

Buffett has shared his investment principles in Berkshire Hathaway's annual letters, numerous interviews, and in speeches at different universities. If you have a goal to replicate Warren Buffett's investment success, you can do it by studying his investment principles and putting them to work for you. His overall investing principle is very simple, but execution of it requires patience and independent thinking. I am not advising you to go ahead and buy the stocks that Warren Buffett buys. Rather, you can learn Buffett's investment principles and buy your own stocks and manage your portfolio the same way he manages his. You will be able to replicate his investment successes and find success in the stock market.

Because I am sure you have your doubts, I am providing the following calculation as an example. Your full-time profession may not allow you to become a fund manager or you may not believe you will be able to build an empire like Berkshire Hathaway, and that is fine. I can understand that. You do not need to be a fund manager or build a wildly successful company. In the following example, you can see how you can invest your own money without outside investors, starting with a modest investment amount of $100,000.

Buffett Partnership generated a 31.6 percent compound annual return for 12 years. You can apply the same return information to your initial investment of $100,000

Final amount = $100,000 \times (1 + .316)^{12}$ = $2.69 million

Berkshire Hathaway generated 20.3 percent
for 40 years (1969 to 2009).

Final amount = $2.69 million $\times (1 + .203)^{40}$ = $4.36 billion

You may have more doubts about these calculations. You could argue that Buffett is a genius and others cannot generate an annual compound return like his. But, in fact, many of Warren Buffett's followers did just that and I will explain this later. So, plan to replicate just 50 percent of his investment successes in your lifetime, a reasonable and attainable goal.

15 percent compound annual return for first 12 years,

Final amount = $100,000 \times (1 + .15)^{12}$ = $535,025

11 percent return, like the Berkshire Hathaway book value,
increased for 40 years.

Final amount = $535,025 \times (1 + .11)^{40}$ = $34.7 million

This example covers Buffett's investing career of 52 years. Not everyone has that kind of time available. Depending on your age, you can adjust your final value depending on how many investing years you have left before your retirement. Just be confident that you, too, can make multimillions of dollars from the stock market, if you invest like Warren Buffett.

You do not need to be a genius to replicate, or at least partially replicate, Warren Buffett's investment success. You do not need a Master's degree in Business Administration (MBA) or even to run your own business. You should, at least, have interest in learning Warren Buffett's investing principles and how to implement those principles. Those factors are explained in this book. Believe in yourself, you can do it.

Before reading books about Warren Buffett, I did not know the basics of stock investing. All of my investment knowledge has come from reading books written about Warren Buffett, Berkshire Hathaway's annual letters, numerous interviews with Buffett, and the reverse engineering of his investments over many years. Each time as Warren Buffett buys new stock, I try to find out why he bought that company's stock at that specific time. Basically, I try to understand his investment reasoning.

After successfully implementing his investing principles into actual trades with my own money, I was very confident that I could handle other people's money and do the same. I did follow Buffett's footsteps and started my own investment partnership fund, GJ Investment Funds, with the same rules that he used when he started his partnership. Nowadays, we call these partnerships *hedge funds* and only accredited investors are allowed into the funds. Normally, hedge funds charge 1-to-2 percent of the management fees and 20 percent of the profit. Even if the hedge fund is down a certain year, it still charges 1 to 2 percent of the management fees on assets under management. Buffett did not use that method; he didn't charge a management fee at all. As general partner, he took 25 percent of the profit above a 6 percent hurdle rate with a high water mark. He believed he did not deserve to get paid if he did not make money for his limited partners above 6 percent. I felt the same way and used those same fund rules. When I started the fund in November 2008 using the Buffett principles, I was very successful. I beat Buffett Partnership returns with a wide margin and got to the top 5 percent of all mutual and hedge fund managers. I am very confident that Warren Buffett's investment principles will continue to guide me to deliver great returns in the future, too. I have found, and so have many others, that it is possible to replicate Warren Buffett's investment success.

For example, Edward Lampart of ESL Investments also used Warren Buffett's investment principles to build his empire. He acquired Kmart from bankruptcy, acquired Sears, and then merged both firms to form Sears Holdings Corporation. He became chairman of the firm. Sears occupies more than 40 percent of his $9 billion dollar hedge fund. The other two biggest positions belong to AutoZone and AutoNation. His employees sit on both companies' boards. These top three positions occupy more than 90 percent of the portfolio. Lampart learned investing by reverse engineering

Warren Buffett's investments. He managed to deliver more than 29 percent compound annual return using Buffett's investing principles. Another example is Appaloosa Management's David Tepper. Using distressed securities and debt, he was able to deliver more than a 28 percent compound annual return. Another example is Ian Cumming. He runs Leucadia National very similarly to the way Buffett runs Berkshire Hathaway. Leucadia stock compounded 33 percent from 1978 to 2004.

The examples are endless. I can keep going with the list, but I believe you get the point. If you are able to implement Warren Buffett's investing principles and execute them properly, you can deliver excellent returns for your investment portfolio. As an individual investor, you are in a more advantageous position than Warren Buffett. Here's why:

1. He manages a $50 billion investment portfolio and he can select only large-cap stocks. He cannot invest in small and mid-cap companies because those investments will not make much difference to his portfolio.
2. You can buy and sell your portfolio holdings faster without affecting the price of the stock; Buffett cannot do that. For example, he owns around 10 percent of Coca-Coca. If he feels that Coca-Cola's stock price becomes overvalued at the current market price and decides to sell at that price, he will not be able to sell all of his holdings at that price. It is not likely there will be a buyer for such a large amount of stock. He needs to sell slowly, without affecting the price of the stock. If he tries to sell all his holdings in a couple of days, his selling alone will knock down the price of Coca-Cola stock.

In this book, I will explain how to implement Warren Buffett's investing principles step-by-step, using actual investment examples. All you need is confidence, and to believe that you can replicate Warren Buffett's investment success. Believe in yourself. You can do it.

Business-Like Investing

If you buy a stock in a business believing that you are a part owner of that company, you behave differently from the stock market crowd. The vast majority of stock market investors believe that the stock exchange is like a big casino and stocks are entry tickets to play the game.

The buying and selling decisions of many investors are totally price myopic and have nothing to do with company fundamentals. They try to predict what the price of the stock will do in a short time and try to profit from that price swing. They think they are investors, but in reality they are traders. They try to predict what the market will do during the short term and buy or sell their holdings depending on those market predictions. Predicting the market is impossible. History proves that "predicting" the stock market simply does not pay off. Still, traders spend tremendous amounts of time and energy trying to do just that.

During the year's end, you can see market gurus and hedge fund managers try to predict the market for the next year. You can go and look back at their predictions for previous years and find out what really happened, and you will find 90 percent of those predictions were wrong. The other 10 percent may be right, but that is because of pure luck, nothing else.

Whenever those market pundits are very bullish on the market, the market actually tanks. Whenever they are worried about the world coming to an end, the opposite happens. For example, just go to the market predictions made by many Wall Street market pundits during the end of 2008, after the financial crisis. You will find they predicted that 2009 would be a horrible year, the sky was going to fall, and everyone should get out of the market. What actually happened? The stock market started to rally starting in March of 2009.

You cannot invest based on those predictions. Millions of market participants are taking action depending on their own perception of the market and what it will do. No one can predict what those millions of individuals think.

Do you want to bet your hard-earned money trying to predict what others will do? In order to avoid this irresponsible behavior, you need to understand a company thoroughly before investing in it. If you want to become a better investor, you need to remove the trader mentality and think like a business owner. Thinking like a business owner before you buy into any business will have you eager to find out everything about the business. You'll research past revenue, profit margin, debt level, competitive forces, sustainability of the business model, market share, management performance, company capability, and so on.

Before investing in a business, find out how that business performed in the last recession. Understand the history of the business and how it performed over the last 10 years. What is its earning growth? What is its owner growth? Gathering as much information about the company before making any decisions is referred to as *fundamental investing*. Once you know all the facts about the company, you can reasonably assume the future cash generation of the company. You can also attempt to calculate the value of the company, which is called *intrinsic value,* a calculation that will be explained in a later chapter. If you buy the stock at less than the calculated intrinsic value of the company and hold that stock for the long term, you can do reasonably well in stocks.

If you are a business owner, you do not sell your business as soon as you can get 10 to 20 percent more money for your business. Instead, you prefer to continue running your business and increasing its economic value over the long term so that you can earn maximum profit from your business. You need to have the same kind of mentality when you invest, even if you are merely purchasing 100 shares of a company.

Below is an example from Warren Buffett's investing career. Buffett started investing Berkshire Hathaway's money in GEICO in 1976.[1] Within five years, he had invested approximately $45.7 million. Due to company share buy-back programs, his stake increased to 51 percent of the company without purchasing any additional shares. In 1996, Berkshire Hathaway paid $2.3 billion to acquire the remaining 49 percent of the company. That means 51 percent of the company's worth was $2.39 billion dollars. For calculation purpose, we assume that he invested $45.7 million in 1976. That means in 20 years, his $45.7 million, increased to $2.39 billion, which is 52.36 times the size of his initial investment.

We can calculate the compound annual return of his investment:

$$I = ((2,393/45.7)^{1/20} - 1) \times 100$$

Compound annual return = 21.88% per year

If he had sold his GEICO shares for a 50 or 100 percent gain, the investment might not have grown to 52.36 percent total return. How was it possible? The answer is because he had the mentality of a business owner, not one of a trader.

GEICO stock might have gone up or down in those 20 years. If he had acted like a trader, he might have sold for a quick gain and moved on to other securities. He might have invested that money in other stocks, which might have lost money. As a business owner, he believed that GEICO had a lot of earning potential. He did not want to leave that great potential reward for short-term profit gain. Because of the business-like approach with a long-term time horizon, Buffett was greatly rewarded.

We can also use Berkshire Hathaway as an example. Buffett took over the company in 1965 with a business-owner mentality. Initially he thought of turning around the textile operation, but found that came with a large number of obstacles. He used the cash flow from Berkshire to buy insurance companies and then used the insurance companies' premiums to buy other businesses. When he liquidated Buffett Partnership, he paid cash or Berkshire Hathaway shares to the limited partners, depending on their preferences. Most of the limited partners stayed with him, and for good reason. The Berkshire Hathaway book value increased 434,057 percent from 1964 to 2009. The stocks traded almost identically to the book value, a 20.3 percent compounded annual return.

If you invested $10,000 in Berkshire Hathaway in 1965 and kept that stock until the end of 2009, that money would be worth $43.4 million. If, however, you acted like a trader and sold your position as soon as it doubled, you would have lost a great fortune. The limited partners who stayed in Berkshire Hathaway became multi-millionaires. I was fortunate to meet a couple of them at one of Berkshire Hathaway's annual meetings.

The business-owner type approach to investing made all of those limited partners a great deal of money. Warren Buffett did not sell any of his shares during those 44 years, because as a business owner he knew the potential of his company and what kind of potential reward he could get in the future.

During Buffett's investing career, there have been many down times, including recessions, real estate bubbles, the 2001 technology bubble, the 1987 crash, and many more. Still, he persisted and generated a 21 percent compound annual return for Berkshire Hathaway shareholders. He did so by owning businesses and buying shares in wonderful companies. Berkshire Hathaway shares have lost more than 50 percent six times over the years since Buffett took over. This did not bother Buffett. He managed to continue thinking like a business owner. He always knew that Berkshire Hathaway's operating companies would earn great amounts of money in the future.

During the recent 2008 recession, revenues of Berkshire's operating companies decreased more than 30 to 50 percent. Berkshire Hathaway shares decreased from around $146,000 per share for Class-A shares in February 2008 to as low as $70,050 per share in March 2009, marking a 52 percent drop. Buffett's net worth decreased 52 percent. The stock price may have bothered him, but he did not panic and sell Berkshire Hathaway shares at the bottom. As a business owner, he knew the economy would begin to recover and his operating companies would increase revenues and earnings. That is just what happened. The Berkshire Hathaway operating companies' revenue started to increase around 30 percent to 50 percent from the low point in two years. Berkshire Hathaway stock also recovered and was trading at around $120,000 in December 2010.

As an investor, if you hold 10 to 20 diverse businesses, you will do fine in the long term. When you have a business-owner mindset, market price swings will not bother you. But that is not human nature. Whenever we see the price of our stocks drop, it is in our wiring to react and sell the stock before it goes down further. As an investor, you need to think like a business owner and restrict that human urge to react. Thinking like a business owner will cause you to behave differently. When you do not see fundamental deterioration in a company, daily price swings should not bother you. When the bargain opportunity exists, you can buy more shares at bargain prices, because the traders of the world will certainly react by abandoning ship and selling.

To provide a recent example, in May 2010 the news of the debt crisis in Greece spread quickly in the financial media, causing the market to free fall. The Dow dropped from 11,151 to 10,380 in five trading days.

On May 6, 2010, the Dow dropped about 1000 points as the result of a technical glitch and closed the trading day around negative 350 points. All the pundits on television were talking as though the world was going to come to an end. They urged us to sell holdings and short securities to earn money from the downturn. If anyone believed in such market prediction and acted, they likely would have lost money on the following Monday. During the following weekend, the European Union announced a $1 trillion bailout and the Dow soared 404 points on May 10, 2010.

If you had a business-owner mindset, you might have raised the following questions:

1. In your portfolio, what percentage of revenue is coming from Greece?
2. Was the company going to generate 7 percent less revenue because of this problem in Greece?

If your company did not do any business in Greece, the revenue and earnings capability of the businesses did not change. Therefore, you should have ignored the market price of your company shares. If your portfolio had no companies with exposure in Greece, you should have left your portfolio alone. Even if your companies had exposure to Greece and earned around 2 to 5 percent revenue and earnings from there, you only needed to adjust your earnings projection and calculate the reduced intrinsic value of the company. If the price of the stock was trading below the intrinsic value, you could have left it as it was. When the market is falling, do not panic and sell your position. If you know the true worth of the business, you can ignore the market prices and take advantage of the opportunity to buy more shares.

Whenever businesses try to institute new initiatives to improve, those changes take multiple quarters or years to reflect the bottom line. Those initiatives might be reducing costs, introducing new products or services, penetrating a new market, spinning off divisions, or acquiring other businesses to grow revenue. Therefore, upon getting word of such initiatives, you cannot buy stock today and expect those changes to happen quickly and increase stock price. Instead, you need to be patient until those initiatives deliver the expected results.

If one of your existing holdings gets into trouble or a temporary downturn, you should not sell that position. If you feel that the problem is temporary, the current management can fix the problem or the business is in the process of fixing the problem, you should hold that stock. Doing so gives you a better return after the business fixes the problem. Below is an example from my investment in Horsehead Holdings Corp., symbol ZINC.

Horsehead Holding Corp. engages in the production and sale of zinc and zinc-based products in North America. The company products include Prime Western (PW) zinc metal, zinc oxide, and special high-grade (SHG) zinc metal. In addition, the company recycles electric arc furnace dust, a hazardous waste product generated by steel mini-mills. An accident happened in one of the company's production plants in Pennsylvania on July 23, 2010. The following is the announcement from the company regarding the accident.[2]

Horsehead Holding Corp. Reports Explosion and Two Fatalities at its Monaca, PA Plant, July 23, 2010

Pittsburgh, PA, July 23, 2010—Horsehead Holding Corp. (Nasdaq: ZINC) reported today that on July 22, 2010 an explosion occurred at its Horsehead Corporation Monaca, PA facility. The explosion, which occurred around 4:30 p.m., resulted in two fatalities and injuries to at least two employees in the plant's refining facility. The Company is honoring the request of the families to not release the names of the deceased and injured employees. Both injured employees were treated and released from local hospitals yesterday evening. The Company's President and CEO, Jim Hensler, said, "We are deeply saddened by the loss of our co-workers and most concerned about our employees and their families; our initial efforts are directed to helping them. The exact cause of the explosion is unknown and is currently under investigation."

The Monaca plant produces zinc metal at its smelting operations and refined zinc metal and zinc oxide at its refining operation. The zinc refinery has been temporarily shut down pending an accident investigation. The Company is assessing the damage and the time it will take to complete repairs. The smelter will continue to produce zinc metal during this period. The Company has notified its insurers and will be actively working with customers to minimize supply disruptions.

After the announcement, on that particular day, the stock lost 9.51 percent and closed the day down 4.5 percent from the previous day's closing. The announcement said the plant was going to shut down temporarily for accident investigation. As soon as negative news was published, the stock lost 9.51 percent and was trading at $7.32 per share. Below is an announcement that was published five days later regarding an update of the incident.

Horsehead Holding Corp. Provides Update on Operations at its Monaca, PA Plant, July 28, 2010

Pittsburgh, PA, July 28, 2010—Horsehead Holding Corp. (Nasdaq: ZINC) today provided an update on the incident that occurred at its Monaca, PA facility on July 22, 2010, which resulted in two fatalities in the plant's zinc oxide refining facility. The zinc refinery remains on temporary shutdown pending completion of an investigation and assessment of the damage. Teams from the U.S. Occupational, Safety and Health Administration (OSHA) and the U.S. Chemical Safety & Hazard Investigation Board (CSB) are investigating the cause and the circumstances that may have contributed to the occurrence of this incident. Horsehead is strongly committed to the safety of its employees, contractors and visitors and is cooperating fully with these investigations. In addition, the Company's insurance underwriters and the Company are conducting their own investigations into the cause and the circumstances that contributed to this incident. The United Steel Workers union is also participating in the investigations.

A preliminary assessment of the damage indicates that each of the 10 columns used to produce zinc oxide and refined zinc metal in the refining facility will need to be rebuilt before production can be safely restarted using these columns. It was further determined that the rebuilding process will be delayed pending results from the accident investigation to assure that all safety measures are considered before production begins. The investigations may take several weeks to complete. It is anticipated that it could take several months for production capabilities in the refining facility to be fully restored. In the meantime, until the full extent and timing of repairs is known, the Company has decided that all employees at the Monaca facility will remain on the payroll and continue to receive benefits.

The Company's President and CEO, Jim Hensler, said, "We are committed to safety and restoration of our operating capabilities and are working hard to provide support to our customers."

While the smelting facility and other operations at the Monaca plant remain active, they are operating at a reduced rate. The smelting facility is currently

(*Continued*)

operating five of its six furnaces producing zinc metal. The operating level of the smelter will be adjusted based on market conditions and as operations at the zinc refining facility are restarted. The full financial impact of this incident is not known at this time. The Company expects that the cost of repairs and the loss of revenue from its zinc oxide sales during the rebuilding period, which historically have represented 40% of the Company's revenues, will be partially offset by increased metal sales and will be subject to recovery under the Company's business interruption and property insurance.

"Our thoughts and prayers continue to go out to the family and friends of Jim Taylor and Corey Keller who were fatally injured in this incident," said Horsehead President and CEO Hensler. "We support the initiative taken by the United Steelworkers in establishing a memorial fund on their behalf. We encourage anyone wishing to make a donation to send a check made payable to the "Keller & Taylor Memorial Fund" and mail it to USW Local 8183, 1445 Market St., Beaver, PA 15009," Hensler added.

The announcement clearly states that five of six furnaces would be operating during the inspection period, and that increased metal sales, along with company insurance, partially offset the revenue loss. Even after the announcement, the stock did not increase much. On July 28, 2010 the stock closed at $7.78 per share. This temporarily fixed the problem and appeared to be a good buying opportunity.

On August 1, 2010 the company announced that it had found the root cause of the accident and was working on fixing the issues. Horsehead announces it would restart the facility on December 21, 2010. The announcement follows.

Looking at Figure 2.1, consider that if you bought the stock after the announcement on July 28, 2010 that confirmed the problem would be fixed in three to six months, you likely could have bought stock at around $7.78 per share. The restarting facility announcement came on December 21, 2010 when the stock was trading at $13.04 per share. This five-month holding period experienced a 67.60 percent return. Thinking like an owner instead of a trader would have given you patience and led you to experience the return. On the contrary, if you panicked and sold your shares when the company announced the bad news, you likely would have lost the upside.

The main focus of mutual fund and hedge fund managers is to generate maximum returns. Those funds report their performances

Horsehead Corporation Announces Return of Zinc Smelter to Full Production, December 21, 2010

Pittsburgh, PA—Zinc producer Horsehead Corporation, a wholly owned subsidiary of Horsehead Holding Corp (Nasdaq: ZINC), today announced that it has re-started a sixth zinc smelting furnace at its facility in Monaca, PA, returning the smelter to full production. The Company has re-started operations at the refinery, with the ability to produce the full compliment of zinc oxide products, and expects to return to pre-incident zinc oxide production capability at its refinery in early January 2011.

Horsehead previously reduced its operations from six furnaces to five in response to the incident on July 22, 2010 at its zinc refinery that resulted in a shutdown of its zinc oxide production process. Since that time, the Company has made significant changes to improve safety and efficiency.

"Our progress in re-building the refinery remains on schedule," said Jim Hensler, Horsehead's President & CEO. "Horsehead is increasing metal production to supply refinery columns that have started into production. Also, we have expanded our customer base since the incident and expect, given current market conditions, to remain at a six furnace operation level for the foreseeable future," Hensler added.

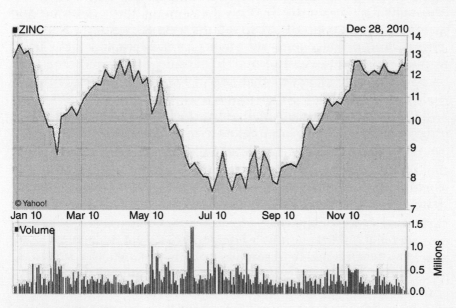

Figure 2.1   ZINC chart

to their investors every month or every quarter. If they do not deliver good numbers, the clients are likely to pull out their money. Because of that pressure, their intention is to generate maximum possible returns before their reporting period. Managers constantly buy and sell large numbers of securities to generate maximum possible return during the short term. Even if they have found the perfect company to buy they are forced to sell too soon and leave the huge upside on the table. Thankfully, those kinds of performance pressures are not there for you. That is another added advantage for you as a regular investor. Your main focus is to generate maximum possible returns from your investments.

I am very confident that when you behave like a business owner, you are able to beat 90 percent of professional mutual and hedge fund managers. Discussing how he behaves like a business owner, Warren Buffett once remarked, "I never attempt to make money on the stock market. I buy on the assumption that they could close the market the next day and not reopen it for five years."[3] Buffett totally ignores the market during the short term. Whenever stocks drop as soon as he buys them, he does not worry or panic; those are just quotation losses. Buffett prefers to monitor his investment successes the same way a company's Chief Executive Officer monitors the company's progress. He looks at the revenue growth, earnings growth, return on equity, return on invested capital, debt level, capital expenditure, and so on. He considers how much the business' net worth increased that year. CEOs do not measure their successes by the stock price increase.

If a business fundamentally improves, the stock price should follow during the long term. Short-term price swings depend more on market news than on fundamental company changes.

Business-like investing will help you make a correct decision in selling also. In *Wit and Wisdom from the World's Greatest Investor*, author Janet Lowe writes:

> Mr. Market was a character invented by Graham to illuminate his student's minds regarding market behavior. The stock market should be viewed as an emotionally disturbed business partner, Graham said. This partner, Mr. Market, shows up each day offering a price at which he will buy your share of the businesses or sell you his share. No matter how wild his offer is or how often you reject it, Mr. Market returns with a new offer the

next day and each day thereafter. Buffett says the moral of the story is this: Mr. Market is your servant, not your guide.[4]

Selecting great stock is one part of the process. If you are right, be patient. You will be rewarded handsomely. Lowe explained this when she wrote:

> One reason for buying excellent companies (in addition to strong growth) is that once the purchase is made, the investor has only to sit back and trust the company's managers to do their jobs. In 1973, Buffett already -size chunk of Berkshire, plus a bank in Illinois, an Omaha weekly newspaper, interest in half a dozen insurance companies, a trading stamp company, and a chain of women's clothing stores and a candy company.[5]

Regarding the ease that results from making wise initial decisions, Sam Thorson, writer for the *Nebraska Journal and Star* once recorded Buffet as saying, "I can almost do it with my hands in my pockets. I really live a pretty easy life."[6]

If you are a business owner and your business doubles, you do not immediately sell the business. You know the true worth of the company and you ride it as much as possible. But Wall Street crowds think the other way. Of course, taking profits never hurts, but missing out on future rewards does. Traders sell their positions as soon as they double their money. Then, they use that money to buy a possible loser.

The business-like investing approach will help you to make intelligent buying and selling decisions. When you are planning to sell stock, do the research and find out the current intrinsic value of the business. Ask yourself what the price of the stock is compared to the intrinsic value of the business. If the price of the stock is less than its current intrinsic value, that is good. Also consider the growth prospects of the company. If the company is still growing, that is great news. Even if you are up 100 percent or 200 percent, do not sell it, because you are going to earn maybe 1,000 percent from that investment. Think like a business owner and behave like one. After all, the greatest investor in the world does:

> Most of our large stock positions are going to be held for many years, and the scorecard on our investment decisions will be

provided by business results over that period and not by prices on any given day. Just as it would be foolish to focus unduly on short-term prospects when acquiring an entire company, we think it's equally unsound to become mesmerized by the prospective near-term earnings when purchasing small pieces of a company, i.e., marketable common stocks.[7]

CHAPTER

3

Long-Term Investing

Long-term investing, also known as *buy and hold,* does not mean buy a company's stock and then forget about the company for 10 to 20 years. You need to buy a growth company and consistently follow its revenue and earnings growth every quarter and every year. As long as the company is growing at a decent rate, keep holding the stocks for long-term gain instead of selling the stock to protect short-term gain. In long-term investing, investors should ignore the stock price variation, which is happening every day depending on the market events. As an investor, you need to judge the investment by its economic progress as a business. Many investors believe that if the stock price increases as soon as they buy it, then they picked a winner and they feel happy. On the other hand, if the stock price goes down, they think that they picked a loser and they feel awful.

When you buy in, you should allow sufficient time to judge whether or not your investment is successful. During the short term, the price variation of the stock is irrelevant to the underlying company's fundamentals. But, during the long term, a company's fundamental changes should reflect the stock price. You need to monitor your investment by following the underlying company's fundamentals.

Here is Warren Buffett's reasoning for his *Washington Post* purchase:

> It's a lot of different going out to Kalamazoo and telling whoever owns the television station out there that because the Dow is down 20 points that day he ought to sell the station to you a lot

cheaper. You get into the real world when you deal with a business. But in stocks everyone is thinking about the relative price. When we bought 8 percent or 9 percent of the *Washington Post* in one month, not one person who was selling to us was thinking that he was selling us $400 million worth for $80 million. They were selling to us because communication stocks were going down, or other people were selling, or whatever reason. They had nonsensical reasons.[1]

In February 1973, Buffett started buying the *Washington Post* at the price of $27 per share. The price of the stock kept going down to as low as $20.75 per share. But, he kept on buying the stock. By October 1973, Berkshire was the largest outside investor in the *Washington Post*. Buffett invested around $10 million in the paper. He still holds that stock and, as of his 2009 annual report, the investment is worth around $357 million. If he felt that he lost money and sold his stock as soon as it dropped 23 percent, he might have had a loss in his investment. Instead, he held it for the long term and generated an excellent result. That is the beauty of long-term investing. That kind of mentality makes Buffett significantly different from the rest of the market.

History shows that long-term investing is a very profitable strategy when compared with short-term investing. Nowadays, there are a lot of articles written about long-term investing stating that buy-and-hold strategies are dead in today's dynamic markets. Market gurus who appear in the media claim that Buffett's kind of investing is an old way of investing and it is not appropriate for today's market.

Today's market is filled with high-frequency trading, day trading, and exchange-traded fund (ETF) investing. Big institutions are using algorithmic trading software to make the buy-and-sell decision rather than depending on emotional humans. Their mantra in these companies is: "To make money in the stock market you have to buy and sell frequently, otherwise you will get killed." But that is not the case in today's market. Long-term investing still yields the best return compared to short-term investing.

Now we look at the recent long-term investing performance of stocks, which we will assume were bought on January 1, 2001, and kept until December 31, 2010, making for a 10-year holding period. We will consider this as a long-term investment. We will look at a couple of the best-performing companies during the last decade.

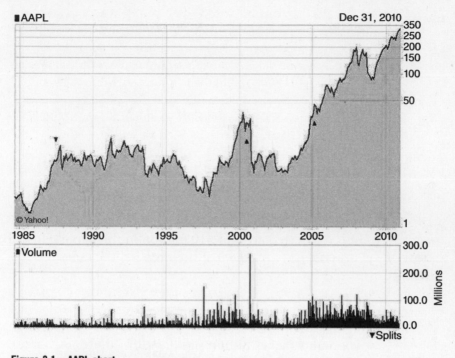

Figure 3.1   AAPL chart

Reproduced with permission of Yahoo! Inc. ©2011 Yahoo! Inc. YAHOO! and the YAHOO! logo are registered trademarks of Yahoo! Inc. Reproduced with permission of CSI ©2009. Data Source: CSI www.csidata.com/

One such company is Apple Computer (AAPL). Everyone knows about this company, and today there are millions of people using its products. Figure 3.1 shows the price chart of AAPL for last 10 years.

AAPL's closing price on January 2, 2001 was $10.81 per share, adjusted for splits. On December 31, 2010, AAPL's closing price was $322.56 per share. The total return was 2,983 percent in 10 years, which is a 40.43 percent compounded annual return. If you had invested $10,000 in Apple stock 10 years ago, that would be worth around $298,300 by year-end 2010. Millions of investors might have bought and sold Apple shares during last 10 years and made profits or lost on their trades. How many people might have gotten 29 times their invested money from the Apple stock? The answer is probably less than 1 percent of the investors. So, why did the other 99 percent of the investors not get that kind of return? The answer is because of their short-term focus. As soon as they doubled or tripled their

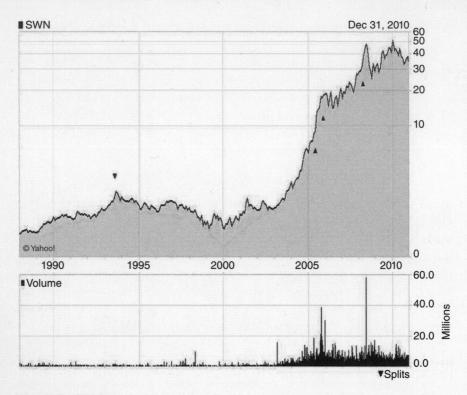

Figure 3.2   SWN Chart

Reproduced with permission of Yahoo! Inc. ©2011 Yahoo! Inc. YAHOO! and the YAHOO! logo are registered trademarks of Yahoo! Inc. Reproduced with permission of CSI ©2009. Data Source: CSI www.csidata.com/

money, they likely sold their shares and left the huge upside on the table.

Now we look at the next example, the energy company Southwestern Energy (SWN). See Figure 3.2.

On January 2, 2001, the SWN closing price was $1.13 per share, adjusted for splits. On December 31, 2010, the closing price was $37.43 per share. The total return was 3312 percent in 10 years, which is a 41.91 percent compounded annual return. If you had invested $10,000 in Southwestern Energy 10 years ago, it would be worth around $331,238 as of the end of 2010. So, the conclusion is long-term investing can most certainly work in this dynamic fast-paced market also. It will work in the future too.

Let's look at another example from Buffett's investing career,

> We owned 5 percent of the Walt Disney Company in 1966. The whole company was selling for $80 million in 1966, debt free. $4 million bought us 5 percent of the company. They spent $17 million on the Pirates of the Caribbean ride in 1966. Here was a company selling at less than five times the ride and they had a lot of rides. I mean that is cheap.[2]

In 1966, Buffett invested in Walt Disney (DIS), his initial investment price was around 31cents per share on a split-adjusted basis. He then sold at around 48 cents for a quick gain. Berkshire Hathaway had a stake in Cap Cities/ABC. After 30 years, Cap Cities/ABC merged with Walt Disney. At that time, Berkshire received $65 per share worth of Walt Disney stock. If he had kept his shares in Walt Disney without selling for a quick gain, he might have generated 209 times his initial investment in 30 years. That is 19.5 percent compounded annual return for 30 years.

On the other side of the rosy pictures I painted previously, if you invested $10,000 in GM or Fannie Mae or Freddie Mac or Lehman Brothers, you might have lost all of your money during 2008 financial crisis. As an investor, you need to differentiate the successful companies from the bad ones. Before buying any company's stock, you have to do thorough research on that company as per the "stock research checklist" which I will explain in from Chapters 5 to 21. After the purchase, you need to monitor how the business is doing each and every year. Consider what the management is doing to improve the bottom line. What are the management's plans for the future expansion? How is the management executing the growth plan? As long as you are satisfied with the company's progress, you can hold the stock. That's why Buffett has a list of stocks as "core holdings," which will be in his portfolio for a long, long time. Of these stocks, Buffett once said, "Charlie (Munger) and I expect to hold our stock for a very long time. In fact, you may see us up here when (we are so old that) neither of us knows who the other guy is."[3]

Apart from the excellent returns explained above, here is a selection of the additional advantages of long-term investing. You can:

1. Reduce the capital gains taxes.
2. Reduce the broker commission.

3. Reduce the expenses for an accountant.
4. Reducing the probability of picking losers.

Capital Gains Taxes

If you sell the stocks before one year, capital gains are taxed at a personal level and may be around 30 percent. If you sell the stock after one year, those capital gains are taxed at 15 percent. If you have capital gains, but do not sell the stock, you do not have to pay anything until you sell the stock. For example, consider two investors, A and B. Both start with a $100,000 initial investment amount. Both are generating 20 percent return every year. But, they invest with different methodologies.

Investor A is a short-term investor. He tries to sell everything as soon as his holdings cross the one-year holding period. Realizing the capital gains, he takes out the money for that year's capital gains taxes and invests the remaining money next year. He generates 20 percent every year. Here are his numbers:

Year	Initial Amount	Return (20%)	Before Tax	Capital Gains Tax (15%)	Final Amount
1	$100,000.00	$20,000.00	$120,000.00	$18,000.00	$102,000.00
2	$102,000.00	$20,400.00	$122,400.00	$18,360.00	$104,040.00
3	$104,040.00	$20,808.00	$124,848.00	$18,727.20	$106,120.80
4	$106,120.80	$21,224.16	$127,344.96	$19,101.74	$108,243.22
5	$108,243.22	$21,648.64	$129,891.86	$19,483.78	$110,408.08
6	$110,408.08	$22,081.62	$132,489.70	$19,873.45	$112,616.24
7	$112,616.24	$22,523.25	$135,139.49	$20,270.92	$114,868.57
8	$114,868.57	$22,973.71	$137,842.28	$20,676.34	$117,165.94
9	$117,165.94	$23,433.19	$140,599.13	$21,089.87	$119,509.26
10	$119,509.26	$23,901.85	$143,411.11	$21,511.67	$121,899.44

Total tax paid was $197,094.98 over 10 year period. The final net amount after 10 years was $121,899.44. The amount profited from 10 years of investing was $121,899.44 − $100,000 = $21,899.44. The net return generated after 10 years of investing was 21.89 percent.

Investor B is a long-term investor. He invested in year one and did not sell any stock for 10 years. His holdings also increased 20 percent annually. He sold the stock and paid the capital gain taxes at the end of the tenth year. Here are his numbers:

Year	Initial Amount	Return (20%)	Final Amount
1	$100,000.00	$20,000.00	$120,000.00
2	$120,000.00	$24,000.00	$144,000.00
3	$144,000.00	$28,800.00	$172,800.00
4	$172,800.00	$34,560.00	$207,360.00
5	$207,360.00	$41,472.00	$248,832.00
6	$248,832.00	$49,766.40	$298,598.40
7	$298,598.40	$59,719.68	$358,318.08
8	$358,318.08	$71,663.62	$429,981.70
9	$429,981.70	$85,996.34	$515,978.04
10	$515,978.04	$103,195.61	$619,173.64

Capital gains tax after the tenth year (15 percent) was $619,173.64 × 0.15 = $92,876.05. The amount profited from 10 years of investing was $526,297.60. The total net return generated after 10 years of investing was 526 percent.

Look at the difference of long-term investing compared with short-term investing, a whopping 504.11 percent! That is one of the many benefits of long-term investing.

Broker Commission

Broker commission is another expense that will eat away at your long-term return. If you use a full-broker service, you will end up paying more commission; discount brokers charge you less for the trade. For example, TD Ameritrade charges $9.99 per trade (of up to 100,000 shares). In a short-term investor scenario, imagine you have $100,000 dollars in your account holding around 20 stocks and with a turnover rate of 100 percent, which means 40 buys and 40 sells. If you trade your full position at one time, that is 80 transactions.

Normally you should not buy and sell your full positions at one time because market prices change all the time. You need to buy or sell incrementally to get better pricing. For our consideration, say you are trading 50 percent of the positions each time, which means 160 transactions per year. That means total expenses would be $1,598/year, 1.59 percent of the initial investment size of your $100,000 portfolio. Multiply this expense over 10 years and you are paying a total of $15,980.

Now consider the long-term investor scenario, 40 transactions for buying and 40 transactions for selling. Total commission is $799.

With long-term investing, you would save around $15,180 dollars in a 10-year period.

The above-mentioned calculation is for 10 years, but think about the expenses for 20 to 40 years of investing duration. In the above calculation, we assumed just 100 percent turnover ratio every year. But in reality, think about the day trader who makes 20 to 30 transactions each day. On an even bigger scale, think about mutual funds' and hedge funds' commission dollars. Those funds make thousands of transactions every year. They are charged about one to three cents per share from bigger brokerage houses like Goldman Sachs. The commission rates for international exchanges are even higher. When you practice long-term investing you can save a lot of money in commission dollars.

Accountant Expenses

When you are filing taxes, each and every transaction needs to be reconciled to calculate the profit and loss of each trade. Think about the day-trader transactions. The accountant needs to spend a lot of time to calculate the profit and loss. They need to consider wash-sale provisions also. Most accountants charge by the hour. If you have more transactions, you have to spend a lot more money for accounting. When you are a long-term investor, you can save on that cost too.

Picking Losers

When you are doing short-term trading, as soon as you get the profit in one of your trades, you like to redeploy that profit to another stock. If you pick the wrong stock at that time, you are probably going to lose the previously gained profit. Even then, you are liable for capital gains tax on the previous profit unless you take a loss on the recent trade. When you are doing too many transactions with too many stocks, your level of research in each one of the companies will be less.

As Warren Buffett puts it,

> I made a study back when I ran an investment partnership
> of all our larger investments versus the smaller investments.
> The larger investments always did better than the smaller

investments. There is a threshold of examination and criticism and knowledge that has to be overcome or reached in making a big decision that you can be sloppy about on small decisions. Somebody says, "I bought a hundred shares of this or that because I heard about it at a party the other night." Well there is that tendency with small decisions to think you can do it for not very good reasons.[4]

To recap: Long-term investing includes buying stock at attractive prices, which are less than the intrinsic value of the business, and holding that stock as long as the company's fundamentals are improving. As Buffett puts it:

Stocks are simple. All you do is buy shares in a great business for less than the business is intrinsically worth, with managers of the highest integrity and ability. Then you own those shares forever.[5]

Permanent Loss of Capital

Warren Buffett's first rules of investing are:
"Rule 1: Never lose money
Rule 2: Never forget Rule No: 1"[1]

An investor's main task is to avoid permanent capital loss. For example, if you have a $100,000 portfolio and $50,000 in permanent capital loss, this means you lost 50 percent of your capital. To make it even, you have to earn $50,000 in investment gain from the available $50,000 capital. That means you need to generate a 100 percent return, which is double the percentage points of what you lost. If you calculate the compound return for a long time into the future, the numbers will be staggering.

In the following scenarios, consider you are generating a 15 percent compound return for the next 20 years.

Scenario 1

You did not lose any capital in the first year. You generate a 15 percent compound annual return for the next 20 years. By the end of the twentieth year, your money would be worth as shown here (you have to use a formula like the one here to calculate the future value).

$$\text{Final amount will be } FV = PV\,(1+I)^N$$

where PV = present value
       I = rate of return
      N = time period
    FV = future value

$$FV = \$100{,}000 \times (1.15)^{20} = \$1.63 \text{ million}$$

Scenario 2

In this scenario, you lost $50,000 in your first year of investing. That means you have only $50,000 capital available when you start to invest next year. You generate a 15 percent compound annual return for the next 19 years. Since you lost the first year, you need to use the remaining 19 years.

$$\text{Final amount will be } FV = PV\,(1+I)^N$$

where   PV = present value
   I = rate of return
   N = time period
   FV = future value

$$FV = \$50{,}000 \times (1.15)^{19} = \$0.711 \text{ million}$$

Because of your first year's $50,000 loss, you might have lost the chance to earn $0.91 million future dollars over the next 20 years. The reason for this kind of calculation is to force you to think about why avoiding permanent capital loss is very important. When you are thinking about a $50,000 loss, you may tend to act a bit casual when you are making investment decision and incurring the permanent capital loss. When you look at the compounded dollar numbers, you may act more seriously when dealing with such losses because of the high numbers.

Here I referred to *permanent capital loss* instead of simply *loss*. There is a reason for that. For example, consider the following scenario. You did thorough fundamental research on a company and you calculated the intrinsic value of the company at around $60 per share (intrinsic value calculation will be explained in Chapter 23. You are buying the shares at around $45 per share, which is around a 25 percent discount to intrinsic value.

Due to market variation or because some brokerage firm downgraded the stock, the shares went below the buy price, down to $35 per share. As per the quotation, your portfolio is at a 22 percent loss. You again check the company fundamentals and you do not see any new fundamental negatives that are going to affect the company's revenue and earnings numbers. The market was reacting to the broker downgrade news, nothing else.

You already lost 22 percent of your money as per the market quotation. At this time, if you panic and sell the stock at $35 per share, then that is a permanent capital loss. Since you already know the true intrinsic value of the company, you should not panic and sell. You should think that the market gave you the opportunity to buy a great company at a cheaper price. You should buy more instead of selling.

When you are experiencing short-term market quotation loss, it does not mean you lost your investment value. You need to allow sufficient time for the market to reflect the true fundamental value of the company. The market does not reflect the changes immediately; it may take a couple of quarters or years, but finally it will reflect the true fundamental value of the company.

This is what happens for normal investors. As soon as they see red in their portfolio, they feel that they made a mistake. That feeling gives them a pain. To avoid the pain, they sell the position at the low price and take a permanent capital loss. To recoup that lost money, they try to look for quick-gain opportunities like other hot stocks or options.

Avoiding permanent capital loss means that you are holding your loss-generating investment for an indefinite period of time and thinking that you will recoup your losses or generate a profit if you hold the stock for a very long time. It does not work that way, either. You may wonder how I differentiate the genuine loser from a market-mispriced stock. You can follow the company closely, check its quarterly earnings, check its balance sheet and cash flow statements, and listen to its conference calls. If the company made progress in those fronts, then you are looking at a market-mispriced security. You can hold on to them or add more shares to your holdings.

On the other hand, you might see earnings reduced, debt increased, cash decreased, and that the management does not have a plan to address those problems for a couple of quarters. Plus, your analysis is pointing out that there is fundamental deterioration in the company's operations. This means the intrinsic value of the company is reduced below your purchase price. The company does not have any turnaround plan, and all the research is indicating that the company will not turn around within a reasonable timeframe, say within two years. If this is the case, then you can sell the stock and use the proceeds to buy another undervalued company.

Here are the ways to avoid permanent capital loss:

- Never react to the short-term price variation because of market gyrations. Analyze the underlying company fundamentals and make a rational decision
- Before buying any security, analyze the downside risk before calculating the upside potential
- Hold a loser for a reasonable time frame—at least two years— before selling it, unless otherwise there is a sudden fundamental-value deterioration in the company
- If there is a challenge to the company and the management is in the process of addressing those challenges, you can buy additional shares at bargain prices so that your average buy price for that stock will be less. When the company turns around, stocks will follow and you can make more profit because of your lower average purchase price.

PART

II

STOCK RESEARCH CHECKLIST

Another main task for investors involves researching the prospective company thoroughly, examining all the aspects of the business, and then deciding what to do with the stock: Buy it, put it on hold for monitoring, or outright reject it.

There are more than 5,000 stocks in the United States alone; if you consider the stocks around the whole world, the numbers are staggering. Investors cannot research each and every stock extensively. Even professional investors cannot do that. Investors need to have a circle of competence and select the companies in those industries. Circle competence is important for many reasons, which will be explained in a later chapter. You should reject companies that are out of your circle of competence. As an investor, you will not be in a position to analyze each and every company in the United States and all around the world. But, you can try to learn each industry slowly and expand your circle of competence.

After the initial interest in the company, investors need to spend a lot of time and energy to research the company and find out if the company is qualified for investment. There are multiple ways an investor needs to analyze the quantitative and qualitative factors of a business. Those factors are included in the checklist that follows in Chapter 5. I suggest you never buy any stock without doing research on every item included in this checklist.

This checklist is formulated from the combined knowledge of teachings from Warren Buffett and Peter Lynch, books written about their investment processes, and my experience with stock market investing.

The stock research checklist items are each explained with Coca-Cola and Goodyear Tire stocks as examples so that investors can better understand them. Some of the checklist items are explained with fund stock picks.

Key Points

- Read the company's 10Ks and 10Qs for many years and research the company as per the checklist. Never buy a stock unless you have researched all the items in the research checklist. You will not find that each and every stock passes all the checklist items. Look for stocks that pass the most number of research checklist items.
- After completing the research checklist, calculate the conservative intrinsic value of the company. Never buy a stock above the calculated intrinsic value of the company.

Stock Research Checklist—
Business Characteristics

When you are investing in a stock, you are part owner of that business, which means you should understand that business thoroughly.

Are You Able to Understand the Business Thoroughly?
Is It a Simple Business?

What are the company products? How is the company generating revenue? How is the company's marketing? What is the competitive landscape? What are the future prospects? Do you understand the business life cycle? If you are able to answer all of these questions, then you understand the business.

Simple Business

Companies that are involved in simple types of business tend to perform better during the long term. For example, Coca-Cola has been in a simple beverage business for more than 100 years and is making shareholders rich. That simple business is easy to understand. Compare this business to some companies in high-tech industries where product life cycles are very short, maybe 18 to 36 months. If the company does not innovate the next product before the end of its current product's life cycle, it will not be able to sustain its revenue and earnings. If you are working in the same industry, then you will be able to understand those life cycles thoroughly, which makes that business a simple business for you. Whether a business is simple or not depends on the investor's circle of competence. Constant product-generating businesses perform better than frequent product-changing companies. This is because the management and research teams are on the forefront of introducing innovative new products, which are better than the competitors'. If they lag behind that process, then the competitors will take away the market share.

Does the Company Have any Moat, which Makes It Difficult for Competitors to Penetrate Its Market Share?

There are two different types of businesses to consider: One is a hard-to-replicate business, and the other is a commodity-type business.

Hard-to-Replicate Businesses

Hard-to-replicate businesses have established brand name products and won the consumers' minds as the best choice.

Brand Name   There are multiple examples for each one of these characteristics. We can cite companies like Coca-Cola for soft drinks, Gillette for razor blades, Hershey for chocolates, and Heinz for ketchup. There are lots of other brand name companies out there. Let's look over some examples.

Even in the fast-changing technology world there are many brand name companies like Google for searching, Microsoft for operating systems, and Oracle for databases. It will be hard for competitors to enter into their territory. It is possible, but it will take billions of dollars and a long time to crack that kind of brand.

Take for example Coca-Cola. Its brand name has been strongly established for over 100 years. Coca-Cola product servings are growing around the world every day. It has won the consumers' minds as the best choice in soft drinks. As Warren Buffett puts it, "If you gave me $100 billion and said take away the soft drink leadership of Coca-Cola in the world, I'd give it back to you and say it can't be done."[1]

That is the importance of a brand name. Pepsi is a second brand name in the beverage industry. Pepsi spent billions of dollars for many years and still could not crack Coke's dominance. A successful brand name company can raise prices without losing customers. This way it can earn more profit, which will reflect in the company's share prices; shareholders will get rich over the long term. That is the advantage of a brand-name business.

Warren Buffett understands these characteristics very well; that is why he invested $1.29 billion in Coca-Cola during late 1980s and still holds those shares. As of 2009, that investment was worth around $11.4 billion.[2] This is one of his permanent holdings.

Consider an example in the technology field. Microsoft started with the operating system DOS, then released Windows operating systems, and then dominated the operating-system field. No other rivals could crack Microsoft's dominance until now. Unix, Linux, and other operating-system companies have tried, but they were not successful. Microsoft was successful in creating similar kinds of products and dominated the original software producers. Think about Sybase, Novell, Netscape, and many other companies, that were all killed by Microsoft. Google is dominating the search and online-advertising business. Even Microsoft was not able to crack Google's dominant position in those fields because Google captured consumers' minds early.

Buffett understood the brand name concept very well. That was the basis of his investment in See's Candy Shops in 1971. The asking price was $40 million; Berkshire Hathaway had $10 million in cash. The true asking price was $30 million and Buffett paid $25 million. See's Candies had an established a brand name on the West Coast. From 1972 to 1999, See's Candy Shops earned $857 million in pretax income. In 1999 alone, See's earned around $73 million without adding any additional capital from the owner. Think about the return on investment of Buffett's $25 million dollars. Berkshire Hathaway still owns that company. It generates cash flow and sends the money to Buffett to reinvest. Apart from See's growth, the company cash flow helped Buffett to reinvest in other businesses. If you add those reinvestment returns, the numbers would be phenomenal. That is why he was able to create his empire.

Patents Patents are another important feature for companies to have because they make it hard for competitors to enter into that company's territory. Normally, pharmaceutical companies have patents for particular drugs. Until that patent expires, brand name drug companies can earn a lot of money with the highest possible profit. Technology companies also have patents for their products and they can license their patents to other companies and earn royalties.

Hidden-Asset-Intensive Companies Competitors cannot replicate certain companies, such as hidden-asset-intensive companies like railroads. They own a lot of assets and cannot be replicated in the modern world. Railroad companies own the land under the tracks. When analyzing the balance sheets of those companies you cannot quantify those assets. As a careful investor, you should take into account those assets when you are analyzing a company. When you find companies that have hidden assets and are being ignored by the market, it gives you a great buying opportunity. You can get great returns from those kinds of companies.

Warren Buffett used to shy away from capital-intensive companies, but he recently bought Burlington Northern Santa Fe (BNI) for $26 billion. Among the important attractions were the hidden assets and high barriers to entry. I was amazed to see that just one gallon of gas can be used for 35 miles of transportation. When you compare that kind of fuel consumption to on-road truck fuel consumption, railroad companies' efficiency is excellent.

Normally, manufacturing companies are crushed because of low-cost manufacturing structure from emerging countries. But in this case, no outside competitor can compete with the railroad business. When the economy does well, these railroad companies post greater profits.

Commodity-Type Business Commodity-type businesses are those that produce products with no difference from the competitor's products. Some examples of commodity-type businesses are air travel, computers, insurance, and metals. When one of the producers finds an efficient way of doing things and can reduce the cost of manufacturing, it can reduce the cost of the products in order to increase market share. Other competitors are then able to copy those cost efficiencies and reduce the price of the product even further. This kind of undercutting can increase market share tactics that will benefit the consumers, not the producers. So, normally, shy away from commodity-type businesses.

For example, take Dell (DELL), the computer supplier. Computers are a pure commodity-type business. Dell innovated supply chain efficiency and sold low-priced computers to the consumers; they called it "Made to order." Another cost-cutting idea was when Dell sold computers directly to consumers and businesses instead of using traditional distribution models. These costs are passed on to the customers. Because of this low-price advantage, Dell became a multi-billion dollar revenue-generating company very quickly. DELL stock delivered a 40,425 percent return between August 1988 and August 2003. DELL's stock price increased from $0.08 per share to $32.34 per share in split-adjusted price. Other computer companies implemented the same kind of efficiency in their models and the low-price advantage disappeared. The company growth has been in question for the past seven years. DELL's share price decreased from $32.42 per share to $14.05 per share from September 2003 to January 2011; shareholders lost 56.6 percent.

If you are interested in commodity-type businesses, search for the companies that have the following characteristics:

- Low cost producer: This is an important factor for commodity-type businesses. Since the business is a low-cost producer, other businesses will not be able to compete on the price and that is the deciding factor for the consumer.
- Size: Company size really matters in commodity-type businesses. Because of a business' bigger size, it can demand the best rates from its suppliers and distributors. It can pass this cost advantage to the consumers so that smaller firms will not be able to compete on the price.

Consider the massive wholesaler Wal-Mart (WMT). Because of its size, Wal-Mart can order huge amounts from suppliers. Because of this, Wal-Mart can get the lowest possible price from suppliers. That low-price advantage gives it an edge with competitors, which is why competitors cannot penetrate the low-priced market territory. Wal-Mart competitors are trying to differentiate themselves with higher-priced goods for higher-paying consumers. Whenever Wal-Mart comes to a particular location, grocers, furniture, and other goods stores disappear quickly.

Wal-Mart has started entering emerging nations like China and India. The company is already doing business in China and has been trying to enter India's market for many years. Wal-Mart started doing joint ventures with Indian companies, but its ultimate goal is to try to own Wal-Mart stores in India. That's why Warren Buffett owns Wal-Mart stock as one of his long-term holdings.

What Is the Nature of the Business? Does It Operate in a Non-Exciting Industry?

Another great investor of our lifetime, Peter Lynch, tries to buy these kinds of companies and generated great returns for Magellan mutual fund investors from 1977 to 1990. When he ran the Magellan fund, he generated 29.4 percent compounded annual returns for 13 years.

Lynch likes to find bargain securities in non-exciting businesses, those companies that operate in boring types of business. The best example is Envirodyne (EDYN), which is in the business of producing plastic forks and straws. His thought process was that there would be a lack of new competitors entering into the boring industries. In the technology field, when a company introduces a new product, it can command a higher profit margin. That profit margin attracts competitors to introduce similar kinds of products. To get market share, the new competitor has to price its product lower than the innovator. Then a price war begins and finally the higher profit margin disappears. Consumers get the benefits, not the companies.

But when a company operates in a boring business, it does not attract many new competitors. If management is very conscious about cost structure, they can grow and capture a greater share of the business. That makes for consistent growth with long-term rewards for the shareholders.

Not many new entrepreneurs want to build these kinds of "boring" companies; they want to go into more exciting businesses, like high technology. That is what happened during the Internet boom, when many Internet businesses were founded in order to participate in exciting types of businesses.

This does not all mean that investors try to hold all the stocks in a dreaded industry. But, investing some percentage of the portfolio in non-exciting businesses can yield long-term and steady returns to the investors. Warren Buffett and his buddy Bill Gates held stakes in Republic Services Corporation for some time. Berkshire Hathaway was holding 11 million shares and sold those shares in the third quarter of 2010, maybe to fund the BNI purchase.

Is the Company Involved in a Dirty Type of Business?

If the company is involved in a "dirty" cleanup kind of business, there will likely not be any new competitors entering into the market. This lack-of-competitor advantage allows for an increase of market share and in turn an increase in revenue and earnings over time. For example, Waste Management (WM) grew from a small operation to today's market cap of $16 billion. Another example is Service Corporation (SCI), which operates in the funeral business. There are multiple businesses like that in the market. If you hold shares in these companies for a long time, you can make a lot of money and build your fortune over time.

With National Chain Companies, Was the Company Successful in Multiple Locations before Expanding Nationally?

Peter Lynch used this test in his investing career many times. This question is very useful when you are thinking of investing in national chain companies. If you get into any of the successful chains in an initial period and hold the shares until they open for business across the nation, you can make a tremendous amount of money. These kinds of national chain companies are available in retail companies like restaurants, shoes, home improvement, groceries, pharmacies, haircutting, furniture, and many more.

The biggest example is the McDonald's Corporation (MCD), which was founded in 1948. Figure 5.1 is a graph with figures from 1970 to 2010.

The stock price was around $0.20 per share on a split-adjusted basis in January 1970. In December 2010, stock was trading around $77.19 per share, which is a 38,595 percent return in 40 years. If you invested $10,000 and left it alone, that money would have been worth around $3.8 million dollars as of December 2010, a 16.05 percent compound annual return for 40 years and no capital gain taxes paid to the IRS.

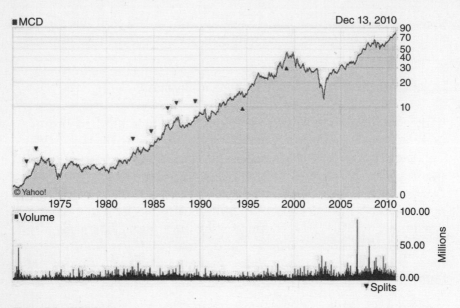

Figure 5.1   MCD Chart

Reproduced with permission of Yahoo! Inc. ©2011 Yahoo! Inc. YAHOO! and the YAHOO! logo are registered trademarks of Yahoo! Inc. Reproduced with permission of CSI ©2009. Data Source: CSI www.csidata.com/

An example of a national chain company in home improvement is The Home Depot (HD). See Figure 5.2.

The stock price was around $0.25 per share on a split-adjusted basis in August 1984. In December 2010, stock was trading at around $34.79 per share, which is a 13,916 percent return in 26 years. If you invested $10,000 and left it alone, that money would have been worth around $1.39 million dollars as of December 2010, which is a 22.83 percent compound annual return for 26 years and no capital gains taxes paid to the IRS.

These businesses both started in one location and, after finding success, opened in multiple locations in the same city, then started to expand to other states, and eventually nationally and internationally. You can wait until the concept becomes successful in multiple locations, then invest. After investing, you can monitor the progress for a couple of years. If the business grows gradually, that is a good sign. It is likely to slowly expand in each state and then complete the nation and start expanding internationally. If you own stock in

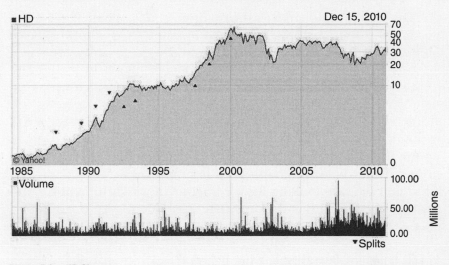

Figure 5.2   HD Chart

Reproduced with permission of Yahoo! Inc. ©2011 Yahoo! Inc. YAHOO! and the YAHOO! logo are registered trademarks of Yahoo! Inc. Reproduced with permission of CSI ©2009. Data Source: CSI www.csidata.com/

a couple of companies like this for the long term, you can very well retire from these investments.

Do not think that because you missed McDonald's and Home Depot that you will not get these kinds of opportunities in the future. There are new chains appearing all the time. We need to look out for those kinds of opportunities. Investors need to wait patiently until a couple of locations become successful and then invest the money. When the chain starts growing in different locations, patiently hold the stock over multiple decades for maximum return possible.

Has the Company Dominated in a Particular Segment of the Market?

When a company concentrates its product or service to address a particular segment of the market that is overlooked by other big and established business, the company can grow bigger. If it is constantly growing in that space, the company can dominate that particular market. Early investors can make a lot of money in these kinds of companies.

The Wal-Mart story is a classic example of this. When Sam Walton was establishing his stores, he started opening in small towns. Sears and other big retailers overlooked small towns. Sam Walton's wife refused to live in a city where more than 45,000 people lived. Because of this condition, he started opening stores only in small towns. That decision gave Wal-Mart early successes. Then he started opening new stores in adjacent towns. He tried to concentrate on those small towns one by one. Before competitors noticed, Wal-Mart was dominating the small-town market. Early investors made a great deal of money if they held the shares for a long time.

When you are looking for a company in which to invest, try to find a particular market segment that dominant players are ignoring and invest in it for the long term.

Is This Company Operating in a Hot Industry?

Investors should shy away from hot stocks in hot industries. Here are the reasons:

- There are lots of competitors coming into the market to take away the market share from the existing hot companies.
- Hedge funds and mutual funds are chasing performances and they trade these stocks heavily, which makes stock prices highly volatile.
- These hot-industry company stocks are always traded at a premium to the intrinsic value of the company.
- The market perceptions of the hot industries are always changing. When that happens, previous hot-industry stock prices will go down faster because investors sell the old hot stocks to raise cash to put into new hot stocks.

Between 1990 and 2000, everything Internet was considered a hot stock. Whoever took their dot-com companies public became an instant multimillionaire. For example, let's look at a graph of Yahoo! Inc. (YHOO) in Figure 5.3.

Yahoo! went public at $1.24 per share, price adjusted for splits, in April 1996. Within three years and eight months, the stock reached $108.17 per share. That is an 8,723 percent return in less than four years. That was an excellent return. December 1999 was the peak of the Internet bubble; the bubble burst in 2000. Yahoo!'s stock

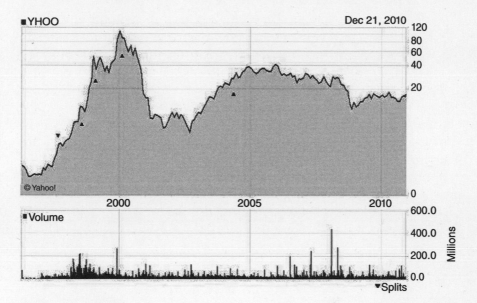

Figure 5.3   YHOO Chart

Reproduced with permission of Yahoo! Inc. ©2011 Yahoo! Inc. YAHOO! and the YAHOO! logo are registered trademarks of Yahoo! Inc. Reproduced with permission of CSI ©2009. Data Source: CSI www.csidata.com/

price started coming down and was trading as low as $4.41 in September 2001.

Investors who bought Yahoo! stock in an initial public offering (IPO) and kept the stock until the peak received an excellent return. Think about the investors who chased the hot stocks in the hot Internet industry, paid $108.17 per share in December 1999, and sold the stock in September 2001. They might have lost 95 percent of their investment.

Stock Research Checklist—Earnings

Examine company earnings growth for the last 10 years. If the company is less than 10 years from its initial public offering (IPO) date, at least examine the earnings growth history from the IPO date.

What Is the Company's Earnings Growth over the Previous 10 Years? Does It Grow Constantly?

Earnings Per Share (EPS) = Company net income ÷ Number of shares outstanding

(When you are using the number of outstanding shares, use the fully diluted shares instead of outstanding shares).
Here is the calculation to get the EPS growth rate

$$I = (FV/PV)^{1/N-1} \times 100$$

$$I = \text{Percentage of EPS growth rate}$$

$$FV = \text{Future EPS value}$$

$$PV = \text{Current EPS value}$$

$$N = \text{Number of years}$$

Here is a sample calculation of EPS growth rate for Company X.

2006: $0.17
2007: $0.25
2008: $0.53
2009: $0.25

$$I = ((\$0.25 \div \$0.17)^{1/4} - 1) \times 100 = 10.12 \text{ percent for four years}$$

In this example, the EPS from 2006 to 2008 looks great. But in 2009, the EPS is reduced. As an investor, you need to find the reason for those downward earnings. Does the company have a temporary problem or is it going to produce reduced earnings in the coming years also? To get the answers, read the annual and quarterly reports; management might have explained the reasons for the revenue and earnings decrease. Or, listen to the company's conference calls; you should be able to get the answers to your questions. Always look for consistent earnings growth from a company so that you can reasonably predict the future earnings of the company. This will help you calculate the intrinsic value of the company.

Warren Buffett looks for consistent earnings history in a company before investing. Here is the example from his permanent holding in Coca-Cola (KO)[1]:

2000: $0.88
2001: $1.60
2002: $1.60
2003: $1.77
2004: $2.00
2005: $2.04
2006: $2.16
2007: $2.57
2008: $2.49
2009: $2.93

Look at the last 10 years of EPS growth. Those numbers are growing in a smooth uptrend. Warren Buffett expects Coca-Cola earnings to grow at the same rate or increased rate into the future.

EPS growth rate I = 12.78 percent for last 10 years.

Warren Buffett always looks for certainty. Here is an incident from his life:

> Marshall Weinberg of the brokerage firm of Gruntal & Co tells about going to lunch with Buffett in Manhattan: "He had an exceptional ham-and-cheese sandwich. A few days later, we were going out again. He said, 'Let's go back to that restaurant.' I said, 'But we were just there.' He said, 'Precisely. Why take a risk with another place? We know exactly what we're going to get.'

That," says Weinberg "is what Warren looks for in stocks too. He only invests in companies where the odds are great that will not disappoint."[2]

Here we can compare Coca-Cola's (KO) numbers with Goodyear Tire's (GT)[3] earnings per share for the last 10 years.

2000: $0.26
2001: (−$1.27)
2002: (−$6.62)
2003: (−$4.52)
2004: $0.63
2005: $1.21
2006: (−$1.86)
2007: $0.66
2008: (−$0.32)
2009: (−$1.55)

For the last 10 years, earnings are up and down a lot. The growth rate of EPS is negative.

Which stock is better in this research checklist item? Obviously, Coca-Cola is the better of the two. We can continue to use the same examples for other research checklist items as well, so that we can have consistency in our research process.

How Does the Company Use the Retained Earnings? Do the Retained Earnings Reflect in the Stock Price?

When the management of a company invests earnings back into the business, that investment should yield a higher return because of those retained earnings. When the management does a great job using retained earnings, it will increase the earnings of that company, and, in turn, earnings per share will increase.

Market price does not always reflect the true value of the company during the short term. But, if you are looking at 10 years or more, market price reflects the true value of the company.

We will examine KO and GT numbers for this checklist item. You need to add the last 10 years of EPS and compare with the market price of the stock in those years.

Coca-Cola

2000: $0.88
2001: $1.60
2002: $1.60
2003: $1.77
2004: $2.00
2005: $2.04
2006: $2.16
2007: $2.57
2008: $2.49
2009: $2.93

Retained EPS earnings of KO for last 10 years = $20.04

Change in market price of the stock from January 2000 to December 2010 is $64.54 − $44.48 = $20.06

$$\text{Calculation} = \text{Market price change/Retained earnings}$$
$$= \$20.06 \div \$20.04 = \$1.0009$$

Each dollar retained by KO generated at least $1 in market value. KO just barely passes this test.

Now look at GT's numbers

2000: $0.26
2001: $1.27
2002: (−$6.62)
2003: (−$4.52)
2004: $0.63
2005: $1.21
2006: ($1.86)
2007: $0.66
2008: (−$0.32)
2009: (−$1.55)

10 years retained earnings = (−$13.38). GT does not even have positive retained earnings.

What Are the Company's Owner Earnings for the Past 10 years? Does It Grow Consistently?

Buffett uses the term "owner earnings." These are the earnings the owner can keep after the capital expenditure. Here is the formula to calculate the owner earnings.

Owner earnings = Net income + Depreciation & Amortization-Capital Expenditure

We can add depreciation and amortization non-cash expenses to the net income and subtract the capital expenditure to yield the owner income. If the owner income trend increases over time, you can project the approximate owner income for the future. But, remember, this number is not going to be perfect.

We can calculate the owner earnings of the examples.

KO owner earnings increase for last 10 years:

$$2000: \qquad \$2,177 + \$773 - \$733 = \$2,217 \text{ million}$$

$$2009: \quad \$6,824 + \$1,236 - \$1,993 = \$6,067 \text{ million}$$

Owner income growth rate I = 10.59 percent for the last 10 years

Coca-Cola's market cap on December 2010 was \$149.77 billion. For this kind of large cap, 10.59 percent growth rate is great. For small caps or mid caps, this kind of growth rate is less ideal and you need to look for at least a 15 percent owner income growth rate.

Now we calculate the owner income growth rate for GT for last 10 years:

$$2000: \qquad \$40.3 + \$630 - \$614 = \$56.3 \text{ million}$$

$$2009: \quad (-\$375) + \$636 - \$746 = (-\$485) \text{ million}$$

Since we calculated a negative owner income for 2009, it does not make sense to calculate the owner income growth rate. The 2008 number was also negative. So, we can look at 2007 numbers in order to be able to calculate the owner income growth rate for the eight years from 2000 to 2007.

$$2000: \quad \$40.3 + \$630 - \$614 = \$56.3 \text{ million}$$

$$2007: \quad \$139 + \$614 - \$739 = \$14 \text{ million}$$

$$I = (-15.96 \text{ percent})$$

Owner income reduced (15.96) percent every year. This does not look to be a great investment.

What Is the Company's Recent Earning Momentum?
Is It Comparable to Its Long-Term Growth Rate?

An investor's portfolio should contain some percentage of large-cap stocks. When the market is in a downturn, these established-company stocks go down less when compared with small- or mid-cap stocks.

When you are researching established companies to invest in, one of the important tasks is to find out if a company's earning momentum matches with its long-term growth rate. When the company is small, its growth rate may be very high. It grows very fast and reaches mid-cap status. After many years of growth as a mid cap, the company reaches large-cap status. When a company is a large cap, its growth rate may not be as high as small- and mid-cap growth, but there will still be growth. The growth may be through internal expansion like expanding to new parts of the world, introducing new products, or entering new markets. The other part of expansion is through acquisition.

When you are researching a company, you need to find out if the company's growth rate in recent years matches with its long-term growth rate. If the company keeps earning momentum, that is great, and the company has passed this checklist item. For an example, we can look at Berkshire Hathaway:

Year	Annual Change—Book Value of Berkshire per Share
1965	23.8%
1966	20.3%
1967	11.0%
1968	19.0%
1969	16.2%
1970	12.0%
1971	16.4%
1972	21.7%
1973	4.7%
1974	5.5%
1975	21.9%
1976	59.3%
1977	31.9%
1978	24.0%
1979	35.7%
1980	19.3%
1981	31.4%
1982	40.0%
1983	32.3%
1984	13.6%

Year Annual Change—Book Value of Berkshire per Share	
1985	48.2%
1986	26.1%
1987	19.5%
1988	20.1%
1989	44.4%
1990	7.4%
1991	39.6%
1992	20.3%
1993	14.3%
1994	13.9%
1995	43.1%
1996	31.8%
1997	34.1%
1998	48.3%
1999	0.5%
2000	6.5%
2001	(−6.2%)
2002	10.0%
2003	21.0%
2004	10.5%
2005	6.4%
2006	18.4%
2007	11.0%
2008	(−9.6%)
2009	19.8%

Compounded annual gain from 1965 to 2009 is 20.3 percent.[4] Overall gain from 1964 to 2009 is 434,057 percent.

Now we can split the average growth rate of book value for every decade.

From 1965 to 1975, average book value growth is 15.68 percent.

From 1976 to 1985, average book value growth is 33.57 percent.

From 1986 to 1995, average book value growth is 24.87 percent.

From 1996 to 2005, average book value growth is 16.29 percent.

From 2006 to 2009, average book value growth is 9.9 percent.

From 1965 to 1975, after Buffett acquired Berkshire Hathaway, he started buying other companies. This was the startup phase, and book growth averaged around 15.68 percent. From 1976 to 1995, there was full-blown growth of 33.57 percent for the first decade and 24.87 percent for the next decade. Starting in 1996, the company entered large-cap space. From 1996 to 2005, growth rate was 16.29 percent. In 2015 we will have the numbers for the decade between 2006 and 2015.

The recent acquisition of Burlington Northern and Santa Fe (BNI) and capital investments in Goldman Sachs, General Electric, and other investments will yield great returns in coming years. All of the operating company's earnings are recovering nicely. Berkshire Hathaway can maintain the earnings momentum it had between 1996 and 2005, but, there is no way it can replicate its 1976 to 1995 growth rate (because, remember, company size drags down its growth rate). The current market cap of Berkshire Hathaway is $196.8 billion and it is unlikely it can grow at 25 percent into the future.

Does the Company Have Any One-Time Event That Recently Increased Earnings?

When you are analyzing a company's stocks, you need to find out if there were any one-time events that increased the company's earnings recently. Because if there are one-time events, you need to remove those earnings from your calculation of historic earnings so you can project the earnings conservatively. One-time events could be a sale of assets, a big order from a particular customer—which maybe increased the earnings for one year or multiple years and might not continue in the future, a big tax refund, or a legal settlement.

For example, look at Sharp Compliance Corp (SMED), which is a medical waste disposal company. The business was founded in 1992 and is a small-cap company with a market cap of around $65 million.

Sharps Compliance Financial Highlights[5]

(In thousands, except per share data)	2008	2007	2006
Revenues	$12,841	$11,956	$10,563
Net Income	$ 82	$ 785	$ 382
Diluted EPS	0.01	0.06	0.03
Total Assets	$ 5,676	$ 4,690	$ 2,190
Debt	–	–	–
Stockholders' Equity	$ 2,885	$ 2,169	$ 252

In February 2009, Sharps Compliance received a five-year contract valued at $40 million dollars from an agency of the U.S. government. The first year, the company received $28.5 million, and the remaining amount was to be received over the next four years for program maintenance. Because of this contract, Sharps Compliance's revenue started to increase from 2009.

(In thousands, except per share data)	2010	2009
Revenues	$39,156	$20,297
Net Income	$ 9.356	$ 4.197
Diluted EPS	0.63	0.30
Total Assets	$31,632	$15,188
Debt	–	–
Stockholders' Equity	$26,941	$ 9,570

Look at the revenue numbers in fiscal year 2009, which are $20.29 million, compared to the $12.84 million from the previous year. In fiscal year 2010 the revenue increased from 2009: $20.29 million to $39.15 million in 2010, which make for a 92.95 percent increase.

The stock price was trading around $2 per share in January 2009. After the $40 million contract announcement, the stock price started to move up and reached $11.16 in December 2009, which is a 458 percent return in 11 months. After that contract, the company did not get that kind of huge contract in 2010 and revenue started coming down sharply. In the first quarter of 2011, revenue decreased to $5.2 million and lost $421,000 in the first quarter.

Below is the content from a company press release.

HOUSTON, Oct. 27, 2010 (GLOBE NEWSWIRE)—Sharps Compliance Corp. (NASDAQ: MED) ("Sharps" or the "Company"), a leading full-service provider of cost-effective management solutions for medical waste and unused dispensed medications generated outside the hospital and large healthcare facility setting, today reported $5.2 million in revenue for the first quarter of fiscal year 2011 ended September 30, 2010. Revenue in the fiscal 2010 first quarter was $15.4 million and included $11.0 million from the product build-out phase from a major contract with a large U.S. Government agency contract.

Net loss for the first fiscal quarter was $421 thousand, or $0.03 per diluted share, which excludes a $570 thousand, or $0.02 per share, special charge related to the retirement of the Company's former CEO. The special charge included a non-cash portion of $73 thousand related to the acceleration of unvested stock options. Including the special charge, net loss for the fiscal 2011 first quarter was $797 thousand or $0.05 per diluted share. Fiscal year 2010 first quarter had net income of $5.8 million, or $0.40 per diluted share.

Sharps Compliance share prices started coming down from $11.16 in December 2009 to $4.42 per share in December 2010.

Think about the investors who bought the stock at $11.16 per share, they might have lost 60.39 percent of their invested amount. This loss likely happened because investors overlooked the one-time event of the $40 million contract in their calculation. Investors need to identify one-time events, determine what caused the earnings increase, and remove those increased earnings from their calculation.

What Is the Company's "Operating Cash Flow"?
Does It Grow at a Constant Rate?

Operating cash flow is the cash generated from the company's operations. Cash flow numbers are calculated from net income, depreciation, and adjustments to net income, changes in accounts receivable, changes in liabilities, changes in inventories, and changes in other operating activities. Cash flow should be positive. But some companies report positive net income and negative cash flow. This means the companies are using aggressive accounting methods to show positive net income. Investors should try to avoid these kinds of companies.

Now we can calculate the cash flow numbers of Coca-Cola for the last 10 years.

2000: $2,950
2001: $4,782
2002: $4,782
2003: $5,197
2004: $5,740
2005: $5,804
2006: $6,018
2007: $6,993
2008: $6,873
2009: $8,060

Cash flow numbers are in millions.

Look at the cash flow numbers for the last 10 years; they show a smooth uptrend. You need to look for that kind of business so that long-term shareholders get rewarded handsomely.

Cash-flow growth = 10.57 percent growth for the last 10 years.

Now we can calculate the cash flow numbers growth for GT.

2000: $671
2001: $433
2002: (−$503)
2003: (−$109)
2004: $744
2005: $869
2006: $345
2007: $753
2008: $583
2009: $261

Cash flow numbers are in millions.

Look at the cash-flow numbers; they are not in a smooth uptrend. The company generated negative cash flow in two years. The company generated $671 million in 2000 and $261 million in 2009. So, there is no positive cash flow growth. Goodyear Tire fails in this checklist item.

How Has the Business Performed in Previous Recessions?

All companies need to perform in all business conditions. When the economy is on an upswing, all businesses do very well. But, you need to identify the company that has done better when the economy is in a state of recession; that company is the real winner.

Here is a scenario to consider. When the economy is on an upswing, businesses generate more revenue and more earnings. The company has cash on its balance sheets and the business is adding cash each quarter. Senior management wants to expand the business as soon as possible. They are formulating aggressive plans to become a big company in a short period of time, either through acquisition or fast-paced expansion.

To support the aggressive growth, they use bank debt, leveraged up as much as possible. The banks also think that the company will generate the same level of increased earnings in the future and allow the company management to leverage up to the maximum possible level. During boom times, the company might have acquired other businesses at an inflated price.

After the economy booms, the stock market soars. Ultimately, stock prices reach bubble levels and finally burst. Then reality comes into the picture. The economy slides back into recession.

Companies' revenues start falling faster. Management might not be able to cut costs fast enough. Because of falling revenues, earnings start to fall. The company's management faces difficulty when servicing acquisition debt, starts to violate the financial covenants, and finally ends up in bankruptcy.

This kind of cycle happens all the time. The 1990s tech boom created a bubble in the stock market. It finally burst in 2000 and the economy slid back into a recession until 2003. In 2003, the real estate bubble started. Banks were lending money to commercial and residential developers and sub-prime borrowers, thinking that real estate prices would never come down. When reality set in, the financial crisis hit in late 2008.

If a company's management is capable or experienced enough to understand business cycles, they act prudently. They conserve cash when the economy is in expansion and run the existing business as usual. When the economy bursts, less well-capitalized companies get into trouble. The well-run businesses acquire the troubled companies at fire-sale prices or take away market share when their competitors end up in bankruptcy.

This is what happened during the last financial crisis; the well-capitalized banks absorbed the troubled banks. When you are researching a company for a possible investment, do the research and find out how the company performed during the last recession. If they came out stronger than before, that kind of company will reward the shareholders very well over the long term.

We can look at how Coca-Cola and Goodyear Tire performed during the last boom and bust cycle. In 2000, the bubble burst and the economy went into a recession. Then in 2004, the economy started booming again and burst in 2008.

The numbers for Coca-Cola are as follows:

Year	Net Income
2000	$2,177
2001	$3,979
2002	$3,976
2003	$4,347
2004	$4,847
2005	$4,872
2006	$5,080
2007	$5,981
2008	$5,807
2009	$6,824

Numbers are in millions.

Look at the net income numbers from 2000 to 2003. There is a growth of 99.6 percent of net income. In 2002, net income decreased around $3 million from 2001. That means net income was flat during that recession.

In 2009, net income increased around 17.5 percent from 2008. From 2007 to 2008, net income decreased by 2.9 percent, which means Coca-Cola was flat and experienced only a small decrease in that recessionary period. That is a great company to own and Coca-Cola passes this checklist item.

Now we can calculate the numbers for GT.

Year	Net Income
2000	$40.3
2001	(–$204)
2002	(–$1,106)
2003	(–$802)
2004	$115
2005	$239
2006	(–$330)
2007	$139
2008	(–$77)
2009	(–$375)

Numbers are in millions.

Look at GT numbers from 2000 to 2003. The company lost around $2.11 billion dollars. During the 2008 recession, GT lost $452 million. Therefore, it fails this checklist item.

As an investor, you need to look for companies that performed well during the last couple of recessions. Suppose a company is flat, or lost around 5 percent of its earnings; that is okay. Investors should not select companies that lost a lot of money in the last couple of recessions. As in our example, if you come across any company that lost around 20 percent earnings in the 2000 recession and did not lose money in the 2008 recession or came out having increased earnings, that company passes the checklist item. This is because the management seems to understand the mistakes they made during the 2000 recession and has learned something in order to plan for future recession periods. That kind of experience with management makes the company capable of earning more money during future recessions (or at least not losing as much). But, if management does not appear to have learned anything in a previous recession, that kind of company will ultimately lose shareholder value over time.

If a Particular Product's Success Attracted You to a Company, What Percentage of That Company's Sales Come from That Product?

This is one of the most important checklist items for investors to complete. Some companies' newly introduced products may be very successful and generate good earnings. However, you should not blindly follow that success and buy those companies' stocks based on those earnings. You need to find out what percentage of sales and earnings come from that product.

If the company is very big and the particular product amounts to less than 10 percent of the company's business and you buy stock because of the particular product's success, you will be making a mistake. You need to find out what the other parts of the business are doing and analyze the company as a whole.

On the other hand, if the successful product makes up more than 25 percent of a company's earnings, that can be a good thing. Sometimes, in small cap companies, 100 percent of the revenue and earnings might come from one successful product. That company can grow fast. At that time, you need to find out the sustainability of that product's success. For example, take Apple (AAPL); the company introduced the iPod to the music world in October 2001. In January 2004, it sold around two million iPods. It was great a success and was followed by the successful iPhone and iPad.

Apple's revenue and net income numbers are below. Revenue and net income numbers are in millions.

Year	Revenue	Net Income	Net Profit Margin (%)
2000	$5,363	(−$37)	(−0.69)
2001	$5,742	$65	1.13
2002	$6,207	$68	1.10
2003	$8,279	$276	3.33
2004	$13,931	$1,335	9.58
2005	$19,315	$1,989	10.30
2006	$24,006	$3,496	14.56
2007	$32,479	$4,834	14.88
2008	$42,905	$8,235	19.19
2009	$65,225	$14,013	21.48

Look at the revenue numbers and net profit margin for the last 10 years. After iPod's introduction, the product was gaining momentum and the company started posting increasing revenue and net

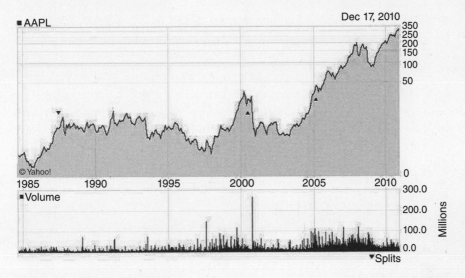

Figure 6.1   AAPL Long-Term Chart

Reproduced with permission of Yahoo! Inc. ©2011 Yahoo! Inc. YAHOO! and the YAHOO! logo are registered trademarks of Yahoo! Inc. Reproduced with permission of CSI ©2009. Data Source: CSI www.csidata.com/

income numbers. How was this possible? The answer is continuous new product introduction. Look at the AAPL chart in Figure 6.1.

Does the Company Have Client Concentration?

Investors need to analyze the company's client base. Suppose the business is earning more than 10 percent to 20 percent of the earnings derived from that particular customer; that is a disadvantage. Here are the reasons:

1. The end customer can demand price reductions, which will affect the profit margin of the company because the big customers already know that the company relies on them heavily.
2. If the end customer's business depreciates, your company revenue will also come down, which is not a good thing.
3. If that customer cancels the contract, there will be a big hit to the company's earnings.

Here is an example of customer concentration problems in Pinnacle Airlines (PNCL).[6]

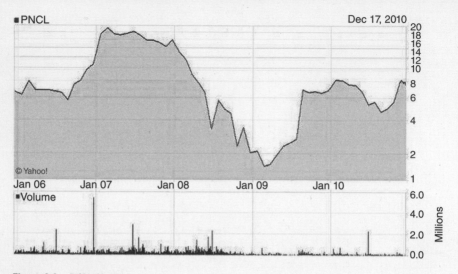

Figure 6.2   PNCL Chart

Pinnacle Airlines provides regional airline capacity to Delta; 78 percent of the company's revenue comes from Delta Airlines. This much concentration always creates problems. Whenever Delta has problems, usually during recessions, it can demand rate reductions. Obviously, Pinnacle needs to do that to make its customers happy; otherwise, it loses those customers, a disaster for the company. There are always contracts between the companies, but the biggest customers can call for renegotiation to reduce the rates. Look at the price chart of PNCL in Figure 6.2.

During the recession period of 2008 and early 2009, PNCL's stock traded around $13.44 per share in January 2008 and dropped to $0.97 per share in March 2009, which is a 92.78 percent loss in less than one year. This happened because of the customer concentration. Obviously, when trading around $1 per share, the company might have been suitable for turnaround play.

Stock Research Checklist—Debt

Debt is an important part of a business. If it is manageable debt, then it is acceptable. But, if the debt load is very high, it will be very hard for that business to succeed; sometimes the company will even end up in bankruptcy. The investors will end up losing all their money. Some industries are capital intensive; they have to use debt to finance their capital investment apart from equity capital. For example, industrial and manufacturing companies need to invest large amounts of money for factories in order to keep them up to date. Auto industries need to spend every couple of years to retool the auto-manufacturing capabilities.

Does the Company Have Manageable Debt?

Normally, I suggest you shy away from heavily capital-intensive businesses. But suppose you find a capital-intensive business at a bargain price. Here you can compare that company's debt level with a direct competitor. If the company can pay off total debt with five years of net income, then that should be a manageable debt.

Find out when the current debt is coming due. If any debt is due within a couple of years, what kind of plan does the company have to pay off that loan? When the company has debt as a bond, it is less risk to the company. Long-term bonds are a good kind of debt to have.

The economy goes through life cycles: recessions, recoveries, and boom periods. If a company loads up on too much debt during boom years, it can generate a higher revenue and be able to service debt. When it enters into a recession, it will be hard to cut costs and reduce the debt as fast as the revenue decreases. It will be hard to handle that debt when the recession period starts.

Does the Company Have Manageable Short-Term Debt?

Short-term debt translates into whatever debt a company needs to pay before one year. It appears on a balance sheet's *current liabilities* section. This may be interest that needs to be paid on long-term debt. If any debt comes due, the company should have money to cover that debt. The company should have cash and cash equivalents, short-term investments, accounts receivables, hidden assets, and cash flow numbers to pay the short-term debt. If the company does not have enough cash to cover that short-term debt, do not even look at the company, because the company may be a sinking ship.

When you are dealing with micro-cap companies, which are trading at more than $1 and less than $5, you may come up with many businesses like these and you need to be aware of them. When you listen to those companies' conference calls, the management may be overly confident, saying that they are in the process of refinancing the existing debt as it comes due or talking to institutional investors to get the capital it needs. Do not invest in those companies thinking they can bring the needed capital; you can start thinking about them after the needed capital is acquired by the company.

If you feel the company may have different assets, and that it can raise the cash selling those assets, you need to do detailed research on that company's assets. For example, the company may have different hidden assets, different divisions, or different separate acquired business. It can sell any of those assets and may be able to pay the debt due. You need to analyze the situation very carefully. If you feel the company can handle that debt situation properly, you can hold that position or buy into a new position. If you invest in those situations, you can make lot of money when those companies start to recover.

What Is the Company's Current Ratio?

Current ratio helps you to find out whether or not a company has the ability to pay current obligations.

The formula for current ratio is

$$\text{Current ratio} = \text{Current Assets} \div \text{Current Liabilities}$$

Current assets consist of cash and cash equivalents, receivables, inventory, and other current assets.

Current liabilities consist of accounts payable, short-term debt, and other liabilities.

If the ratio is below 1, that is a bad sign. This means that the company does not have enough current assets to meet the current obligations. Investors need to dig deeper with these kinds of companies. If the ratio is more than 2, this means that the company is in excellent condition and can meet the short-term obligations easily. Investors need to focus more on businesses that have a current ratio of more than 1.

If the current ratio is less than 1, it does not necessarily mean that the business will go into bankruptcy. You can dig deeper and discover if there are any other hidden assets that the business can use to meet its short-term obligations.

When this kind of situation happens, most investors dump the stocks. The stock may end up losing a lot of value and go into extreme bargain value.

Bargain value alone is not sufficient for an investor to invest in a particular stock. Investors need to work through all of the checklist items explained in this book before feeling confident that the company in question will be able to meet its short-term obligations. These kinds of opportunities can yield excellent returns, but you should not invest more than two to five percent of your portfolio in them. Sometimes, the company may not be able to monetize the particular assets before the debt comes due, or business conditions might deteriorate very quickly. Again, a word of caution: even if you are very confident the company can pay the short-term debt before the due date, only move forward as far as other checklist research items dictate.

For example, take the Las Vegas Sands (LVS) situation shown in Figure 7.1. Because of the financial crisis, Las Vegas Sands' revenue started decreasing very quickly. The company was in the middle of many development projects around the world.

The stock used to trade around $133 per share in September 2007 and then crashed down to $1.38 per share in March 2009 because of decreasing revenue and debt load. LVS founder Sheldon

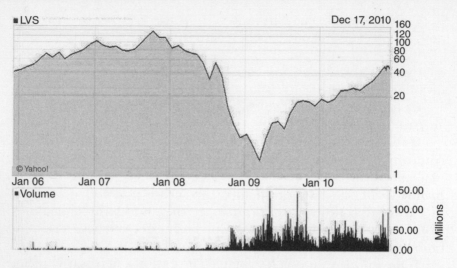

Figure 7.1   LVS Chart

Gary Adelson injected around $475 million dollars into the company via convertible senior notes in a private transaction. The stock started to recover. After the capital injection, I got the confidence that the company would not end up in bankruptcy. I got in at $6 per share in April 2009. I held the shares until May 2010, and sold them for around $24 per share. That is a 400 percent return in 13 months.

If I had bought when the stock was around $1.30 per share in March 2009 and held it until May 2010, I might have earned an 1800 percent return. In March 2009, I did not have enough evidence to think that the company could service its debt. I knew LVS had assets and it could monetize the holdings, but I was not sure how soon it could do so. But, after the founder invested the money, I was fairly confident that the company would survive. Now that the downside was minimal, I was willing to invest the money and got a 400 percent return for the fund that I managed.

Now we can calculate the current ratio for our example companies.

Third quarter 2010, Coca-Cola's (KO) current ratio is:

$$\text{Current ratio} = \$23.10 \text{ billion} \div \$17.27 \text{ billion} = 1.33$$

Coca-Cola's current ratio was 1.33, which is good. Investors do not need to worry about the short-term liquidity issues.

We will calculate for Goodyear Tire (GT), at the end of third quarter of 2010:

$$\text{Current ratio} = \$8.40 \text{ billion} \div \$4.93 \text{ billion} = 1.70$$

GT's current ratio is good. They have good short-term liquidity.

What Is the Company's Long-Term Debt? Is It Manageable?

As a first choice, investors should look for companies that do not have long-term debt. The companies may not have long-term debt for of any of the following reasons.

1. The company is operating in an industry where it does not need to spend a lot of money on capital expenditures. For example, services industries do not need to spend a lot of money on capital expenditures, so they do not get into long-term debt. Specific companies include software companies like Microsoft or Oracle, outsource service providers like Infosys and Cognizant, data providers like Moody's, and financial services companies like Fiserv.
2. Warren Buffett likes to search for these kinds of companies because they can create more shareholder value over the long term. There is no risk of default because they have no long-term debt. Plus, company earnings are not reduced because of interest payments on long-term debt.
3. The company may be in a sustainable competitive position to earn a higher profit and, in turn, generate a higher cash flow every year. Management can fund the growth of the company from existing cash flow rather than relying on debt. This kind of business is good and generates higher shareholder value over the long term.
4. When the input costs increase, sustainable-competitive-position companies can raise the prices and still maintain a decent profit. That is, management can expand the company via internal growth and spend capital expenditures from company

profits rather than depending on debt. Companies like this can generate excellent value for shareholders over the long term. If you can identify companies with no long-term debt and a competitive position at attractive pricing, you should invest and hold those companies for the long term to generate a great return.

You should not have a rule of investing only in companies with no long-term debt. If you do, you will eliminate many wonderful businesses that have manageable long-term debt. In some industries, like manufacturing, you cannot run a business without long-term capital investment. As such, investors also need to look out for those companies that have a reasonable debt level.

So, what is reasonable debt? It means the company should be able to repay the whole long-term debt with four or five years of net income. That is reasonable debt. The company should have at least two times the cash flow each year to meet the principal and interest payments to service that long-term debt. There should be a sufficient cushion in the cash-flow figure and debt-service figures.

The investor needs to analyze what kind of long-term debt the company has. Callable bank debt and commercial paper debt are the worst kinds of debt. Bank loan agreements contain many financial covenants, and the whole debt is callable if the bank decides the company may not be able to service the debt or because of a sudden revenue decrease in the company. Investors need to analyze what percentage of the long-term debt falls into this kind of high-risk-debt category. If the company has a consistent history of cash flow for the last 10 years, investors do not need to worry much about this.

The advantageous kind of debt is in corporate bonds with long-term maturities and low interest rates. Investors cannot demand the principal payments immediately and also management can defer the interest payments.

Now we calculate the long-term debt levels and net income levels for KO and GT.

KO's long-term debt levels for the last 10 years:

Year	Long-Term Debt	Net Income	Payoff from the Net Income
2000	835	2,177	5 months
2001	1,219	3,979	4 months
2002	2,701	3,976	8 months
2003	2,517	4,347	7 months
2004	1,157	4,847	3 months
2005	1,154	4,872	3 months
2006	1,314	5,080	3 months
2007	9,329	5,981	1.6 years
2008	2,781	5,807	6 months
2009	5,059	6,824	9 months

Numbers in millions.

If you look at Coke's pay-off duration, it is mostly less than one year, so the long-term debt is very reasonable.

Now we calculate the long-term debt level and pay-off factor for GT.

Year	Long-Term Debt	Net Income	Payoff from the Net Income
2000	2,350	40.3	58 years
2001	3,204	−204	NA
2002	2,989	−1,106	NA
2003	4,826	−802	NA
2004	449	115	4 years
2005	4,742	239	20 years
2006	6,563	−330	NA
2007	4,329	139	31 years
2008	4,132	−77	NA
2009	416	−375	NA

Numbers in millions.

Look at GT's long-term debt numbers and compare them with Coke's long-term debt. Investors should prefer the Coca-Cola long-term debt numbers, as GT failed this test.

Does the Company Pay Little or No Interest Expense?

Durable, competitive companies pay little or no interest expenses for their short- and long-term debt. If a company does not spend money on its interest expenses, that is good because it is a zero-debt company.

On the other hand, investors should not totally eliminate interest-paying companies from their research list. A reasonable percentage of interest expenses is acceptable. When that percentage goes higher, then investors need to examine those companies. Find out what percentage of the operating income is spent as an interest expense. Investors can calculate for the last 10 years to determine if interest expenses are a consistent percentage or going down. However, if the percentage of interest expenses is going up, that is a bad sign.

Now we calculate the percentage of interest expenses from the operating income for KO.

Year	Interest Expense	Operating Income	Interest Expense/ Operating Income (%)
2000	$447	$4,464	10.10
2001	$289	$6,155	4.69
2002	$199	$6,264	3.17
2003	$178	$6,071	2.93
2004	$196	$6,591	2.97
2005	$240	$7,017	3.42
2006	$220	$7,246	3.03
2007	$456	$8,532	5.34
2008	$438	$9,862	4.44
2009	$355	$9,780	3.62

Numbers are in millions.

Average interest expenses for the last 10 years is 4.36 percent.

If you look at the interest expense, it was around 2.5 to 4 percent consistently, which is great. Durable, competitive companies should have little or no interest expenses.

Now we calculate the same percentage of interest expenses in terms of operating income for Goodyear Tire.

Year	Interest Expense	Operating Income	Interest Expense/ Operating Income (%)
2000	$283	$1,173	24.13
2001	$292	$926	31.53
2002	$241	$915	26.34
2003	$296	−$549	NA
2004	$369	$1,457	25.33
2005	$411	$1,706	24.09
2006	$451	$1,256	35.91
2007	$566	$1,677	33.75
2008	$397	$1,434	27.68
2009	$311	$900	34.56

Numbers are in millions.

Average interest expenses for the last 9 years is 29.26 percent.

Look at the average interest expense of GT, which is 29.26 percent. Compare this number with KO's average interest expense of 4.36 percent and it is easy to determine which is the better choice in this category. In 2003, GT did not even generate positive operating income. GT is in a highly competitive and capital-intensive business, which is why the interest expenses were so high. Investors need to avoid this kind of business.

Does the Company Have Preferred Stock?

Preferred stockholders have a higher claim on the capital structure of the company. They get paid a fixed dividend and have conversion rights to common stock. If the company is in liquidation, preferred stock holders have claim before the common shareholders get paid. If the company pays a dividend, preferred stockholders also get paid first. This form of preferred stock is a costly form of the debt for the corporation, because the company needs to pay the interest *and* have an equity-appreciation potential for the preferred stockholders. You need to look for companies that do not have, or have very little, preferred stock. That does not mean investors should outright reject companies that issue preferred stock. If a company is able to pay the interest and have a plan to pay off preferred stock capital, that is acceptable.

During the financial crisis, Warren Buffett invested $5 billion with a 10 percent dividend every year and received a warrant to buy Goldman shares at $115 each. He got the dividend and also the price-appreciation potential of Goldman Sachs common shares. He invested $3 billion in General Electric (GE), with a 10 percent dividend and the option to buy $3 billion worth of common shares at $22.50 each.

A company's management will often try to issue preferred stock when they are having a difficult time raising capital. Companies should have sufficient cash on hand to handle unknown situations. Buffett always keeps a cash cushion in Berkshire Hathaway. Shareholders often question him about cash and cash equivalents in the annual meeting. His usual response is something along with lines of, we should have enough cash at hand to handle any unexpected cash need for our operating companies so that another person cannot determine our future. That kind of cash cushion helped him get juicy deals, like Goldman Sachs, which will reward Berkshire Hathaway shareholders. Investors need to find such a company without preferred stock so that the company does not need to pay the interest and dilute the stock of existing shareholders.

CHAPTER 8

Stock Research Checklist—Equity

In simple terms, return on equity (ROE) is how much profit the company is generating with the shareholders' money. As a shareholder, you can earn lot of money over time with a company that has a high ROE.

What Is the Company's ROE for the Last 10 Years?
Does It Trend Upward?

Here is how to calculate ROE:

$$ROE = \text{Net income} \div \text{Share holder equity}$$

Warren Buffett monitors ROE compared with earnings per share (EPS). In EPS, management can do some financial engineering to increase the figure over time, without increasing the earnings numbers. If they want to improve the earnings numbers, they can buy back shares, which causes the EPS to start to increase. Buying back shares is a good thing for the company and shareholders. But the intention to increase the EPS alone is not a good thing. If the company uses more debt, it can generate a higher ROE too. Generating a high return on equity with reasonable debt is a good thing.

Now we can calculate the ROE for both of our company comparisons; Coca-Cola's (KO) ROE for the last 10 years are as follows:

2000: 23.1%
2001: 38.5%
2002: 34.3%
2003: 33.6%
2004: 32.3%
2005: 30.2%
2006: 30.5%
2007: 30.9%
2008: 27.5%
2009: 30.2%

Average ROE for last 10 years = 31.11 percent

Look at the consistency of the ROE every year; it is right around 30 percent. That is a great number. The company is generating an average 31.11 percent profit from shareholder-invested money. That money will also be compounded for many years into the future. That is the reason Warren Buffett is holding Coca-Cola shares as a permanent holding.

Now we can check the ROE of Goodyear Tire (GT).

2000: 1.1%
2001: NA
2002: NA
2003: NA
2004: 565.5%
2005: 325.2%
2006: NA
2007: 13.3%
2008: NA
2009: NA

For the numbers listed as "NA," there was no net income, and therefore there was no positive ROE. In 2004 and 2005, the ROE is extremely high. GT generated six years of negative ROE and four years of positive ROE (out of those four years, two were very high). There is no consistency at all. Therefore, GT failed this checklist item.

Does the Company Have More Equity When Compared with Long-Term Debt?

Debt-to-equity ratio is one of the most important figures to examine. You need to look for companies with more equity than debt. That kind of company has a strong balance sheet, and investors do not need to worry about leverage problems. This kind of company makes more money for long-term shareholders.

When a company has more debt than equity, especially when the economy starts to slow, the company may feel financial pressure to make the interest payments or run the risk of violating the financial covenants. Situations like that quickly reduce stock prices, and long-term shareholder values can be destroyed in a short period of time. When a company uses leverage, it can generate more revenue and that revenue flows to the bottom line as earnings. If those extra earnings are sufficient enough to service the debt, pay down the principal debt balance, and also add more earnings to the company, that is good. That kind of company will create more shareholder value over time.

If the company has enough cash to cover the short-term debt, we can omit the short-term debt and use the long-term debt as the debt for our calculations. The debt-and-equity ratio varies for different industries. For capital-intensive businesses, the debt-and-equity ratio will be higher; less capital-intensive businesses will have a lower ratio. When comparing this kind of ratio, investors need to compare with competitors in the same industry so that investors can be the winners. Warren Buffett tries to pick companies with low debt-to-equity ratio every time.

Now we can calculate the debt-to-equity ratio for KO over last 10 years. Remember, a lower debt to equity ratio is better.

Year	Long-Term Debt	Equity	Debt/Equity Ratio
2000	835	9,316	0.08
2001	1,219	11,366	0.10
2002	2,701	11,800	0.22
2003	2,517	14,090	0.17
2004	1,157	15,935	0.07
2005	1,154	16,355	0.07
2006	1,314	16,920	0.07
2007	9,329	21,744	0.42
2008	2,781	20,472	0.13
2009	5,059	24,799	0.20

Debt and equity numbers are in millions.

The average debt-to-equity ratio for the last 10 years is 0.15. This kind of ratio is excellent.

Now we calculate the debt to equity for GT during the last 10 years.

Year	Long-Term Debt	Equity	Debt/Equity Ratio
2000	2,350	3,503	0.67
2001	3,204	2,864	1.11
2002	2,989	651	4.59
2003	4,826	(−13.1)	NA
2004	449	72.8	6.16
2005	4,742	73	64.9
2006	656	(−758)	NA
2007	4,329	2,850	1.51
2008	4,132	1,022	4.04
2009	4,167	735	5.66

Debt and equity numbers are in millions.

We can omit 2003 and 2006 because of negative equity. The average debt-to-equity ratio for last eight years is 11.09.

Compare the debt-to-equity ratio for KO and GT. Obviously, in this category, investors need to pick Coca-Cola when compared with Goodyear Tires.

Stock Research Checklist—Profit Margin

Net profit margin is a simple calculation that tells investors how much net profit is generated from each dollar of revenue.

Net profit margin as a percentage = (Net income ÷ Revenue) × 100

If a company increases its earnings, that is obviously a good thing. The next thing you need to identify is whether or not a company can maintain that profit margin. A company can increase revenue and earnings by undercutting the competitors, but that is not profitable for the shareholders. The company cannot do that for the long term.

What Is the Company's Net Profit Margin for the Last 10 Years? Does the Company Generate a Consistent Upward-Trend Profit Margin or at Least Maintain an Average Profit Margin?

For example, take Company X. It earned $100 million net income from $1 billion in revenue in one year:

Net profit margin: ($100 ÷ $1,000) × 100 = 10 percent

Next year, the company increased earnings to $150 million from $2 billion in revenue:

Net profit margin: ($150 ÷ $2,000) × 100 = 7.5 percent

Company X's net profit margin decreased from 10 percent to 7.5 percent, which is not a good thing.

Now we can calculate the net profit margin for Coca-Cola (KO) for 10 years.

2000: 10.6%
2001: 19.8%
2002: 20.3%
2003: 20.7%
2004: 22.1%
2005: 21.1%
2006: 21.1%
2007: 20.7%
2008: 18.2%
2009: 22.0%

KO's average net profit margin for the last 10 years is 19.66 percent.

Look at the consistent net profit margin for the last 10 years; it was around 20 percent, which is great.

Let us now look at Goodyear Tire's (GT) net profit margin for the last 10 years.

2000: 0.3%
2001: NA
2002: NA
2003: NA
2004: 0.6%
2005: 1.2%
2006: NA
2007: 0.7%
2008: NA
2009: NA

NA means there was no net income in that year, which means the company was operating at a loss. Obviously, a company that is producing a 20 percent net profit margin is better than a less-than-1-percent net profit margin company.

What Is the Company's Gross Profit Margin for the Last 10 Years? Does it Consistently Grow, or at Least Maintain an Average Rate?

A gross profit is how much money is left after the cost of goods sold is subtracted from the revenue numbers.

$$Gross\ Profit = Revenue - Cost\ of\ Goods\ sold.$$

$$Gross\ Profit\ Margin = Gross\ Profit \div Revenue$$

Investors need to look for companies with higher gross profit margins. Normally, sustainable competitive businesses have a higher percentage of gross margins when compared with competitive-industry companies.

Durable, competitive companies generate a 60 percent or higher profit margin. If a business generates a 40 percent gross margin or less, this probably means it operates in a highly competitive industry. Investors should try and avoid businesses in highly competitive industries. Different industries should have different ranges of gross profit margins. You need to compare companies with competitors in similar types of industries.

Now we can calculate the gross profit margin for Coca-Cola during the last 8 years. I am using 8 years here, because 10 years worth of data was not available.

Year	Gross Profit	Revenue	Gross Profit Margin (%)
2002	$12,459	$19,564	63.68
2003	$13,081	$20,857	62.72
2004	$14,068	$21,742	64.70
2005	$14,909	$23,104	64.53
2006	$15,924	$24,088	66.11
2007	$18,451	$28,857	63.94
2008	$20,570	$31,944	64.39
2009	$19,902	$30,990	64.22

Numbers are in millions.

Average gross profit margin for the last eight years is 64.29 percent, which is good.

Now we calculate the gross profit margin for GT during the last 10 years.

Year	Gross Profit	Revenue	Gross Profit Margin (%)
2002	$2,550	$13,856	18.40%
2003	$2,621	$15,102	17.36%
2004	$3,557	$18,353	19.38%
2005	$3,563	$18,098	19.69%
2006	$3,025	$18,751	16.13%
2007	$3,733	$19,644	19.00%
2008	$3,349	$19,488	17.18%
2009	$2,625	$16,301	16.10%

Numbers are in millions.

The average gross profit margin at GT for the last eight years is 17.91 percent

Compared with Coca-Cola, Goodyear Tire failed this gross-profit-margin checklist item.

Does the Company Have a High Pretax Profit Margin?

Pretax income is calculated after interest expenses, and deducted from the earnings before interest and taxes (EBIT) and before income taxes are paid. If you concentrate on taxable income, companies have a different strategy to manipulate net incomes. So, to be safe, calculating pretax income will give you the true picture.

Always look for companies with high pretax profit margins. When the economy is in a recession, normally a company will reduce the price of its products to attract customers. If a company has a higher pretax profit margin, it can reduce the price and still post a decent profit margin. On the other hand, if the company already has a low pretax profit margin when the economy enters a recession, the company will usually start generating losses. Multiple years of recession can put a company under financial distress and ultimately land it in bankruptcy. When you are calculating the pre-tax profit-margin percentage, compare companies in the same industry.

When a company posts a higher pretax profit margin, it can invest that income for business expansion, acquiring new businesses, paying dividends, or buying back shares.

$$\text{Pretax profit margin} = \text{Pretax income} \div \text{Revenue}$$

Now we can calculate the pre-tax profit margin for KO for the last 10 years.

Year	Pretax Income	Revenue	Pretax Profit Margin (%)
2000	$3,399	$20,458	16.61%
2001	$5,670	$20,092	28.22%
2002	$5,499	$19,564	28.11%
2003	$5,495	$21,044	26.11%
2004	$6,222	$21,962	28.33%
2005	$6,690	$23,104	28.96%
2006	$6,578	$24,088	27.31%
2007	$7,873	$28,857	27.28%
2008	$7,439	$31,944	23.29%
2009	$8,946	$30,990	28.87%

Numbers are in millions.

Average pretax profit margin for the last 10 years is 26.31 percent. Look at the consistency of the pretax profit margin (with the exception of the year 2000).

Now we can calculate the pretax profit margin for GT for the last 10 years.

Year	Pretax Income	Revenue	Pretax Profit Margin (%)
2000	$92	$14,417	0.64%
2001	–$273	$14,147	–1.93%
2002	$38	$13,850	0.27%
2003	–$655	$15,119	–4.33%
2004	$381	$18,370	2.07%
2005	$584	$19,723	2.96%
2006	–$113	$20,258	–0.56%
2007	$464	$19,644	2.36%
2008	$186	$19,488	0.95%
2009	–$357	$16,301	–2.19%

Numbers are in millions.

Average pretax profit margin for the last 10 years, including negative pretax income, is 0.03 percent.

To make the average better, we can remove the negative pretax income and then calculate the average pretax profit margin. The pretax profit margin of GT is 1.54 percent.

Compare GT's number, 1.54 percent, with KO's consistent 26.31 percent. Which company is going to make more shareholder value over the long term? No question about it, Coca-Cola is going to generate more shareholder value than Goodyear Tire.

CHAPTER

Stock Research Checklist—
Capital Investment

Here is the calculation formula for return on assets (ROA):

$$ROA = Net\ income \div Total\ asset$$

Total assets consist of debt and equity.

This percentage gives you, the investor, the percentage of net income generated for the money invested, which includes both debt and equity capital. As long as the ROA is high, company shareholders will be greatly rewarded.

What Is the Company's ROA for the Last 10 Years? Is It Growing Constantly or at Least Maintaining an Average ROA for the Last 10 Years?

Now, say for example, that Company X is generating $10 million of net income, and total invested assets (including debt and equity) equal $100 million.

$$Company\ X's\ ROA = (\$10 \div \$100) \times 100 = 10\ percent$$

Company Y is generating the same $10 million net income, and total invested assets (including debt and equity) equal $50 million.

$$Company\ Y's\ ROA = (\$10 \div \$50) \times 100 = 20\ percent$$

Which company is better for the shareholders? Obviously, Company Y is the better choice because it generated 20 percent out of the total invested assets. As with many of the other checklist items, you need to compare the ROA with competitors in the same industry.

Now we can calculate the ROA for Coca-Cola (KO) and Good-year Tire (GT). I understand that Coca-Cola and Goodyear are in different industries and that their total invested assets will be different. Normally Goodyear should have more capital expenditures when compared with a company like Coca-Cola.

As an investor, you need to identify which industries are offering a higher ROA. As a first step, it will be helpful to use the examples of Coca-Cola and Goodyear. Then, you can compare Coca-Cola's ROA with a competitor in the same industry, like Pepsi, and choose the best company from there.

ROA for last 10 years for KO:

2000: 10.3%
2001: 18.4%
2002: 16.9%
2003: 16.8%
2004: 16.5%
2005: 16.0%
2006: 17.1%
2007: 16.3%
2008: 13.9%
2009: 15.3%

The average ROA for the last 10 years is 15.75 percent, which is an exceptional number.

We calculate the ROA for GT for last 10 years.

2000: 0.3%
2001: NA
2002: NA
2003: NA
2004: 0.7%
2005: 1.5%
2006: NA
2007: 0.8%
2008: NA
2009: NA

The average ROA for the last 10 years is −1.40 percent
It is clear that KO is the much better choice.

Does the Company Have Consistent ROIC Numbers?

Here is the formula to calculate the Return on Invested Capital
(ROIC).

$$ROIC = (Net\ income - Dividends) \div Total\ Capital$$

Total capital includes long-term debt and common and preferred shares. The higher the ROIC, the better it is for the investors.
If the ROIC is very high, it means management is doing a great job
of allocating capital profitably. Since we can easily capture the ROIC
numbers from the Evaluator section in the Evaluator Quotes &
Research section of http://investing.quicken.com, we do not need
to calculate for each year for our example companies.

ROIC for KO: The average ROIC for the last 10 years is 26.20
percent.

ROIC for GT: The average ROIC for the last 10 years is −4.80
percent.

Because KO has a much higher ROIC, KO is better in this regard
than GT.

Does the Company Need to Spend Large Amounts of Money as a Capital Expenditure to Stay Competitive?

When you are researching companies, examine capital expenditures
over time. If a company is spending large amounts of revenue as a
capital expenditure, then it is not a great business. If a company is
not spending large amounts of money, it is unlikely that it can be
competitive in its industry. This especially applies to the manufacturing, textile, and auto industries.

After capital expenditures, there will be less money available for
other good things to increase shareholder value, such as expanding
the business, buying back shares, acquiring other businesses, and
paying dividends. If a company is spending large portions of its
revenue for capital expenditures, it will be difficult to spend money
to increase shareholder value over time.

When Warren Buffett acquired Berkshire Hathaway, the company was in the textiles business. The firm demanded a high level of capital expenditures to upgrade the plant. Even after the expense, return on investment was negative. After a few capital investments, Buffett resisted the urge to invest additional amounts into the textile business. He finally closed down the textile operation after many years of operating at a loss. For good reason, Warren Buffett used to invest in less capital-intensive businesses all the time.

For example, if you look at his investment holdings in Moody's, Fiserv, the *Washington Post*, American Express, Wells Fargo, and See's Candies, they are not high capital-intensive businesses. Recently, Buffett acquired a capital-intensive business in Burlington Northern. The reason is that Berkshire had grown very big and it needed a bigger deal to improve the bottom line. Plus, the economic characteristics of the railroad business are very bright. As mentioned earlier, railroads are more efficient than other transportation methods. Again, you might not believe it, but only one gallon of oil is used for 400 miles of transportation. When the economy is growing and the population is growing, BNI needs to ship large amounts of goods and other commodities so that Berkshire Hathaway shareholders will be earning profits for a long time into the future.

Now we can calculate the capital intensity for our examples. We can calculate the percentage of pretax income spent as a capital expenditure.

Capital expenditure percentage = Capital expenditure
÷ Pretax income

Coca-Cola's expenditure is

2000: 21.5%
2001: 13.5%
2002: 15.4%
2003: 14.7%
2004: 12.1%
2005: 13.4%
2006: 21.3%
2007: 20.9%
2008: 26.4%
2009: 22.3%

Average capital expenditure percentage of operating income: 18.14 percent

KO is spending 18.14 percent of its pretax income as a capital expenditure.

GT's capital expenditure percentage for last 10 years:

2000: $614 ÷ $92.3
2001: $435 ÷ (−$273)
2002: $458 ÷ $37.9
2003: $375 ÷ (−$655)
2004: $519 ÷ $381
2005: $634 ÷ $584
2006: $671 ÷ (−$113)
2007: $739 ÷ $464
2008: $1,049 ÷ $186
2009: $746 ÷ (−$357)

Numbers in millions.

If you look at the last 10 years, GT's capital expenditure was more than the operating income. Therefore, that is not a good business in which to invest because holding the stock for a long time will not reward shareholders. GT failed this research checklist item.

What Is the Company's Investing Strategy? Is the Company Investing in Its Area of Expertise?

When a company earns income for its owners every year and increases that income, the cash is going to pile up. You need to find out what a company is going to do with that cash. When a company tries to invest those earnings back into growth, you need to identify where it is sinking its investment dollars. If its strategy is growing through acquisition, you need to find out how the company management plans on acquiring companies. Also, is the business that management hopes to acquire related to existing business, or is it a totally different business?

You need to also examine whether or not a company invests in its area of expertise. This is important. If a company tries to buy totally different kinds of businesses and then tries to integrate the new companies, that is a bad move. History teaches us that most management does a lousy job of integrating companies with different cultures. After many years of trying, they fail to integrate the companies and finally write off those investments.

However, there are businesses out there that thrive on acquiring different kinds of companies. That is the concept behind holding companies. That is how Warren Buffett built Berkshire Hathaway. If you are examining this kind of company, this test of employing a same-expertise restriction will not apply. There is a difference between Warren Buffett's holding company and normal businesses that are trying to buy a new business in order to expand. The difference is:

- Warren Buffett buys around 80 percent to 100 percent of the business. When he buys 80 percent of a business, the remaining 20 percent continues to be owned by the company's founders or previous owners so that they can drive growth of the business as usual. There is an alignment of interest.
- Buffett does not interfere with existing management's decisions. They can run the business as they like. If the existing managers are interested in entering into discussions with him, he will discuss with them; otherwise, he will not disturb them in day-to-day operations. All they really need to do is send internally generated financial statements to him monthly or quarterly. When they have more cash, they can send that cash back to Buffett to invest somewhere else. Since there is no micromanagement, whoever sold the business acts the same way as they did before the sale.

That kind of confidence produces a positive effect on the management since Warren Buffett puts his confidence in the existing managers. That confidence drives the existing managers to perform even better.

Here is an example from a GEICO incident with Jack Byrne.

A Fortune 500 company made a serious bid to acquire GEICO. Jack Byrne called Buffett and asked what he thought. Buffett said, "It's up to you." Byrne said, "Oh, come on—you gotta give me more than that." Buffett said nothing but agreed to accompany Byrne to a late-night bargaining session at the Waldorf-Astoria in New York. The suitor addressed themselves to Buffett, the controlling stockholder. Buffett said, 'You are talking to the wrong guy. He (Byrne) is the one you have to convince.' Byrne took Buffett aside and pleaded, "At least whisper a price in my ear." Buffett stayed mum. "It was amazing," Byrne said. "We were talking billion dollars or so. He left it in my hands." Finally Byrne named a price that was out of the buyers range and the talks ended. No doubt, Buffett wanted Byrne to know that he trusted him.[1]

Even if Buffett did not want that deal to happen, he did not say anything. That kind of confidence makes existing management work harder.

- Lifetime partnership—When Warren Buffett buys a company, he likes to continue the business for a lifetime. If one of the businesses Buffett has bought loses money in one quarter or a year or multiple years, it does not bother him. If he thinks the business has a good economic future and is just going through some temporary problems, he tries to ride it out. After a reasonable amount of time spent working to turn the company around, if Buffett believes he will not be able to generate positive income from the business, obviously he will sell that business. That is what he did during his partnership and Berkshire Hathaway's early years.

Most companies fail when they try to acquire other businesses from different industries.

Here are the difficulties of integrating different businesses under one roof:

- The acquirer tries to change the acquired company's culture.
- The acquirer changes senior management personnel or at least changes the future plans of the existing company.
- The acquirer might have paid a higher price for the acquired company.
- After the acquisition, the founder or previous chief executive officer (CEO) might have left the company.

    Normally, when acquiring a company, the acquirer puts in the contract that the acquired company's CEO or founder must stay with the company for at least a couple of years. In those years, the acquiring company's management may undercut the previous CEO's decisions or plans. When that happens, the acquisition is highly likely to fail. After the non-compete agreement expires, the CEO may leave with the best talents of senior management to start a new company. This is what happened with GM's acquisition of Electronic Data Systems (EDS). After the expiration of the non-compete agreement, the former EDS CEO started Perot Systems with other members of the previous senior management.

- To save costs, the acquirer tries to eliminate important people, which obviously affects the existing business. If the acquirer does a good job in this task, they can eliminate the excessive cost and generate higher earnings. This is where integration skills come into the play.

If you are looking for a company for an investment, analyze that company's previous acquisitions and find out how they executed the integration. What was the outcome of previous acquisitions? Did the revenue and earnings increase the way they projected or did the acquiring company end up writing off that investment? If they did a good job with acquiring other companies and increased the revenue, then that is great. If it is not a holding company concept and the business is investing in other areas where they do not have expertise, be suspicious and monitor how the integration is going. What is the outcome of the diversification? If it is not successful, that company fails on this checklist item.

What Percentage of Revenue Is Spent on Research and Development?

Research and development (R&D) is an important task for most businesses because it allows the business to invent new products, upgrade existing products, increase efficiency, and decrease production costs.

R&D is a very important task for technology companies. If technology companies do not invent new products all the time, competitors can kill them and take their market share. Even companies with monopoly products need to kill their own product to deliver a new product in order to increase revenue. This is what happened with Microsoft. MS-DOS was a moneymaking machine for many years, but Apple was in the process of releasing graphical-based operating systems in Mac machines. Microsoft released the Windows operating system to compete with Mac's graphical-based operating system. Subsequently, DOS lost revenue. If Microsoft had not delivered the Windows operating system, Apple might have gained more of its market share.

Take Intel, which introduces high speed central processing units (CPUs) every year to maintain market share. Even consumer-product companies need to invent new products on an ongoing basis to maintain existing market share and increase revenue over time. For example, Gillette keeps inventing new products to keep and increase its market share. Coca-Cola introduced multiple flavors of Coke and Coke Zero to increase company revenue and keep introducing new products.

Investing a certain percentage of the revenue in R&D is important for a company's growth. Spending alone does not increase the revenue of the company. As an investor, you need to identify how effective the current management is at generating returns on their investment. They have to generate a good return on their investment. Of course, some products are going to fail; it is part of the R&D process. You need to find out what percentage of the investment is successful and what kind of revenue is being generated from those new products.

When you are analyzing companies, compare similar companies in the same industry and their previous new-product inventions and the revenue generated from those products. Apple Inc. was very successful for the last 10 years because of its new product inventions like the iPod, iTunes, the iPhone, and the recently launched iPad. Take another example, 3M; it has invented hundreds of new products to increase market share in many different industries.

Warren Buffett likes to invest in a company that supplies the same product for many years. He likes the certainty of the earnings. That is why he invested in Coca-Cola, Gillette, American Express, and the *Washington Post*. Even these companies need to spend a little bit of money on R&D to develop new products and improve existing products. These companies do not need to deliver new products every year like Apple or Microsoft. The pace of innovation is very slow. Once the product is launched it will be there for many years. For example, Coke has lasted for more than 100 years.

As compared to these companies, innovation needs to be constant for technology companies. The life cycle of previously introduced products is very short. If the company is not introducing new products all the time, it is in danger of losing revenue. That kind of uncertainty leads Buffett to reject technology companies. Also, Buffett does not have the technical skills to assess technology companies' future prospects. When you are looking at a company, pay special attention to find out how effectively its previous R&D activities delivered revenue. If you find a company that does not have R&D expenses and has also grown more than 15 percent for the last five years (at least) then you have found a good company and should do the research for other checklist items.

Stock Research Checklist—Management

When you are dealing with fast growing companies, pay special attention to how the business has been growing recently and what plans the management has in place to grow the business in the future.

What Is the Company's Growth Recently? What Plans Does Management Have to Grow the Business?

Let's consider a restaurant. When the business is small and successful, the owner can expand from one restaurant to multiple restaurants in the same city simply by using the cash flow from the business and the help of a bank loan and credit lines. When that expansion is successful, the owner can look for private equity money to expand to the state level and open up many more restaurants. After that expansion is successful, the next step is to raise money from the public market and start opening many restaurants in other states.

If the restaurant was growing at around 20 percent in those early years, that would be excellent. If senior management lets success go to their heads, they may feel that they want to grow even faster. They may want to reach the national level within three years. However, the economy may have been stronger when the restaurant was in its infancy. To compensate, management starts borrowing money and trying to open new restaurants as soon as possible. When businesses are growing that fast, management tends to make costly mistakes, such as hiring the wrong people, choosing the wrong locations, not anticipating supply chain problems, or providing inadequate training to new employees. Because of this, customer service starts to falter. Company revenue might increase because of new restaurant locations, but bottom line profit margin starts to decrease because of debt interest and expansion expenses. When the economy starts to slow down, these issues start to damage the company. Its revenue starts to fall and it cannot reduce costs as fast as revenue is decreasing. The company starts to violate the financial covenants on its debt. Because of this, the company's stock gets hammered and finally the company files for bankruptcy. There have been countless failed companies that followed similar business cycles over the history of the stock market.

As an investor, you need to look for companies that are growing slowly and steadily. If companies use the company cash flow to fund their expansion, then that is great. If companies use moderate debt, that is also acceptable. When a business expands slowly, it can execute its plan methodically. Management can spend enough time finding great locations for new restaurants. They can hire excellent managers to run the new locations and hire new people and provide them better training. Those processes, in turn, improve customer service. The company revenue and net earnings can start to improve and that growth will reflect in the stock price. These kinds of slow and steady companies generate great shareholder returns over the long term.

Take, for example, Buffalo Wild Wings, Inc. (BWLD), which is opening around 25 restaurants every year. As I write this book, BWLD has 652 restaurants in 42 states and has a plan to reach 1,000 restaurants nationally in five years. This kind of slow and steady process should be a winner. They have around $39 million in cash and cash equivalents and $63 million in short-term investments, totaling around $102 million as of September 2010. BWLD carries short-term debt of $32 million and no long-term debt. This kind of slow growth will yield healthy results for long-term investors.

Does the Company Have Related-Party Transactions with the Family Members or Relatives of the Senior Management or Board of Directors?

You need to take time to review at least three or four years of annual reports in order to research any related-party transactions. If the company is doing business with any of the company's senior management or relatives who are involved in other companies, you need to avoid this company. Whenever relative companies act as suppliers, they are likely paid top dollar for their products or services. That will affect the profit margin of the company, and in turn, decrease the share price of the stock.

You need to compare at least three or four years of annual reports and research the number of pages allocated to related-party transactions. If the number of pages is increasing every year, be cautious. You need to dig farther in order to fully understand the situation. Companies as gigantic as Enron have collapsed in large part due to related-party transactions.

Another point to examine is whether the company is lending any money to senior management or directors. If the answer to that question is yes, you need to sell that stock so that you can avoid losing money. A situation like this is what destroyed MCI WorldCom.

Are You Able to Understand the Footnotes of the Company's Financial Statements?

When you are reading the financial statements of prospective companies, be sure to read the footnotes. If you are reasonably good at reading financial statements, you should be able to understand the footnotes. But, if you are not able to understand the footnotes, move on to another company; management may be writing the footnotes in such a way that you do not understand them because they do not want you to understand for one reason or another. As Warren Buffett puts it,

> It's not impossible to write (an accounting) footnote explaining deferred acquisition costs in life insurance or whatever you want to do. You can write it so you can understand it, if it is written so you can't understand it, I'm very suspicious. I won't invest in a company if I can't understand the footnote because I know they don't want me to understand it.[1]

For practice, you can read the Coca-Cola (KO) and Goodyear Tire (GT) footnotes and try to understand them.

Is Management Candid in its Performance Reporting?

You can judge management's transparency by looking at the company's annual and quarterly reports. If management only trumpets successes or tries to hide poor results, that will give you an idea about their openness. You need to find a company where the shareholders are treated like owners. If the management thinks shareholders are owners, they try to talk about the positives and negatives openly. When you are listening to company conference calls, you can really get a feel for what is going on in a company by the way the management treats the shareholders. If questions about negatives of the business come up and management answers honestly, then you can likely trust the management.

Warren Buffett does candid reporting in his annual reports. When one of his company's portfolios does well, he openly praises that company's Chief Executive Officer (CEO). When Buffett himself makes mistakes, he openly admits them in the annual reports and also in shareholders meetings.

Here is an example:

> Of course some of you probably wonder why we are now buying Capital Cities at $172.50 per share given that this author, in a characteristic burst of brilliance, sold Berkshire's holdings in the same company at $43 per share in 1978-80. Anticipating your question, I spent a lot of time working on a snappy answer that would reconcile these acts. "A little more time please."[2]

When he bought ConocoPhilips, he admitted his mistake openly in the annual report, stating that he bought at the wrong time when the price of oil was much higher.

If management is open about their mistakes, they show that they want to treat their shareholders as owners of the company. That is what Warren Buffett does in Berkshire Hathaway annual meetings, and that is why 60,000 people show up to Berkshire Hathaway annual meetings.

Is Senior Management Success Oriented?

Success-oriented people want to win in whatever they do. If you find a company that passes all of the checklist items explained in this book *and* it is being run by highly successful senior management, that will be a jackpot. If you look at any successful business, it was likely started from scratch and has grown into a multibillion-dollar business because it is run by a successful CEO or founders of the company. There are countless examples in the market to support this claim. Some examples: Bill Gates built Microsoft, Warren Buffett built Berkshire Hathaway, Sam Walton built Wal-Mart, Richard Branson built the Atlantic-Virgin empire, Walt Disney built Walt Disney, and Steve Jobs built Apple. All these individuals are very competitive by nature. Whatever they do, they want to win. Even in games, Bill Gates wants to win; he is very competitive at company annual events. Buffett wants to win in the investing game. He piles up money not to spend it, but because it identifies him as a winner, and that makes him happy.

Buffett's daughter once said, "The whole thing is a big game to him. Dollars are the mark of the winner. He doesn't spend anything. He will drive his car and wear his clothes until they fall apart."[3]

As a shareholder, if you are a partner with the kinds of companies where success-oriented people run the company, you will be end up making a lot of money in the long term. Success-oriented leadership attracts success-oriented employees, and those employees will build a great company. Success-oriented people want to work with a company where their leader has the same characteristic; they want to feel proud to work for the company. We can look at some of the companies' stock performance at this point.

Wal-Mart's stock performance is shown in Figure 11.1.

Wal-Mart (WMT) was trading at around $0.05 per share on a split-adjusted basis in August 1972. In December 2010, the stock was trading at around $54.16 per share. That is a 108,320 percent return in 38 years. If you had invested $10,000 in 1972, it would have been worth $10.8 million in 2010, which is a 20.18 percent compounded annual return. In December 2010, WMT's market cap was $195.86 billion. You cannot invest now and expect 1,083 times your initial investment in another 38 years. You need to search for the next business that is likely to grow like Wal-Mart.

Walt Disney's stock performance is shown in Figure 11.2.

Walt Disney Co. (DIS) was trading at around $0.07 per share on a split-adjusted basis in February 1962. In December 2010, its stock was trading at around $37.24 per share. That is a 53,200 percent return in 48 years. If you had invested $10,000 in 1962, it would have

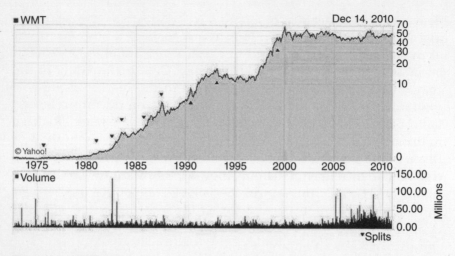

Figure 11.1   WMT Chart

Reproduced with permission of Yahoo! Inc. ©2011 Yahoo! Inc. YAHOO! and the YAHOO! logo are registered trademarks of Yahoo! Inc. Reproduced with permission of CSI ©2009. Data Source: CSI www.csidata.com/

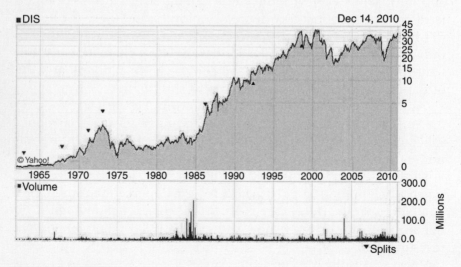

Figure 11.2   DIS Chart

Reproduced with permission of Yahoo! Inc. ©2011 Yahoo! Inc. YAHOO! and the YAHOO! logo are registered trademarks of Yahoo! Inc. Reproduced with permission of CSI ©2009. Data Source: CSI www.csidata.com/

been worth $5.32 million in 2010, which is a 13.96 percent compounded annual return. In December 2010, DIS's market cap was $70.29 billion.

A 30-year-old can invest in a company like the next Wal-Mart or Disney and hold it for another 30 to 40 years. Then, before he or she retires, he or she will have a great nest egg waiting for that retirement. Investors can hold a couple of positions as permanent holdings in their portfolio forever. That is what Buffett is doing with his some of the permanent holdings like the *Washington Post,* Wells Fargo, and Coca-Cola. The reason for these permanent holdings is that he likes the CEOs who are running those businesses.

Do the Financial Numbers on the Company's Earnings Release Match the Numbers on the Documents That Are Submitted to the SEC (Especially Income Taxes Paid)?

The simple test to check the integrity of the management is to compare the income tax paid numbers, which are indicated on the earnings release and the documents that are submitted to the Securities and Exchange Commission (SEC) as a 10-Q or 10-K. The numbers should match. If, for any reason, the numbers do not match, I suggest you reject the company and move on.

Does Management Deliver What It Promises?

When you are researching companies, you need to find out if management has delivered what they have promised in previous years. Promises can come in different forms, most notably:

- Future earnings outlook
- Company profitability plan
- Setting target growth rate of the companies
- What they want to achieve in five years.

Future Earnings Outlook

Warren Buffett's Berkshire Hathaway never does earnings outlooks, which is okay. When the company is investing, it wants to increase the long-term benefit to the company, which means it does not need to worry about the short-term earnings.

Most companies do provide earnings outlooks. If you are researching companies that provide earnings outlooks, you need to search for those that under-promise and over-deliver results. That is good for the investors. When the company promises less, the investors' expectations are also less. When they deliver results above what they promised, investors think that the company beat the expectations. Headlines are written as "earnings beat" or "earnings surprise" and the media's positive coverage can fuel the stock price to jump 10 to 20 percent immediately.

Some bullish CEOs normally give higher ranges of earnings outlooks for the year without considering the possibility of economic contraction at any time. Those companies over-promise and miss the already announced earnings outlook. When the companies under-deliver, "earnings miss" headlines appear in the media, causing the price of the stock to decrease 10 to 20 percent immediately.

Look at the positive side of the under-promise and over-deliver scenario. For example, take Cognizant Technology Solutions (CTSH), which under-promises and over-delivers all the time. Cognizant Technologies reported second quarter earnings on August 3, 2010. Quarterly revenue rose 15 percent sequentially and 42 percent from the year-ago quarter. The stock price closed at $55.42 per share on August 2, 2010. After the earnings announcement, the stock closed at $60.62 per share, which is a 9.38 percent jump. You can look at the company's earnings history; the company beat the earnings numbers most of the time. Figure 11.3 shows the CTSH price chart for the last year.

Stock increased from $45.33 per share in December 2009 to $72.20 per share in December 2010, which is a 59.27 percent increase in one year. When the company consistently beats earnings estimates, existing shareholders make money.

Big money managers such as mutual fund and hedge fund managers try to deliver maximum short-term results to their investors. These people chase the positive surprise companies and ride the momentum stocks. After the earnings announcements, the company stock increases 10 to 20 percent immediately. But the stock price slowly starts to come down after a couple of weeks of buying pressure.

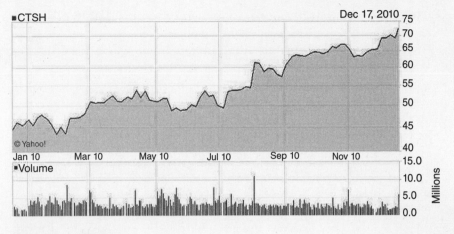

Figure 11.3   CTSH Chart

Reproduced with permission of Yahoo! Inc. ©2011 Yahoo! Inc. YAHOO! and the YAHOO! logo are registered trademarks of Yahoo! Inc. Reproduced with permission of CSI ©2009. Data Source: CSI www.csidata.com/

If you are an existing shareholder, hold the stock. If you are planning to buy, do not buy during the spike period; wait for a couple of weeks before you buy the stock. Each company has its own announced profitability plan to achieve. You need to find out if management has delivered the announced gross and net profit margins recently.

For example, consider iGATE Corporation (IGTE). Its announced profit model is 40/20 percent, which means they want to do the 40 percent gross margin and 20 percent net profit margin. The company has consistently hit that target. Look at the price chart shown in Figure 11.4.

Every company announces its growth rate. You need to find out if the company consistently delivers that performance. If they always deliver that performance, that is good news. Investors can estimate reasonable expectations of the company's owner income into the future.

Look again at Buffalo Wild Wings (BWLD). Its plan is to grow the company's net earnings at least 20 percent per year. BWLD has consistently delivered that kind of growth rate in net earnings. If it misses one quarter, that is acceptable. At those times, the stock price

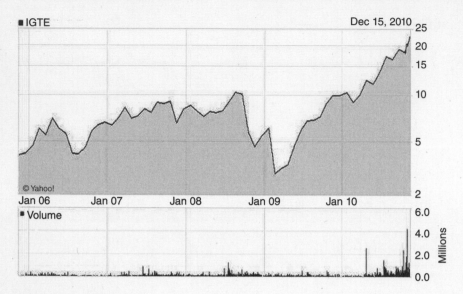

Figure 11.4   IGTE Chart

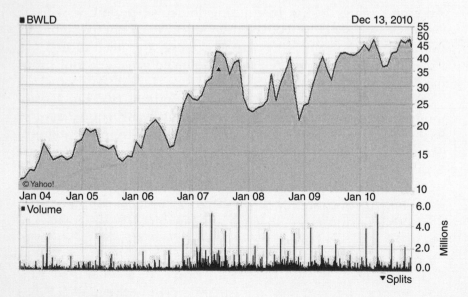

Figure 11.5   BWLD Chart

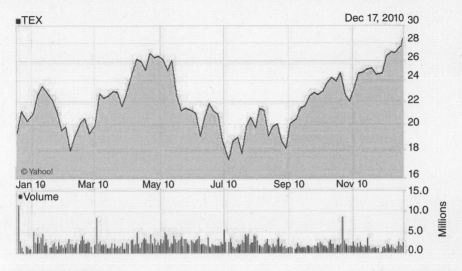

Figure 11.6   TEX Chart

Reproduced with permission of Yahoo! Inc. ©2011 Yahoo! Inc. YAHOO! and the YAHOO! logo are registered trademarks of Yahoo! Inc. Reproduced with permission of CSI ©2009. Data Source: CSI www.csidata.com/

gets hit heavily, and long-term investors use that opportunity to add more stocks to their portfolio.

Look at the chart of BWLD in Figure 11.5.

Some companies announce expected earnings for three to five years into the future. You can monitor their progress each quarter. For example, Terex Corporation (TEX) announced they can double their business before the end of 2013, which would be $13 billion in revenue with a 12 percent operating profit. They are marching toward that figure. During the financial crisis in 2008, the business came down sharply. In late 2010, the business started to turn around and the earnings started to increase.

Figure 11.6 is the price chart of TEX; notice that the stock price increased from $19.81 per share in December 2009 to $28.64 per share in December 2010, which is a 44.57 percent increase in one year.

CHAPTER

12

Stock Research Checklist—Dividend

If a business operates with stable cash flow and pays cash every quarter and the management does not have the opportunity to reinvest in the business, they can pay the dividend to the shareholders. If you are looking for income from your stock portfolio, you can select companies that pay conservative dividends and hold those stocks for the long term.

If You Are Buying the Stock for Dividend, Make Sure the Company Pays the Dividend Without Interruption and Has a History of Raising Dividends

When you are looking for good dividend companies to invest in, look for the following characteristics:

- The company should be an established company and should produce stable cash flow for a long time.
- The company should not have rejected or reduced its dividends at any time in its history. Businesses have to go through different economic cycles all the time—like economic expansion, slow downs, recessions, and depressions—and the company should have survived in all the difficult economic cycles.
- If the company has a history of repeatedly raising dividends, it is a great company to invest in for dividends.

For a higher dividend yield, dividend investors need to look for market sell-off to buy stock in dividend-paying companies. In the fourth quarter of 2008 and the first quarter of 2009, a lot of dividend-paying stocks were reduced to very low prices. Whoever bought the shares at those low prices might have captured the highest dividend yield.

There are many great dividend-paying companies out there. Here, we look at Coca-Cola's (KO) dividends:

Year	Dividend
2000	$0.68
2001	$0.72
2002	$0.80
2003	$0.88
2004	$1.00
2005	$1.12
2006	$1.24
2007	$1.36
2008	$1.52
2009	$1.64

The dividend increased 9.2 percent per year compounded annually for the last 10 years. The dividend has been paid since 1893 and the dividend yield is 2.70 percent. Coca-Cola is still a growth company and investors can get capital appreciation from stock holdings.

Now we look at Goodyear Tire's (GT) dividend information. I wanted dividend information for the last 10 years, but GT has not paid a dividend since 2002.

Year	Dividend
2000	$1.20
2001	$1.02
2002	$0.48

Look at the dividend trend; it decreased instead of increasing. GT failed on this checklist item.

What Is the Percentage of Earnings Paid as a Dividend?
Is It a Small Percentage of the Revenue?

When investors try to analyze the dividend stocks, they need to search for the companies that pay out a smaller percentage of their revenue as dividends to the shareholders. This is because when the business goes through a hard time, it should have a cushion of earnings to meet the dividend payments. If not, it needs to cut the dividends to preserve cash to fight the downturn. This is called the payout ratio.

$$\text{Payout ratio} = \text{Dividend per share} \div$$
$$\text{Earnings per share as a percentage}$$

The lower the payout ratio the better. For example, if you come across a payout ratio at around 50 percent, this means the company has to pay 50 percent of the earnings as a dividend to the shareholders. You have a 50 percent cushion in earnings to withstand any business downturn. On the other hand, if the business payout ratio is around 80 to 90 percent, that is very dangerous because there is only a 10 to 20 percent cushion available. When the business goes through a recessionary economic cycle, business earnings might decrease more than 20 percent. At those times, the dividend needs to be cut. That is not a good position for dividend investors. When the company announces dividend cuts, the stock price gets hammered. As dividend investors, that is like getting hit on both sides, losing dividend income and also losing principal invested amount.

Now we look out the payout ratio for Coca-Cola for the last 10 years.

Year	Payout Ratio
2000	77%
2001	45%
2002	50%
2003	50%
2004	50%
2005	55%
2006	57%
2007	53%
2008	61%
2009	56%

The average payout ratio for Coca-Cola over the last 10 years is 55.4 percent.

This is a good payout ratio. Coca-Cola has been paying dividends since 1893 and dividends have increased 9.2 percent over the last 10 years. Coca-Cola passes the dividend checklist item with flying colors. Coca-Cola is still a growth company, so there will be capital appreciation well into the future too.

CHAPTER

13

Stock Research Checklist—Assets

Trying to identify companies that have hidden assets that are over-looked by Wall Street is beneficial because those stocks trade cheaper, meaning you can get more reward by investing in them.

Does the Company Have Any Hidden Assets
That Have Been Overlooked by Wall Street?

For example, look at natural resource companies that specialize in resources such as gold. During 2009 and 2010, gold prices soared. The reason for the price hike was Federal Reserve quantitative easing, which increased demand from China and India and caused a lack in supply. Because of the gold price increase, gold mining stocks soared.

Sometimes, Wall Street does not recognize the value of those reserves and it misprices the securities. For those situations, you need to use the opportunity to buy the securities at discount prices. When commodity prices are in a downturn, people think that prices are going to stay the same. So, tired of waiting, they sell their stocks at the lowest prices. When the commodity prices start to recover, whoever bought the shares at the lowest prices is going to earn a high return on their investment.

Established brand names are another form of hidden assets Take Coca-Cola (KO), for example. When you are looking at the Coca-Cola balance sheet you do not see the dollar figure for Coke's brand name. But, think about the value of Coke's brand name, which has been around for more than 100 years and is the result of many pricey marketing campaigns. In my opinion, Coke's brand name is going to dominate for another 100 years in the soft-drink market.

Another form of hidden assets is real estate. For example, take McDonald's again; we know it is a fast-food company serving burgers. But, whenever it started its franchise operation, McDonald's owned the land beneath its restaurants and leased the land to the franchises. McDonald's then watched the land value appreciate over time. Also, McDonald's collected rent over the years while its many land parcels appreciated. On the balance sheet, those real estate investments might already have been written off.

During the 1960s, 1970s, and 1980s, newspapers also had these kinds of hidden assets. Consider single-newspaper towns; the towns' readers needed to subscribe to them and the towns' advertisers needed to use them to advertise their products and services. The newspapers were able to raise the prices and still not lose customers. But, as we all know, newspapers' dominance have changed because of the technology.

Warren Buffett wants to own businesses with hidden assets:

> A sore point was the rumor that Buffett had said owning a monopoly newspaper was like owning an unregulated bridge. When the comment came up in court, Buffett said:
>
> "I have said in an inflationary world that a toll bridge would be a great thing to own if it was un-regulated."
>
> "Why?" asked the opposing attorney.
>
> "Because you have laid out the capital costs. You build the bridge in old dollars and you don't have to keep replacing it."[1]

Does the Company Have a Low Percentage of Net Receivables?

The money owed to a company by customers is referred to as *receivable*. Net receivable means total receivables minus bad debt.

If the company is in a sustainable competitive position, it should have fewer net receivables as a percentage of revenue because it can collect the receivables from the customers faster.

On the other hand, if the company is in a competitive business, it can give more time to the customers to pay back the receivables in order to keep the customers happy. For example, take the information technology (IT) consulting field. Vendors supply the contractors to the customers. The consultants provide the time sheet to the consulting company at the end of every month. The company needs to send invoices to the customers. The customer pays back that money in 30 days, which is the norm in the IT consulting industry. The company needs to pay the consultant biweekly or monthly as per the contract with the consultant. So, what does the consulting company do? They borrow the money from the bank credit line in order to the pay the consultant. When they receive the payment from the customer, they pay back the bank credit line.

This is a very competitive industry; there are no high barriers to entry. Anyone can start a consulting company and supply the contractors as long as they have contact with the customer. Suppose another vendor comes to the customer and says they can supply the contractors and are willing to give 60-day invoices. The customers will like that because they can pay slowly.

Now, what can the previous company do? They have to match the 60-day invoices or provide the consultants a lower rate than the new vendor. Otherwise the current vendor is going to lose the customer to the new vendor. To gain new business, the new vendor can also reduce his consultants' rates below those of the existing vendor. The competitive war continues; the vendors lose all their profit margins and even get into loss. So you see, it would behoove you to avoid this kind of competitive business.

If you see a high amount of net receivables as a percentage of the revenue, try to examine that company's situation carefully. If you see a sudden increase in receivables, that is a problem because the company's products may not be in great demand. The company needs to give more time to dealers or distributors to pay back their invoices in order to stock their products.

Another thing you need to calculate is the rate of net-receivable growth compared to sales growth. For example, if the sales grow at 10 percent per year, the receivables should also grow at the same percentage. But, if the sales grow at 10 percent a year and the net receivables grow at 20 percent a year, then that is a problem because the company is giving more time to their customers to pay back the invoice in order to increase sales. That is not a good sign.

Now we can calculate KO's net receivables as a percentage of revenue for the last eight years. I am using eight years here because 10 years worth of data was not available.

Year	Net Receivables	Revenue	Net Receivables/Revenue (%)
2002	$2,152	$19,564	11.00
2003	$2,152	$20,857	10.32
2004	$2,313	$21,742	10.64
2005	$2,353	$23,104	10.18
2006	$2,650	$24,088	11.00
2007	$3,373	$28,857	11.69
2008	$3,141	$31,944	9.83
2009	$3,813	$30,990	12.30

Numbers are in millions.

Average percent of net receivables/revenue for the last 8 years is 10.87 percent

If you look at the last eight years' net receivables as a percentage of revenue, it was around 10 to 12 percent and averaged around 10.87 percent, which is great.

Now we can calculate the rate of revenue growth and net receivables growth for the last eight years.

Percent of revenue growth rate is 5.91 percent.

Percent of receivables growth rate is 7.41 percent.

There is difference between net receivables and revenue growth rate, which is 1.5 percent (7.41 percent – 5.91 percent).

Now we can repeat the same exercise for Goodyear Tire (GT).

Year	Net Receivables	Revenue	Net Receivables/Revenue (%)
2002	$1,540	$13,856	11.00
2003	$2,745	$15,102	18.18
2004	$3,542	$18,353	19.30
2005	$3,288	$18,098	18.17
2006	$2,898	$18,751	15.46
2007	$3,191	$19,644	16.24
2008	$2,610	$19,488	13.39
2009	$2,650	$16,301	16.26

Numbers are in millions.

If you look at the last eight years, net receivables as a percentage of revenue was around 11 to 19 percent and averaged about 16.01 percent.

Now we can calculate the rate of revenue growth and net receivables growth for the last eight years.

Percent of revenue growth rate is 2.05 percent

Percent of receivables growth rate is 7.02 percent

There is difference between net receivables and revenue growth rate, which is 4.97 percent (7.02 percent − 2.05 percent).

Now we can compare KO's numbers with those of GT.

Percent of net receivables divided by revenue:

KO is 10.87 percent

GT is 16.01 percent

The difference between net receivables and revenue growth rate is rate:

KO is 1.5 percent

GT is 4.97 percent

You can easily see that KO is better than GT in this checklist item.

Does the Company Have More Pension Assets than Vested Benefits?

Certain companies provide pension and health benefits to their former employees after their service with the company. These kinds of benefits improve the loyalty and retention of existing employees, which is great for the employees but not for the shareholders. When U.S. companies are factoring these costs into their finished products, they are not competitive enough to win the market share or withhold their existing market share internationally (not all countries provide these kinds of benefits). If a company operates in a competitive industry, that makes it even more difficult for the company's survival.

For example, GM filed bankruptcy in 2009 to save the pension costs, which add $2,700 to the cost per vehicle. Japanese and Korean companies do not provide these kinds of benefits, causing their cost structure to be more effective when compared to U.S. auto manufacturers. That is one major reason why Toyota and Honda have gained market share in the United States and around the world, while GM and Chrysler filed for bankruptcy. Ford was a survivor because it could negotiate smaller benefit contracts with employee labor unions.

Nowadays, tech companies and other service industries do not provide pension benefits. That is why their liabilities are less. You can look for a company that does not have pension plans. Or, if you like a company with a pension plan and it is one that passed the other checklist items, that is acceptable. But, make sure the pension assets are higher than the vested benefits. When the company's pension assets are less than the vested benefits, the company needs to pay that difference, which is pure liability for the company.

Normally, pension assets are invested in the equity and debt markets. When the market mood swings, the value of pension assets decreases or increases. You need to read the annual report to find out the amount of pension assets and vested benefits and how much money the company contributed to the pension assets last year.

KO contributed around $269 million to the pension assets in 2009 because pension plan assets had decreased. Here is the content from KO's 2009 annual report:

> The significant decline in the equity markets and in the valuation of other assets precipitated by the recent global credit crisis and related financial system instability affected the value of our pension plan assets. In spite of improving asset values in 2009, the fair value of our plan assets remains lower than pre-crisis levels, and this could lead to higher pension expense in the future. As a result of the decline in the fair value of our pension plan assets and a decrease in the discount rate used to calculate pension benefit obligations, we made contributions of $269 million to our U.S. and international pension plans in 2009 and will consider making additional contributions in 2010 and beyond.

Now we can look out how much GT contributed to pension assets in 2009. Here is the information from GT's 2009 annual report:

> During 2009, our domestic pension fund experienced market gains, which increased plan assets by $699 million and decreased net actuarial losses included in Accumulated Other Comprehensive Loss ("AOCL") by $464 million. As a result, annual domestic net periodic pension cost will decrease to approximately $200 million to $225 million in 2010 from $300 million

in 2009, primarily due to expected returns on higher plan assets and amortization of lower net actuarial losses from AOCL.

A significant portion of the net actuarial loss included in AOCL of $2,311 million in our U.S. pension plans as of December 31, 2009 is a result of 2008 plan asset losses and the overall decline in U.S. discount rates over time. For purposes of determining our 2009 U.S. net periodic pension expense, our funded status was such that we recognized $154 million of the net actuarial loss in 2009.We would recognize approximately $135 million of net actuarial losses in 2010. If our future experience is consistent with our assumptions as of December 31, 2009, actuarial loss recognition will remain at an amount near that to be recognized in 2010 over the next few years before it begins to gradually decline.

Are Any Large Shareholders or Raiders Working to Uncover the Value of the Under-Valued Asset Plays?

As discussed earlier, when you are looking at asset plays, there may be hidden assets in the company, as but, the market may value the business less than it is actually worth. The market might not be able to identify the hidden asset or assets that you identified (or the value might have been ignored by Wall Street). If you get into those asset plays, you might not be able to reap the benefits, because the market may take years to reflect the true value of the company.

Suppose a large shareholder or raider is working to uncover the value of the company; this can be a good thing. The shareholder or raider may engage in a legal battle or takeover war with the company. The board and management are pressured to act in order to unlock the value of the company. When that happens, as a fellow shareholder you can reap the benefits sooner and use the money to invest in other under-valued opportunities.

CHAPTER

14

Stock Research Checklist—Inventory

In business, inventory is an incredibly important part of the process. After the manufacturing process is completed and the product is ready to market or sell to the customers, a business is left with inventory.

What Is the Inventory Buildup?

As an investor, you need to calculate the inventory level as a percentage of sales and compare that with multiple year numbers. Suppose inventory grows faster than sales. That should raise a red flag because it means the sales growth rate is slowing. To reduce the inventory, the company needs to offer higher discounts on their products, which will affect the bottom-line earnings of the company.

In the retail business, you need to pay special attention to the inventory levels compared with those of previous years. If the inventory grows faster than sales for a particular product, it means customers might have lost interest in that product. The company needs to improve the product or sell at fire-sale prices to reduce the inventory.

For example, look at Skechers (SKX), shown in Figure 14.1; it introduced toning shoes and claimed that when people wore them and walked, they would lose more weight. That market slogan created a higher demand for Skechers toning shoes. The company revenue increased and stock reached a multi-year high in June 2010 at $44.90 per share.

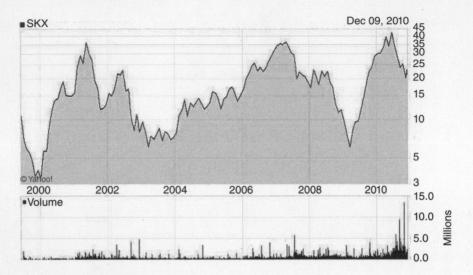

Figure 14.1   SKX Chart

Because of the toning-shoe success, big competitors started to introduce toning shoes of their own, which put pressure on the Skechers brand. When the demand was great, the company manufactured more shoes. When the competition came in, demand fell and big customers cancelled previously placed orders. Due to cancellations, the level of inventory was very high.

The inventory was around $189 million in March 2010, $219 million in June 2010, and around $326 million in September 2010. That is a 72 percent jump from March 2010 to September 2010. The stock fell from $44.90 per share in June 2010 to $19 per share in October 2010, a 57 percent drop in stock price within five months.

During a conference call, the company announced it would take a couple of quarters to clear out the excess inventory. As usual, Wall Street overreacted and knocked down shares to $19 per share. The stock was trading at a price-to-earnings (P/E) ratio of around 6.5. That was very cheap for a fast grower like Skechers. Long-term investors should use this kind of opportunity to buy stock in Skechers. I got into the position at around $20 per share in November 2010. In a couple of quarters, the inventory buildup will clear and the company should be able to maintain appropriate inventory levels.

Stock Research Checklist—
Share Buybacks

Market capitalization is calculated using the number of diluted shares multiplied with the share price of the stock.

Market cap of the company = Diluted share count × Share price

For example, the market cap for a company with a $1 million diluted share count at $10 per share would be $10 million because $1 million multiplied by 10 is $10 million.

When a company is expanding or getting into trouble, it can raise capital by issuing equity or debt. When a company issues new shares, share dilution occurs. This can be detrimental to the existing shareholders. On the other hand, when a company is successful and generating enough profit, it can finance its expansion plans through its cash flow. You should be interested in that kind of company.

Are the Company's Total Outstanding Shares Decreasing over Time?

Dilution can also occur because of existing senior management's option grants. When a company's senior management's compensation consists of salary plus incentive-option grants, senior management and shareholder interests are aligned. But, in some companies the compensation committee approves a boatload of options to the senior management without increasing the bottom line of the company. In order to determine if this is happening, you need to read the proxy statements very carefully. When the board of directors and management are shareholder friendly, they have an option plan tied to improving the company's bottom line. The company at least buys back the management's option dilution so that outside shareholder shares will not get diluted. When a company does not buy back, that can be acceptable too; up to three percent dilution per year is acceptable.

Shareholder-friendly companies do not allocate a higher level of option grants to their senior management. Look at Berkshire Hathaway; the company does not have an option plan for senior management. Buffett's operating company managers receive cash bonuses based on their performance. They in turn invest that cash in Berkshire Hathaway shares. Therefore, management's intention is to improve shareholder value.

Average diluted shares outstanding for Coca-Cola (KO):

2006: 2,350 million shares
2009: 2,329 million shares

There were 21 million fewer shares in 2009 than in 2006, which is a good thing. Existing shareholders gained more ownership of the company in 2009 with existing shareholders' ownership increasing by 0.29 percent annually.

Average diluted shares outstanding for Goodyear Tire (GT):

2006: 177.3 million shares
2009: 241.5 million shares

There were 64.2 million more shares in 2009 when compared with 2006. Existing shareholder ownership was diluted more. Existing shareholder ownership diluted 10.85 percent annually.

When comparing KO and GT, KO existing shareholder ownership increased 0.29 percent annually, which is a small percentage, but compared to GT's 10.85 percent dilution, KO's increase is a good thing. KO passed this checklist item.

Has the Company Bought Back Shares Recently?

When a company generates a high cash flow for many years, cash and cash equivalents will increase, which allows it to do multiple things with the earnings. For instance, a company could do the following:

- It can invest in existing business and generate above average return.
- When management does not have the above opportunity, it can elect to pay the dividend to shareholders, though the dividend will be taxed at 15 percent to the investors.
- It can acquire other businesses and improve its earnings, which increases the price of stock so that shareholders get rewarded by way of capital appreciation.
- It can buy back shares.

If a company's return on invested capital is better than historical average and it has the opportunity to earn more than at least 15 percent, it should invest the money to improve the existing business. That is the prudent decision. That is why each and every large-cap company is grown from small operations. But, after reaching a certain size, the companies do not have sufficient opportunities to compound the dollars at a high rate. In those situations, companies need to look for other opportunities.

The next thing for the business is to acquire other businesses and grow. But, the business should have the skills and management expertise to integrate the acquired company and effectively manage the combined business.

When a company does not have any opportunities to acquire above-average returns by generating new business or through the existing business, and it is not generating a great return on its invested capital, returning money to the shareholders is a prudent thing to do. But the shareholders will have to pay a dividend tax on their income. After the tax, the shareholders can invest that money into another business, possibly one that generates more than a 15 percent return on their invested capital.

The next best thing is for the company to buy back shares, if, of course, the existing business is generating an above-average return. This way, the total count of diluted outstanding shares will reduce and existing shareholder ownership will increase. This is the easiest way to improve the shareholders' return. During the market sell-off, most of the stocks reached extremely low levels irrespective of a company's fundamentals. At those times, the company can buy back the shares to improve shareholder ownership. This is what happened in the fourth quarter of 2008 and the first quarter of 2009.

The companies that bought back shares during those turbulent times invested that capital prudently.

You can identify the prudence of a company's management by examining at what price management is buying back the shares. If they are paying *more* than intrinsic value of the business, that is not a good thing. If they are buying back the shares at *less* than the intrinsic value of the business, that is a great thing.

During Berkshire Hathaway's annual meetings, the same question about buying back Berkshire Hathaway shares nearly always gets repeated. Buffett's constant reply is something along the lines of, *if I feel Berkshire Hathaway trades at a deep discount to the intrinsic value and if I do not have any other opportunity to invest or acquire other businesses to generate more of a return than Berkshire Hathaway, then I would buy back the shares.*

Does the Company Have Any Treasury Stock on its Balance Sheet?

Treasury stocks can be created in two ways:

1. A company can buy back the shares from the open market and keep it in the Treasury for later use.
2. The company shares are initially issued, but not all the shares are issued to the public.

To determine this, you can look at the balance sheet. If the company has any treasury stock, that is usually a good thing because the existing shareholder ownership should be increasing. If you find that numbers of the treasury stocks are increasing over a period of a time, that is an added advantage. This means the company has a history of share buybacks. It does not mean you have to reject that company if it does not own treasury stock. When the company generates a positive cash flow, it can invest in the business and improve the future earnings of the company or it can buy back the shares to increase existing shareholder ownership in the company.

Now we can calculate the treasury stock information for KO for the last three years (these data are readily available):

2007: $23,375
2008: $24,213
2009: $25,398
All the numbers are in millions.

Look at the treasury stock information; it was growing from 2007 to 2009, which is a good thing because it means the company is buying back shares regularly.

The growth rate of treasury stock for the last three years is 2.80 percent per year.

These kinds of buybacks increase shareholder value over the long term; no wonder Buffett keeps KO as one of his permanent holdings.

We cannot look at the GT balance sheet for this item because there is no treasury stock present from 2007 to 2009. The company did not buy back any shares in the last three years.

Does the Company Have a Retirement of Stock on Its Balance Sheet?

This is related to the share buybacks. After a company purchases stock from the open market, instead of keeping it in the Treasury, it can retire the stock. If it keeps it in the Treasury, those shares can be reissued later to raise capital.

If you see the retirement of stock value on a company's balance sheet, that is a good thing because the company is confident that it does not need to issue new shares to raise capital in the near future.

I could not find any entries for the retirement of stock in either KO or GT, which is a negative, but not a large negative.

CHAPTER

Stock Research Checklist—Insiders

No one knows a company better than insiders. Therefore, you need to give special attention to insider buying activity.

Did an Insider Buy the Stock Recently?

Insiders buying the company stock may mean one of the following:

- Insiders feel that the company's stock is undervalued compared to the company's intrinsic value.
- The company stock price is fairly valued, but the insiders feel that the company's future prospect is going to improve significantly. Therefore, the current price is going to be a bargain when you are considering future earnings.

Basically, insiders think that the current price of the stock is undervalued and that is why they are buying their own company's stock. You need to take these activities as a positive event. When you are analyzing companies, if you see that many insiders bought the stock recently, that is a great thing. This information is easy to come by; you can get insider activity on all of the major financial web sites.

On finance.yahoo.com, type the stock symbol, click "Get Quotes", go to the *ownership* section, and then *insider transactions*, and you can get information on transactions performed by the insiders. You can click on the insider's name and you can check that insider's

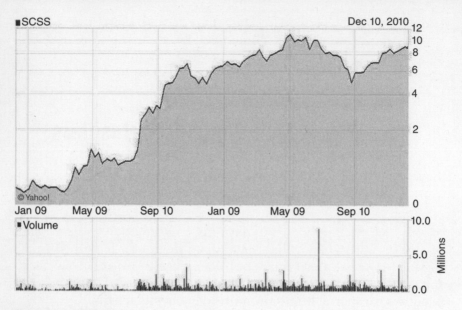

Figure 16.1   SCSS Chart

historic transactions. Most of the time, the stock price improves within 3 to 12 months of the insider purchase date.

Here is a real life example: I generated about 20 times my fund's initial investment in Select Comfort Corp. (SCSS), which I bought during the financial crisis. I got into the position for an average purchase price of around $0.45 per share during the fourth quarter of 2008 and the first quarter of 2009. I sold those shares at around $9 per share in July 2010, which made for a 2,000 percent return in 18 months. (See Figure 16.1.)

After I sold the shares at $9 per share in July 2010, SCSS stock kept coming down even though there was nothing wrong with the company. Remember, there were non-company events such as the Europe debt crisis and fears of a double-dip recession that made the market go down. I was closely monitoring the stock, which reached $4.92 per share in August 2010.

On August 27, 2010, insider Jean-Michel Valette bought 25,000 shares at the average price of $5.25 per share by investing around $130,000. I took notice and researched the company based on the checklist items described in this chapter. I got into the position around $6.25 per share in September 2010. At the writing of this chapter in December 2010, the stock was trading at around $9.18 per share, which is a 46.88 percent increase within four months of my second purchase price. If you had bought at the same price as the insider price at $5.25 per share, the return would have been 74.85 percent in four months. This checklist item does not mean you should blindly follow insider purchases; a company still needs to pass the stock research checklist items.

Similarly, insider selling should not automatically be considered a negative activity, because insiders might have sold for different reasons, such as personal expenses, divesting from one investment to another, or to raise cash to buy a company's stock options. Insiders have a stock-option plan that allows them to sell only a certain percentage of their options each year. Also, the Securities and Exchange Commission (SEC) restricts them to selling only during a particular timeframe because they need to use that timeframe to raise cash for their personal needs. But, insider-buying activity indicates that they think the current price of the stock is undervalued and it is going to go up. That is why they are investing their personal money in that stock.

Do the Insiders Own a High Percentage of the Company?

You can check insider ownership information on most of the major financial web sites. When you are dealing with small-cap and mid-cap companies, the founder (or founder's family) most likely owns the major portion of the company. But when you are dealing with large-cap companies, insider ownership will be small.

When the insiders own a major portion of a company's stocks, it is usually very good for the existing shareholders. Here are the some of the reasons:

- Insiders' and shareholders' interests are totally aligned. Since they own a higher percentage of the company, they feel like they are running their own company and work hard to improve the bottom line of the company. When they invest, they invest for the long term. Those kinds of initiatives make the revenue and bottom-line earnings grow faster. Obviously, that growth reflects in the stock price. Their net worth increases with the existing shareholders' net worth.

- Normally founders and insiders do not trade their holdings frequently; they have a restricted time period and also they know the long-term potential of the company. When the largest shareholders hold their stock, there is a smaller percentage of stock floating in the marketplace. When the demand picks up, the stock price increases very fast.
- There will be stability in the company. There will not be any hostile takeover situations to deal with because fighting back hostile takeover situations is a time-consuming and costly process.

For example, take iGATE Corporation (IGTE),[1] one of the best stocks in the information technology service sector, which generated a great return to the fund.

Major shareholders:[2]

Breakdown	
Percent of Shares Held by All Insider and 5 Percent Owners:	49%
Percent of Shares Held by Institutional and Mutual Fund Owners:	45%
Percent of Float Held by Institutional and Mutual Fund Owners:	88%
Number of Institutions Holding Shares:	102

Major Direct Holders (Forms 3 and 4):

Holder	Shares	Reported
TRIVEDI ASHOK	10,714,082	Nov 2, 2010
WADHWANI SUNIL	10,106,551	Nov 2, 2010
MURTHY PHANEESH	217,829	Jul 22, 2010
TRUSSELL JASON	118,124	Oct 19, 2010
NARAYANAN SEAN SURESH	71,282	Oct 19, 2010

Look at the company's major shareholders: they are all insiders, and 5 percent of stock owners collectively hold around 49 percent of the company, with the company founders owning the bulk of this stock.

Ashok Trivedi and Sunil Wadhwani are the founders of this company and built it from a small information technology consulting company to a billion-dollar company. The company growth increased after they hired Phaneesh Murthy from Infosys, and in 2011, iGATE acquired 75 percent of Patni Computer Systems LTD, another offshore solution provider with a market cap of $1.35 billion.

IGTE clearly satisfies the following three advantages:

1. Shareholders' and insiders' interests are aligned. Company management tries to increase the share price as much as possible because their net worth is tied up with the company.
2. There is less stock floating around in the market place.
3. No hostile takeover is possible.

IGTE is a mid-cap kind of company (as mentioned earlier, you do not find large insider ownership percentages in large-cap stocks). Because the company market cap was so high, the founders' and insiders' percentages will be much lower. At Berkshire Hathaway, Warren Buffett owns 36 percent of the company's stock. He worked all his life to increase the net worth of the company and himself. During that time, existing shareholder net worth also increased. When you keep three or four companies in your portfolio for the long term and the companies grow at a decent clip, you can earn a fortune in your lifetime.

Now we can look at the insider ownership information for Coca-Cola (KO):

Breakdown	
Percent of Shares Held by All Insider and 5 Percent Owners:	5%
Percent of Shares Held by Institutional and Mutual Fund Owners:	64%
Percent of Float Held by Institutional and Mutual Fund Owners:	67%
Number of Institutions Holding Shares:	1,344

Major Direct Holders (Forms 3 and 4):

Holder	Shares	Reported
KEOUGH DONALD R /NY	4,537,338	Dec 31, 2009
ALLEN HERBERT A	N/A	Mar 1, 2010
DILLER BARRY	1,401,000	Nov 11, 2010
ISDELL E NEVILLE	785,365	Feb 19, 2009
REYES JOSE OCTAVIO	88,050	Feb 18, 2010

Now look at the insider information for Goodyear Tire (GT):

Breakdown	
Percent of Shares Held by All Insider and 5 Percent Owners:	0%
Percent of Shares Held by Institutional and Mutual Fund Owners:	81%
Percent of Float Held by Institutional and Mutual Fund Owners:	81%
Number of Institutions Holding Shares:	313

Major Direct Holders (Forms 3 and 4):

Holder	Shares	Reported
KEEGAN ROBERT J	403,578	Sep 30, 2010
KRAMER RICHARD J	179,591	Feb 25, 2010
RUOCCO JOSEPH B	111,875	Aug 26, 2010
COHADE PIERRE E	104,070	Feb 25, 2010
HARVIE C THOMAS	76,611	Aug 7, 2009

Five percent insider ownership in Coca-Cola is higher than the negligible ownership in Goodyear Tire.

17

Stock Research Checklist—Institutional

As an investor, you need to find the undervalued stocks that are being ignored by the Wall Street analysts. This does not necessarily mean that highly followed companies are not good investments, though. When you find the small- and mid-cap companies that are ignored by Wall Street, their stocks might be selling for bargain prices, and that kind of entry price can lead to higher investment returns.

Is the Company not Followed Closely by Wall Street Analysts?

Warren Buffett and Peter Lynch are two great investors who are very interested in finding under-followed companies rather than widely followed companies. When Warren Buffett ran his partnership, he invested in under-followed companies, which generated great returns for his partnership because the entry prices were very low. For example, he invested in Sanborn Maps with the stock priced at $45 but the company portfolio alone was worth $65 per share; the map business was thrown in for free. The company was under followed and no one noticed the bargain price because the institutions and investing public are always busy chasing hot sectors and highly followed companies. Buffett bought enough shares to gain seat on the board, where he pressed the company to liquidate its portfolio. The company agreed to use portfolio proceeds to buy out stockholders and Buffett made a 50 percent profit.

When Warren Buffett attended a Columbia Business School event with Bill Gates in late 2009, he was asked how he finds out about under-valued companies. Buffett responded by saying that, in early years, he read Moody's manual page-by-page at least twice. No one is going to tell you about those under-valued companies; you have to search for and find the great investment opportunities yourself. If you would like to replicate Warren Buffett's success, you should put that kind of hard work into searching for under-valued companies.

Peter Lynch used to visit companies as part of his stock research process. He was (and still is) very interested in finding under-valued companies. When he liked a company on paper, he visited it to try and understand more about the company and meet the management in person. Whenever he learned that no analysts recently visited the company, he would become even more excited. He knew that if he could get the stock at cheap prices, he might also get the opportunity to join the board early. When you get in at the bottom of a growing company, before Wall Street takes notice, you can gain at least 10 times your initial investment if you hold it for the long term. When a company's success grows and reaches $1 billion in revenue, many Wall Street firms are going to publish analyst reports for that company, and suddenly institutions will want to own a part of it. Therefore, stock prices go up.

On the other hand, look at the over-followed companies like Wal-Mart and Google. More than 30 Wall Street firms follow these companies and publish analyst reports. Each and every detail of the company is made available to the prospective institutions and general public. Finding under-valued securities in this space is more difficult than under-followed companies. That does not mean over-followed companies are not suitable for investment. Because of stock-market euphoria, discount to intrinsic value opportunity exists, but the percentage of discount to intrinsic value will be less when compared with under-followed companies.

Does the Company Have a Small Percentage of Institutional Ownership?

You need to look for a company that has a low institutional holding because institutions mean bigger hedge funds and mutual funds. These institutions act in lemming-like patterns. All these hedge fund and mutual fund managers work to intimidate one another. If any one of the bigger hedge funds or mutual funds starts dumping a particular stock in a certain industry, everyone will try to do the same. Because these fund managers own vast amounts of stock, when all of them start dumping it, the stock drops very quickly. That is what happened during the recent financial crisis. When Lehman Brothers failed, a great many hedge fund and mutual fund managers started selling all kinds of stocks at the same time, especially financial stocks. There was fear in the market, a feeling that all the failing banks were going to go bankrupt or be taken over by the government. Some of these hedge funds might have been highly leveraged. When the market was coming down, highly leveraged hedge funds might have started dumping the shares to avoid margin calls, in spite of the prices.

Take, for example, the price changes in Citigroup stock. In September 2008, the stock was trading at around $20 per share; in March 2009 it was trading around $0.97 per share. These kinds of price swings happen when all the institutions are selling at the same time. After the government injected money into the company, the stock was trading at around $5.02 per share in September 2009. Whoever bought the stock at $0.97 per share might have made a 517 percent return in six months. Whenever you find less institutional ownership in a stock, that is a good thing because when the market is in a downturn, you do not see a high percentage of loss in your stocks.

CHAPTER

18

Stock Research Checklist—Inflation

Inflation is a kind of tax in this world. As Warren Buffett puts it:

> The arithmetic makes it plain that inflation is a far more devastating tax than anything that has been enacted by our legislature. The inflation tax has been enacted by our legislature. The inflation tax has a fantastic ability to simply consume capital. It makes no difference to a widow with her savings in a 5 percent passbook account whether she pays 100 percent income tax on her interest income during a period of zero inflation, or pays no income taxes during years of 5 percent inflation. Either way, she is "taxed" in a manner that leaves her no real income whatsoever. Any money she spends comes right out of capital. She would find outrageous a 120 percent income tax, but doesn't seem to notice that 5 percent inflation is the economic equivalent.[1]

Is the Company Able to Raise the Price of the Product or Service According to Inflation?

In the normal course of business, the input of raw materials, people's wages, cost of maintenance, and capital investment in the infrastructure increase over time because of inflation. If you are looking at a company that can raise the price of its products to reflect the input costs, then you are looking at a good business.

Most businesses operate in competitive industries and will not be able to increase the price of their products. If they do, they will lose market share to their competitors. In those situations, the company needs to absorb the increase of input costs that will reduce the profit margin. If a business is able to increase the price of its final product or service and it can maintain the profit margin, that is great. If they can increase the price of the profit to more than the inflation rate, then that will be excellent and shareholders will reap the rewards for a long time to come.

For example, commodity businesses like air travel, insurance, and computers are not able to increase the price of their products or services to reflect the increase in inflation price. But, if you take brand name products like Coke or See's Candies, those companies can raise the price of their products more than inflation and not lose market share.

CHAPTER 19

Stock Research Checklist—
Cyclical Company

If you looking at a cyclical stock as a possible investment, you need to first understand the company's cycle and how it relates to the economic cycles. Some companies perform very well when the economy does well and fall rapidly when the economy falls. Those are cyclical stocks.

Do You Understand the Relationship of the Company's Revenue Cycle in Relation to Economic Cycles in a Cyclical Company?

We can divide goods or services into two different categories: necessities and luxuries. Companies that are involved in creating or providing services as necessities are called non-cyclical companies. For example, food, health care, auto and home insurance, electricity, water, and gas are necessities.

Companies that produce luxury items or services are cyclical companies. People can postpone the purchase of these kinds of products. Cyclical products include automobiles, vacations, jewelry, furniture, and many more.

Cyclical stocks perform well during early economic recovery and economic expansion. Revenue starts to fall during the start of an economic slowdown and during a recession and reaches bottom before the economy starts to recover.

To make money in cyclical stocks, you need to get in at the early part of the recovery, hold the shares until the economy begins to expand, and sell the shares before the economy starts to slow, when the company is in peak. You may lose some of the stock's upside, but that is acceptable because you do not want to lose the gains that you already made.

When the economy starts to slow, revenue at these cyclical companies drops faster. Before that happens, your cyclical stock might have lost most of its gains, because the market tries to predict what will happen six months into the future. But not everyone is able to predict the economic cycle perfectly. You do not want to sell when everyone is selling; you want to sell the stock when everyone wants to own.

Let's look at the net income numbers for Ford (see Figure 19.1) during the economic expansion years and recession years so that you can see how the stocks of cyclical industries behave in relation to economic cycles.

Year	Net Income
2000	$5,410
2001	−$5,453
2002	$284
2003	$921
2004	$3,634
2005	$2,228
2006	−$12,615
2007	−$2,764
2008	−$14,580
2009	$2,694
2010	$6,667 (Fourth Quarter 2010 is estimated)

Numbers are in millions

Look at the net income numbers, which decreased from $5.4 billion from year 2000 to a loss of $5.4 billion in 2001 because of the recession. If you would have waited until the company posted a real loss, you might have lost 50 percent of your stock price within one year. The economy was improving from 2002 to 2005, but in 2006, Ford lost $12.6 billion dollars and went on to lose $14.5 billion dollars in 2008.

After the first quarter of 2009, the government introduced the "cash for clunkers" program and the auto industry started showing signs of life. GM and Chrysler filed for bankruptcy and requested help from the government; Ford did not request it. The economy

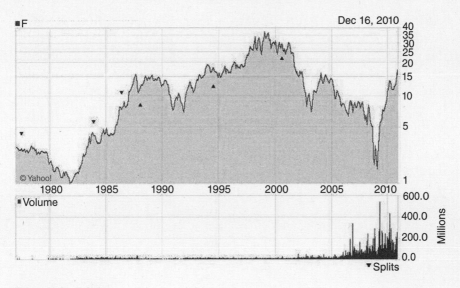

Figure 19.1   F Chart

Reproduced with permission of Yahoo! Inc. ©2011 Yahoo! Inc. YAHOO! and the YAHOO! logo
are registered trademarks of Yahoo! Inc. Reproduced with permission of CSI ©2009. Data Source: CSI
www.csidata.com/.

started recovering during the second quarter of 2009 and slowly
increased in 2010. Ford released three quarters of financial numbers
in 2010, and is yet to release the fourth quarter of 2010 (as of the
writing of this book). Based on a fourth-quarter estimate, Ford is
likely going to earn $6.6 billion for the full year.

The stock price increased from as low as $1.01 in October 2008
to as high as $17.42 per share in November 2010. That is a 1,724
percent return in 13 months. If you know the economic cycles and
cyclical industries, you can make a great deal of money by buying
and selling at the appropriate times. To make money, you do not
need to buy at the exact bottom and sell at the exact highest price,
if you buy and sell within the range of values, you can make lot of
money.

You need to sell cyclical stocks during the peak because everyone
wants to own these stocks because the underlying companies are
generating maximum revenues and earnings numbers at that time.
If you stay firm for a long time, you will almost always lose your
capital gains, and also part of your invested capital. Even if the stock
goes up after you sell the position, do not kick yourself; it will ultimately come down. When you are buying, buy before the economy

starts to recover. At that time, your main concern should be whether or not the company was able to avoid bankruptcy. If you are confident that the company has sufficient assets to withstand a couple more brutal years, then you can invest at that time. If you are not sure, you can wait until signs of an early economic recovery begin to appear. You may lose some bargain entry price, but that is okay as long as you buy during the slow economic-recovery cycle.

CHAPTER

20

Stock Research Checklist—Turnaround

You can make a great deal of money if you are able to get into successful turnaround situations and hold the stock until the business returns to a normal operating environment. When a company deteriorates from a successful company to a difficult situation, everyone wants to get out. No one will be there to buy the stocks and the price declines will be enormous. Sometimes, prices can fall more than 90 percent from a previous peak. If the company survives from that downturn, whoever got in at the bargain price stands to earn a great deal of money.

Has the Company Taken the Following Steps to Turn the Business Around?

Consider a company that has stock trading at around $10 per share when it is operating in a normal environment. When the economy falls into a recession and the company falls into a difficult situation, it loses 90 percent of the stock price and is trading at around $1 per share. After careful analysis, you feel that the company will survive the downturn and you get into the position at $1 per share. The company slowly starts to recover. The rate of recovery tells you that it will take another three years before the company is able to generate the same kind of revenue it did pre-recession. You can reasonably assume that the market will give the same kind of valuation as a normal revenue generating capacity, so that a $10 per share price reached in three years is a total return of 900 percent, which is a 115.44 percent compounded annual return.

You may believe the recovery in the previous scenario is overly aggressive and that the company will probably generate only half of the revenue in three years when compared with its pre-recession level. So, you are considering the stock trading at around $5 per share in three years, which would be a 400 percent return in year years and a 70.99 percent compounded annual return.

This return is possible because you invested during a severe downturn situation after you determined the company would survive the downturn. You then patiently held the shares until the company came back into a normal business environment. But, if you were wrong, you might have lost 100 percent of your invested capital.

One of the main questions you need to answer is whether the company can survive the current downturn. Find out, is the company doing the following to turn the company around and survive the downturn?

1. Is management cutting costs according to the reduced revenue?
2. Is management putting the company into cash-conservation mode?
3. Is the company able to service existing debt?
4. What is management doing to increase sales in the current environment?
5. If the company has debt with a high interest rate, is management trying to refinance existing debt to a lower interest rate?
6. Is the company selling or spinning off any non-profitable divisions to raise cash to pay down its debt so that it can spend less in interest costs?
7. To handle the company debt problems, is management trying to do a secondary offering to raise equity to pay down the debt?
8. If the company is not able to go to the public market, is management trying to raise equity or subordinated debt from private equity investors?
9. Is the company able to issue long-term maturity bonds and use the proceeds to the pay down existing debt?

If you can answer these nine questions, you can assess whether or not the current management can turn around the company.

If you are able to spot the successful turnaround companies, you can make a tremendous amount of money in a short period of time. The following example applies the nine questions to a turnaround company. Figure 20.1 shows the balance sheet numbers for Select Comfort (SCSS) for year-end 2008.

As per its 2008 annual report, Select Comfort had only $13 million cash on hand, with total current assets of $69.15 million, and

	2008	2007
Assets		
Current Assets:		
Cash and cash equivalents	$ 13,057	$ 7,279
Accounts receivable, net total allowance for doubtful accounts of $713 and $876, respectively	4,939	18,902
Inventories	18,675	32,517
Income taxes receivable	25,900	—
Prepaid expenses	4,109	9,816
Deferred income taxes	1,323	6,796
Other current assets	1,150	3,833
Total current assets	69,153	79,143
Property and equipment, net	53,274	80,409
Deferred income taxes	5,941	25,543
Other assets	7,045	5,394
Total assets	$135,413	$190,489
Liabilities and Shareholders' (Deficit) Equity		
Current liabilities:		
Borrowings under revolving credit facility	$ 79,150	$ 37,890
Accounts payable	40,274	69,775
Customer prepayments	11,480	8,327
Accruals:		
Sales Returns	2,744	3,751
Compensation and benefits	14,575	14,865
Taxes and withholding	2,938	4,812
Other current liabilities	8,256	9,723
Total current liabilities	159,687	149,143
Non-current liabilities:		
Warranty liabilities	5,956	6,747
Capital lease obligations	621	—
Other long-term liabilities	10,779	10,473
Total non-current liabilities	17,356	17,220
Total liabilities	177,043	166,363
Shareholders' (deficit) equity:		
Undesignated preferred stock; 5,000 shares authorized, no shares issued and outstanding	—	—
Common stock, $0.01 par value; 142,500 shares authorized, 44,962 and 44,597 shares issued and outstanding, respectively	450	446
Additional paid-in capital	4,417	—
(Accumulated deficit) retained earnings	(46,497)	23,680
Total shareholders' (deficit) equity	(41,630)	24,126
Total liabilities and shareholders' (deficit) equity	$135,413	$190,489

Figure 20.1   SCSS Balance Sheet[1]

current liabilities of \$159.6 million, and shareholder deficit of \$41.6 million. The company was operating in a difficult situation. Company management was in the process of raising equity from private equity investors and they also received a tax refund of \$25.9 million.

Here is the management discussion about the situation as per the 2008 annual report:

In 2008, following several years of generating positive net income, we realized a net loss of \$70.2 million, including \$34.6 million of asset impairment charges and a \$26.8 million charge for the establishment of a deferred tax valuation allowance. Our 2008 operating results were significantly affected by an industry-wide decrease in consumer spending. While we generated \$3.0 million of operating cash flows in 2008, the decline in our operating performance and the acceleration of the decline of consumer demand in the fourth quarter of 2008 has affected our liquidity.

As of January 3, 2009, we had outstanding borrowings of \$79.2 million, plus \$5.9 million under letters of credit, with an additional \$5.0 million available under our \$90 million credit facility. Pursuant to a series of amendments of our Credit Agreement, the Lenders have deferred to March 31, 2009 a reduction in the amount available under our line of credit from \$90 million to \$85 million that was previously scheduled to become effective as of December 1, 2008. Also pursuant to these amendments, the Lenders have waived compliance, through the close of business on March 30, 2009, with certain financial covenants under the Credit Agreement applicable to fiscal periods ending on or about December 31, 2008, January 31, 2009 and February 28, 2009. In early March 2009, we received a federal income tax refund of approximately \$23.0 million. Pursuant to the terms of the Credit Agreement, these funds have been placed in a cash collateral account with the Lenders. Upon expiration of our most recent amendment on March 30, 2009, we will not be in compliance with certain financial covenants under the credit agreement. If we are unable to continue to obtain amendments from the Lenders that waive compliance with these financial covenants, the Lenders could place us in default under terms of our credit agreement. Even if we obtain amendments to our credit agreement, our business may require additional capital in order to fund our operating needs. A default under the Credit Agreement would enable the Lenders to seek immediate payment in full of any amounts outstanding under the credit facility and to exercise various remedies as secured creditors, which may severely or completely constrain our ability to continue to operate our business and may require us to seek protection from creditors through bankruptcy proceedings. Our uncertain financial position may also disrupt relationships with our suppliers.

We expect macro-economic trends and consumer confidence to remain weak throughout 2009. We have taken significant actions designed to return the company to profitability and generate positive cash flows to fund our business, including: corporate workforce reductions, reduced capital spending, development of plans to close stores, supply chain cost reduction initiatives, reduced media spending, reductions in fixed and discretionary marketing and selling expenses, and ceasing all activities associated with the implementation of SAP®-based information technology applications. We recently introduced lower product price points and initiated an enhanced promotional strategy designed to stabilize sales. However, further expense reductions may be necessary should our 2009 net sales decline at a steeper rate than we currently expect. In addition to actions to align our cost structure with expected sales declines, we have been exploring a range of strategic and financing alternatives to enhance our financial flexibility.

Our ability to continue as a going concern is dependent on various factors, including: macro economic trends, the successful execution of our cost reduction plans, successful negotiation with the Lenders and successful efforts to raise additional capital. Some of these factors are not entirely within our control. These conditions raise substantial doubt about our ability to continue as a going concern.

Our financial statements have been prepared on the going concern basis, which assumes the realization of assets and liquidation of liabilities in the normal course of operations. The consolidated financial statement do not include any adjustments relating to the recoverability or classification of recorded asset amounts or the amounts or classification of liabilities should we be unable to continue as a going concern.

In June 2006, we entered into a Credit Agreement (the "Credit Agreement") with a syndicate of banks (the "Lenders"). The Credit Agreement, as amended to date, provides a revolving credit facility in an aggregate amount of $90 million to be used for general corporate purposes, which amount decreases to $85 million as of March 31, 2009 and to $80 million as of July 1, 2009. The Credit Agreement terminates in June 2010.

The Credit Agreement was amended on February 1, 2008 and on May 30, 2008 to allow greater flexibility under the existing financial covenants, provide additional financial covenants and monthly measurement of financial covenants, modify the credit limit and maturity date, increase the cost of borrowing, provide the Lenders with a collateral security interest in substantially all of our assets and those of our subsidiaries, and impose additional restrictions and covenants with respect to our operations.

We had outstanding borrowings of $79.2 million and $37.9 million, under the credit facility as of January 3, 2009, and December 29, 2007, respectively. We also had outstanding letters of credit of $5.9 million and zero as of January 3, 2009, and December 29, 2007, respectively. Outstanding letters of credit reduce the amounts available under the credit facility. At January 3, 2009, and

(Continued)

December 29, 2007, $5.0 million and $62.1 million, respectively, were available under this credit facility. In early March 2009, we received a federal income tax refund of approximately $23.0 million. Pursuant to the terms of the Credit Agreement, these funds have been placed in a cash collateral account with the Lenders. We are in discussions with the Lenders regarding the potential use or application of these funds to address our near-term liquidity needs.

At January 3, 2009, borrowings under the credit facility bore interest at a floating rate and could be maintained as base rate loans (tied to the prime rate, plus a margin of up to 4.00% or the federal funds rate plus 5.00%) or as Eurocurrency rate loans (tied to LIBOR, plus a margin up to 5.0% depending on our leverage ratio, as defined). We also pay certain facility and agent fees. As of January 3, 2009, and December 29, 2007, interest rates on borrowings outstanding under the Credit Agreement were 6.0% and 5.2%, respectively. We are subject to certain financial covenants under the agreement, including a maximum leverage ratio, a minimum interest coverage ratio, minimum EBITDA requirements, and capital expenditure limits.

By reading this annual report, you can find what the company is doing to turn around from its dire situation. In summary, Select Comfort stated it was:

- Reducing the workforce
- Reducing capital spending
- Closing underperforming stores
- Reducing supply chain cost structure
- Reducing media spending
- Reducing marketing and selling expenses
- Reducing information technology (IT) expenses
- Reducing the product price to increase the revenue
- Talking to private equity investors to raise capital
- Able to get the credit waiver agreement not to violate the existing financial covenants

The company was doing all the necessary actions to turn around. I was closely monitoring how much money the company could save from all of these cost-reduction initiatives

Here is the content from first quarter financial announcement.

Cost Reduction

The company:

- Reduced general and administrative expenses in the quarter by $2.8 million on a year-over-year basis, and reported general and administrative (G&A) expenses as a percent of net sales of 9.6 percent, flat with the prior year;
- Closed 30 stores during the quarter, with plans to close another 25 stores by the end of 2009. These actions, cumulatively, are expected to reduce fixed store costs by approximately $10.0 million in 2009;
- Made significant progress on 2009 supply-chain restructuring initiatives that drive savings of more than $6.0 million in 2009, including logistics resizing and closing the company's Omaha, Neb., facility; and
- Reduced first quarter marketing expense as a percent of net sales from 24.6 percent in 2008 to 17.8 percent in 2009, a 6.8 percentage point improvement.

Preserving Cash

The company:

- Significantly reduced capital expenditures in the quarter by suspending store openings and discontinuing major IT projects. Capital expenditures in the first quarter of 2009 were $1.2 million compared with $10.3 million in the prior-year period.
- "Our progress during the first quarter affirms that we have the right strategies in place for 2009," McLaughlin continued. "While we have accomplished a great deal during the past several months, the Select Comfort team continues to pursue incremental ways to reduce costs, sustain and build our brand, and preserve cash. We believe these efforts also will significantly strengthen the company's prospects for future success when an economic recovery ultimately takes hold."

Cash flows from operating activities were $24.1 million in the first quarter of 2009, which included a $23.0 million tax refund associated with prior-year losses. This compares to operating cash flow in the first quarter of 2008 of $14.6 million. The company reduced capital expenditures to $1.2 million in the first quarter of 2009, compared to $10.3 million in the first quarter of 2008. As of April 4, 2009, cash and cash equivalents totaled $3.1 million, cash restricted under debt agreements totaled $23.0 million, and outstanding borrowings under the company's revolving credit facility totaled $74.3 million. Subsequent to the end of the first quarter, the $23.0 million tax refund that previously had been restricted was used to pay down debt, and current availability of debt under the company's credit facility was reduced by $18 million.

Financial Position

The Company continues to operate under and rely on short-term waivers to comply with certain ongoing bank covenants. During the fourth quarter of 2008 and first quarter of 2009, it entered into amendments to its existing credit agreement and has continued to operate under its borrowing limits as a result of modifications to that agreement. The current amendment under which the company is operating remains in effect through May 8, 2009.

As previously stated, the seasonally low second quarter is expected to increase cash requirements, which will require continued support and future accommodations from the company's bank syndicate. The company has worked closely and cooperatively with its bank syndicate over the past several quarters and expects to continue to do so during the coming months. The company also continues to pursue a range of strategic and financing alternatives to enhance both its short-term and long-term financial flexibility. While the company cannot provide assurance that it will be successful in these pursuits, any strategic or financing alternative has the potential to increase the company's cost of capital and/or be dilutive to existing shareholders.

When Select Comfort announced the $35 million agreement in May 2009, I was confident that bankruptcy was not an option.

Here is the third quarter press release in which Select Comfort announced the agreement:[2]

Select Comfort Announces Definitive Agreement for $35 Million Investment by Sterling Partners

MINNEAPOLIS, May 26, 2009 (BUSINESS WIRE) – Select Comfort Corporation (NASDAQ: SCSS), the nation's leading bed retailer and creator of the SLEEP NUMBER® bed, today announced it has entered into a securities purchase agreement with Sterling Partners, a leading growth-oriented, U.S.-based private equity firm. Under the terms of the agreement, Sterling Partners will purchase 50 million shares of common stock at $0.70 per share, for a total investment of $35 million. These shares will represent a 52.5 percent ownership interest in the company. The investment is subject to shareholder approval and customary closing conditions.

The purchase agreement also contemplates the execution of an amended credit agreement with the company's existing lenders. The amended credit agreement would provide maximum availability of $70 million, include new covenants, and extend the maturity from June 2010 to December 2012. The combination of the equity infusion and the amended credit agreement would provide longer-term financial flexibility for the company. The amended credit agreement is subject to final lender approval and definitive documentation.

Cost Reduction The company:

Closed 21 stores during the quarter and 51 stores year-to-date, with plans to close at least 15 additional stores by the end of 2009. These actions are expected to reduce fixed store costs by approximately $14.0 million in 2009;

Enhanced effectiveness and efficiency of marketing spend, with second-quarter marketing expense as a percent of net sales down from 25.4 percent in 2008 to 17.7 percent in 2009, a 765 basis-point improvement; and

Reduced general and administrative and research and development expenses in the quarter by $2.5 million on a year-over-year basis.

Reigniting the Sleep Number Brand   The company:

Continued to support the company's value strategy, benefiting from first-quarter product line redesign and refining successful promotional programs;

Continued to advance results from core direct marketing and the new local radio campaign, which highlights the differentiated benefits of the Sleep Number bed and the location of the company's retail stores; and

Experienced sequential improvement in same-store sales to an 11 percent decline in the second quarter from a 14 percent decline in the first quarter of 2009.

Preserving Cash and Improving Capital Structure   The company:

Maintained strict discipline on capital spending in the quarter. Capital expenditures in the second quarter of 2009 were $0.7 million compared with $10.6 million in the prior-year period; and

Reached an agreement with Sterling Partners for a $35.0 million investment, subject to shareholder approval and other closing conditions, which also would result in an amended credit agreement with new covenants and extended maturity from 2010 to 2012.

> "We are pleased with the impact of our efforts on our overall financial position, and our team remains focused on pursuing incremental ways to reduce costs, build our brand, and preserve cash and improve our capital structure," continued McLaughlin. "These efforts will help ensure we have adequate capital and are well positioned for future success as our programs gain momentum and the macro-economic environment ultimately improves."

Cash flows from operating activities totaled $35.6 million for the first six months of 2009, which included $25.8 million in tax refunds associated with prior-year losses. This compares to $10.4 million of operating cash flow for the first six months of 2008. The company reduced capital expenditures to $1.9

million for the first six months of 2009, compared to $20.9 million in the first six months of 2008, which reflects actions taken to significantly reduce investments in store expansion and IT infrastructure. As of July 4, 2009, cash and cash equivalents totaled $4.5 million, and outstanding borrowings under the company's revolving credit facility totaled $43.8 million.

Outlook

"We do not anticipate a significant economic recovery or improvement in consumer confidence for the balance of the year, which will likely result in continued sales volatility in the near term," said Jim Raabe, senior vice president and CFO, Select Comfort Corporation. "That said, we expect sales declines to moderate in the second half of 2009, as we lap the impact of the significant economic downturn we experienced during the second half of 2008."

In the second half of the year, the company anticipates it will remain cash flow positive and achieve break-even or slight profitability, before the impact of charges associated with the Sterling Partners transaction and subsequent actions. The combination of the $35.0 million investment and the amended credit agreement would improve the company's current capital structure, allowing the company to address its liquidity needs and pursue long-term opportunities that become available.

Financing Update

The Company continues to operate under and rely on short-term waivers to comply with certain ongoing covenants associated with the $75.0 million available under its revolving credit facility. On May 26, 2009, the company announced that it had entered into a securities purchase agreement with Sterling Partners, a leading growth-oriented, U.S.-based private equity firm. Under the terms of the agreement, Sterling Partners would purchase 50 million shares of common stock at $0.70 per share, for a total investment of $35.0 million. These shares would represent a 52.5 percent owner-ship interest in the company. The investment is subject to shareholder approval and customary closing provisions, and the company expects the shareholder meeting and the closing of the transaction to occur in late August or early September. The company believes there is uncertainty with respect to its ability to secure a longer-term amendment to the credit agreement without consummation of the transaction with Sterling Partners, and a likelihood of significant cost, dilution, limited financial flexibility and limited term in the event such an amendment could be secured. In conjunction with the purchase agreement, the company's existing lenders have agreed to negotiate in good faith to amend and restate the company's current credit agreement. The amended credit agreement would provide maximum availability of $70.0 million, include improved operating covenants and extend the maturity from June 2010 to December 2012. The amended credit agreement is subject to final lender approval and definitive documentation.

On June 25, 2009, the company announced that Sterling Partners intended to seek the appointment of a new CEO, Pat Hopf, following closing of the transaction.

The company shareholders rejected the Sterling partner's transaction in a small margin:

MINNEAPOLIS–(BUSINESS WIRE)–Sep. 1, 2009– Select Comfort Corporation (NASDAQ: SCSS), one of the nation's leading bed retailers and creator of the SLEEP NUMBER® bed, today provided additional information concerning the special meeting of its shareholders held on August 27, 2009. As Select Comfort reported on August 27, 2009, its shareholders did not approve the transactions contemplated by the Securities Purchase Agreement (the "Sterling Stock Purchase Agreement"), dated May 22, 2009, between Select Comfort and Sterling SC Investor, LLC ("Sterling"), which would have included the issuance and sale to Sterling of 50 million shares of the Company's common stock at a price of $0.70 per share (the "Sterling Transaction").

In September 2009, the company announced third quarter results, in which same-store sales increased 9 percent:

Select Comfort Announces Third Quarter Results
Company Reports Net Income of $0.15 per Share; 9 Percent Increase in Same-store Sales

MINNEAPOLIS–(BUSINESS WIRE)–Oct. 22, 2009—Select Comfort Corporation (NASDAQ: SCSS), the nation's leading bed retailer and creator of the SLEEP NUMBER® bed, today announced results for the fiscal 2009 third quarter ended October 3, 2009. Net sales for the quarter totaled $147.5 million, a decrease of 6 percent compared to $157.2 million in the third quarter of 2008. The company reported third-quarter net income of $6.9 million, or $0.15 per diluted share, compared to net income of $1.0 million, or $0.02 per diluted share, in the third quarter of 2008. The company generated $17.4 million in cash flow from operating activities during the quarter. Third-quarter results include a one-time charge of $3.3 million, or $0.05 per share, associated with the terminated financing activities year-to-date.

"Third-quarter results improved significantly as our focus on controlling costs, building our brand for improved sales, and preserving cash helped mitigate the impact of ongoing market volatility," said Bill McLaughlin, president and CEO, Select Comfort Corporation. "While our business has begun to stabilize and we're beginning to experience its longer-term potential, economic and market conditions remain uncertain. Therefore, we are planning and managing conservatively, while prepared to capitalize on growth as we see opportunities."

After the shareholders rejected the previous $35 million deal, Sterling Partners agreed to invest $10 million dollars at the price of at $4 per share in November 2009. The company also announced completing the public offering.

After the $10 million investment from Sterling Partners and $16.4 million public offering, the company paid down the entire debt. Now the company is totally debt free.

This was a successful turnaround story. As shareholders, you can make a great deal of money in successful turnaround situations.

Figure 20.2 shows the stock performance.

The stock fell as low as $0.19 per share in December 2008 and increased to $12.06 per share in April 2010. That is a 6,347 percent return in 17 months. Obviously, no one bought at the absolute minimum and sold at the absolute maximum. Even if you bought the shares after the May 2009 private-equity-agreement announcement, the max price for that month was $1.21 per share. In that

MINNEAPOLIS, Dec 14, 2009 (BUSINESS WIRE)—Select Comfort Corporation (NASDAQ: SCSS), today announced the closing of its previously announced underwritten public offering of 3.8 million shares of its common stock at a public-offering price of $4.75 per share. Piper Jaffray & Co. acted as the sole manager for the offering. Net proceeds from the sale of the shares, after underwriting discounts and commissions and other offering expenses, are expected to be approximately $16.4 million (excluding $1.6 million, which the company would receive if Sterling SC Investor exercises its contractual preemptive rights).

The company stated it will use the proceeds of the public offering to improve working capital and pay down debt. "The close of this public offering represents another significant milestone in our efforts to strengthen our balance sheet and improve financial flexibility," said Bill McLaughlin, president and CEO, Select Comfort Corporation. "The combination of the recent Sterling Partners investment and the proceeds from this public offering allows us to eliminate our currently outstanding debt. The closing of this offering fulfills our obligation to raise equity capital under our credit agreement and we have no present intention to raise any additional equity capital."

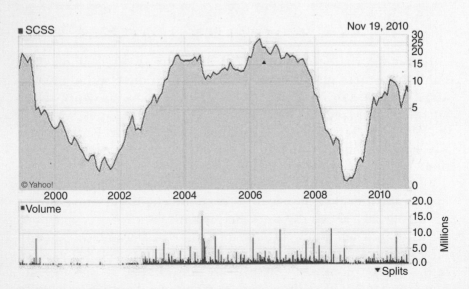

Figure 20.2   SCSS Chart

case, the return would have been 996 percent. For my fund, I did purchase the shares in different time periods, with the average purchase price of $0.45 per share. I sold at $9 per share, which was a 2,000 percent return in 17 months.

Turnaround situations are very profitable if you invest money after you are convinced that the company will survive. If you are not comfortable and have any doubt that the company will not survive, do not invest. If you hold at least one or two turnaround positions in your portfolio, and they are successful, it will generate a great return and worthwhile investment.

Stock Research Checklist—Stock Price

Does the Company Trade at a P/E Ratio That Is Less than Its Growth Rate?

Price-to-earnings (P/E) ratio = Price of the stock ÷ Earnings of
the company previous year

If you buy stock at too high of a P/E multiple—even after all the research checklist items are passed—you will not be able to make a profit on your purchase. To determine this, first calculate the company's growth rate for the last 10 years. The simple calculation should show that the P/E ratio is less than the company's long-term growth rate. If the company is growing at 20 percent over the last five years, consider buying the stock for less than 15 times conservative future earnings. Never buy stock at or above 20 times conservative future earnings.

When you are dealing with high-growth stocks, this simple calculation should be remembered at all times. The stock of high-growth companies trades in higher multiples most of the time. Whenever there is any bad news that is related to the company, the industry, or a severe market sell off, the high-multiple stocks sell off badly. You should use that opportunity to buy the stocks when the price is low and earnings multiples are less than the growth rate. If the stock does not fall enough, do not buy the stock.

When you are calculating the P/E multiple, do not rely on the current P/E ratio, which is calculated using the previous year's earnings. To get the proper calculation, consider using the historic average earnings multiple so that one particular year's events will not affect the purchasing decision. When you are dealing with cyclical stocks, be sure to consider this scenario. When the earnings are depressed, the denominator is less, causing the P/E ratio to come out very high. Don't worry about that kind of situation because you can get the low and high P/E numbers from annual reports or Standard & Poor's reports. Then, you can calculate the average P/E.

Here, we calculate the average earnings information for Coca-Cola (KO) during the last 10 years.

Year	P/E-Low	P/E-High	P/E-Average
2000	49	76	62.5
2001	26	39	32.5
2002	27	36	31.5
2003	21	29	25
2004	19	27	23
2005	20	22	21
2006	18	23	20.5
2007	18	25	21.5
2008	16	26	21
2009	13	20	16.5

The average P/E ratio of KO for the last 10 years is 27.5

The earnings-per-share (EPS) growth for the last 10 years is 12.8 percent as per our calculation in the earnings growth checklist item. KO stock is trading at a higher P/E than its long-term growth rate.

Now we calculate the average P/E information for Goodyear Tire (GT) during the last 10 years.

Year	P/E-Low	P/E-High	P/E-Average
2000	NA	NA	NA
2001	NA	NA	NA
2002	NA	NA	NA
2003	NA	NA	NA
2004	11	24	17.5
2005	9	15	12
2006	NA	NA	NA
2007	32	56	44
2008	NA	NA	NA
2009	NA	NA	NA

Except for 2004, 2005, and 2007, GT does not have positive earnings, so there is no positive P/E ratio.

The average P/E ratio for those three positive years is 24.5.

GT does not have positive EPS growth for the last 10 years.

In December 2010, GT was trading at $11.60, and the P/E ratio was 41.33. The P/E ratio was too high because EPS was at $0.28 per share.

These calculations are done using the previous year's earnings; you need to concentrate on future earnings. As Warren Buffett puts it, "Of course, the investor of today does not profit from yesterday's growth."[1] You need to invest based on the future earnings of the company, but, from the previous year's earnings growth, you can reasonably calculate the future earnings potential of the company. That will be helpful when calculating the intrinsic value of the company. You can listen to conference calls and read the annual and quarterly reports to learn what management says about the company's projected earnings. Also, you will be able to find out what kind of new initiatives the company is exploring right now. If you feel that the new initiatives are going to improve the earnings substantially, you can act accordingly.

When you are looking at very high-growth companies—for example, companies growing at 30 percent or more—analyze how the company is able to grow as fast as it is. If a particular product is the reason, find out more about the product and the product's shipment trends. Newly introduced products grow very fast during their initial periods, but then lose momentum. You need to follow the company and product for a long time before. If the particular product fades, try to find out if the company will be introducing any new products to keep the momentum. Also, what is the company's recent growth rate and what is its recent profit margin? Because high-growth companies attract more competitors into their space, a price war will likely appear.

Does the Stock Trade at a Discount to the Company's Intrinsic Value?

After all of the checklist items have been explored, the important thing to find out is if the stock trades at less than it's calculated intrinsic. The details for calculating the intrinsic value of the business are explained in Chapter 23. You need to look for at least a 25 percent discount to intrinsic value. If you get a 50 percent discount to the intrinsic value, that is ideal. Even if the company passes all the checklist items, you should never buy the stock if the shares trade above the intrinsic value. The rule is to never buy a stock without at least a 25 percent discount to intrinsic value. Even if the business is successful, you cannot make a great return. In fact, you will likely lose your money if your entry price is higher than the intrinsic value of the business.

Does the Stock Trade at a Discount to Its Book Value?

You should not use book value as an ultimate deciding factor for your investment decisions. Some people say that if the price of a stock is less than its stated book value, it is automatically undervalued, but that is not the case.

To illustrate this point, consider the following scenario: an industrial company invested $10 million to upgrade its machines five years ago. It depreciated a certain amount every year over the last five years, say $1 million depreciation every year. As per the balance sheet, those machines are worth $5 million. If new machines are introduced into the field, those old machines are equal to nothing, or the business might be able to sell them for a scrap value of maybe 10 to 20 percent of the stated book value.

Even accounts receivable, which is the money owed to the company, cannot be considered at full value, because the company may not be able to collect all the pending accounts receivable. I have experienced this in my own business when I experienced collection problems with a software company I ran for many years. I was never able to collect 100 percent of the company's accounts receivable in a year. If, as a business owner, you are not successful after many attempts to collect pending receivables, you need to give those accounts to a collection agency to pursue. If the agency collects successfully, it takes a commission of between 18 and 25 percent of the recovered money. Following this course of action may cause you to lose the company's profit margin. However, if you are unable to collect, you will need to go to court and file legal claims. If the attorneys are successful, they will take 50 percent of the recovered money.

To give an example, when Warren Buffett acquired Berkshire Hathaway during the 1960s, he bought company shares that were less than the stated book value, and book value consisted of textile machine assets. But when he liquidated the textile operation, he got 10 percent of the stated book value for the machines.

In technology companies, on the other hand, the stated book values are much less. You cannot eliminate the businesses whose market cap is higher than the book value. In technology companies, you do not need to do a high-capital investment. The business will be worth the future owner income that can be derived from the business. For example, take Oracle Corporation (ORCL), which had a market cap of $159.23 billion and shareholder equity of $32.1 billion in December 2010. Market cap was around 4.96 times the shareholder equity. Therefore, you should not reject stock in terms of book value alone.

Does the Company Have Any Catalysts?

When the stock price is trading below a company's intrinsic value, try to find out if there are any catalysts available to unlock the value in the company. A catalyst could be the particular company's events, such as a new product introduction or the acquisition or sale of a particular division or the whole company. Other catalysts could include entering into a new market, waiting for a big contract, or a corporate raider trying to take over the company. When these kinds of catalysts are available, you can realize your stock gain as soon as the event occurs.

Stock Research Checklist—Infosys

To understand the stock research checklist a bit better, here is an example that uses Infosys Limited.[1] In this example, we will look at how the company scores against each of the research checklist items. Infosys Technologies Ltd. was founded in 1981. It provides information technology (IT) development and consulting services worldwide through onshore and offshore execution methods. The company performs most of the offshore development activities from India. The shares trade on the Nasdaq market under the symbol INFY as an American Depository Receipt (ADR). The stock price of the stock was $74.53 per share in December 2010.

Are You Able to Understand the Business Thoroughly?
Is It a Simple Business?

This checklist item has two questions. First, does the company operate a simple business? Infosys is operating in the technology field providing information technology services, but the nature of the business is very simple. Companies need to have an information application to manage the business effectively and improve the productivity of the business. Even when the company is small, it needs software applications to manage the business effectively. Companies need a service provider to develop those applications and maintain them. Since most of the software development activities are performed in India, they can reduce the cost of the company compared with the U.S.-based IT firm.

When the company satisfies a particular checklist item, we will call it **Pass.** When it does not satisfy the checklist item, we will call it **Fail.** Infosys passed the previous question, so the result for this checklist item is **Pass**.

Second, do you understand the businesses? Yes. Infosys provides software development and consulting services from onshore and offshore development centers. It provides services worldwide. Company revenue is either project-based or time-based. It needs to compete with other U.S.-based IT firms and offshore IT firms from India and the Philippines. It needs to compete with other IT firms from India to hire technical talent.

Result for this checklist item: **Pass**.

Does the Company Have Any Moat, Which Makes it Very Difficult for Competitors to Penetrate the Company's Market Share?

Here is the analysis to find out the moat factors for Infosys:

- **Brand Name:** Infosys has a recognized brand name. It is the leader in offshore IT outsourcing. It operates 63 offices and development centers in India, Australia, Poland, the United Kingdom, and the Czech Republic. Infosys has a well-recognized brand name in corporate America, with most of the Fortune 500 companies as its customers. There are other offshore IT companies that offer IT services at lower rates than Infosys, but it still maintains leadership in the industry and commands higher prices than other competitors from India.
- **Size:** Infosys and its subsidiaries had 122,468 employees as of September 30, 2010. Because of its size, Infosys can obtain larger projects when compared with other offshore IT providers.
- **High switching costs:** When a company outsources its IT applications to Infosys, Infosys then develops custom-based applications after thoroughly understanding the customer's business and needs. The company cannot switch to a new vendor immediately, as it is very difficult for another vendor to take over a project in the middle of project development.

The company would need to spend a great deal of time, effort, and money for the new vendor to catch up on business processing and the old vendor's software development methodologies and logic. Because of this, it is not easy for customers to switch to new vendors.

- **Customer loyalty:** Infosys works with customers for a long time during application-development and implementation stages. This way, it can slowly build customer loyalty. That relationship will generate more revenue for Infosys well into the future. You can research customer loyalty from the company's revenue-generating pattern. Infosys generates 97 percent of its revenue from existing customers and only 3 percent from new customers, which means the company is building customer loyalty very well.

There is MOAT around the solution side of the Infosys business. The other part of the business is providing IT contractors to the clients' contracted projects on a per-hour basis. This is a kind of commodity-type of businesses, and many U.S. IT consulting companies can effectively compete with the business. In this division, Infosys' profit margin will be less when compared to the IT solution side of the business.

Result for this checklist item: **Pass**.

What Is the Nature of the Business? Does It Operate in a Non-Exciting Industry?

The IT business is an exciting and growing industry. Management and technical people need to upgrade their skills to match IT industry trends and provide those services, otherwise their services will be outdated and rejected by prospective customers.

Result for this checklist item: **Fail**.

Is the Company Involved in a Dirty Type of Business?

IT businesses are high-margin and exciting, not dirty.

Result for this checklist item: **Fail**.

With National Chain Companies, Was the Company Successful in a Couple of Locations before Expanding Nationally?

The company was initially very successful in providing IT services throughout India and then moved forward to international locations and obtained customers all over the world. The company has offices in 63 locations and development centers in India, China, Australia, the Czech Republic, Poland, the United Kingdom, Canada, and Japan.

Result for this checklist item: **Pass**.

Has the Company Dominated in a Particular Segment of the Market?

Infosys does not operate in a niche market; it provides general IT outsourcing services. It has developed brand loyalty, but is not a niche market player.

Result for this checklist item: **Fail**.

Is This Company Operating in a Hot Industry?

The offshore IT industry was hot in the early 1990s, but not anymore. Infosys just provides the IT services for corporations.

Result for this checklist item: **Fail**.

What Is the Company's Earnings Growth over the Previous 10 Years? Does It Grow Constantly?

Below is the formula used to find out the growth rate. This formula is used throughout this chapter for growth and compounded annual return calculations.

$$I = ((FV \div PV)^{1/N} - 1) \times 100$$

I = Percentage of earnings-per-share (EPS) growth rate

FV = Future EPS value

PV = Current EPS value

N = Number of years

Here is the EPS information for Infosys during the last 10 years:

Year	Earnings per Share
2001	$0.25
2002	$0.31
2003	$0.37
2004	$0.51
2005	$0.76
2006	$1.00
2007	$1.50
2008	$2.02
2009	$2.25
2010	$2.30

Look at the consistent earnings growth for the last 10 years. There were two recessions in the last 10 years, but still the company posted increased earnings every year. That is a great business and better execution.

EPS growth rate is 24.84 percent growth for the last 10 years.

Result for this checklist item: **Pass**.

How Does the Company Use Retained Earnings? Are Retained Earnings Reflected in the Stock Price?

Here is the EPS information for Infosys during last 10 years:

Year	Earnings per Share
2001	$0.25
2002	$0.31
2003	$0.37
2004	$0.51
2005	$0.76
2006	$1.00
2007	$1.50
2008	$2.02
2009	$2.25
2010	$2.30

Total retained EPS is $11.27 per share for the last 10 years.

Infosys stock price change for the last 10 years is $74.20 − $27.11 = $47.09

Calculation: $47.09 ÷ $11.27 = $4.17

Each dollar retained by Infosys generated $4.17 in market price. That is an excellent number.

Result for this checklist item: **Pass**.

What Are the Company's Owner Earnings for the Last 10 years? Does It Grow Consistently?

Here is the formula for owner earnings:

Owner earnings = Net income + Depreciation and amortization – Capital expenditure

Here is the owner earnings detail of Infosys during last 10 years:

Year	Net Income	Depreciation and Amortization	CapEx	Owner Income
2001	$132.00	$24.50	$96.80	$59.70
2002	$164.00	$33.60	$68.30	$129.30
2003	$195.00	$39.40	$43.20	$191.20
2004	$270.00	$52.30	$93.20	$229.10
2005	$419.00	$66.00	$186.00	$299.00
2006	$555.00	$99.00	$246.00	$408.00
2007	$850.00	$118.00	$336.00	$632.00
2008	$1,155.00	$157.00	$374.00	$938.00
2009	$1,281.00	$165.00	$285.00	$1,161.00
2010	$1,313.00	$199.00	$192.00	$1,320.00

Look at the owner earnings, which trend upwards for last 10 years.

Percentage of owner income increase is 36.28 percent per year.

This kind of owner income growth is excellent.

Result for this checklist item: **Pass**.

What Is the Company's Recent Earning Momentum? Is It Comparable to Its Long-Term Growth Rate?

Due to the recent recession, the company's earning momentum slowed from 2008 when compared with the long-term growth rate.

Result for this checklist item: **Fail**.

Does the Company Have Any One-Time Event That Recently Increased Earnings?

There is no one-time event that recently increased the earnings.
    Result for this checklist item: **Pass**.

What Is the Company's "Operating Cash Flow"?
Does It Grow at a Constant Rate?

Here are the operating cash flow numbers for Infosys over the last 10 years:

Year	Operating Cash Flow
2001	$162
2002	$212
2003	$258
2004	$345
2005	$522
2006	$698
2007	$970
2008	$1,308
2009	$1,539
2010	$1,659

Numbers are in millions.

    Look at the nice uptrend of operating cash flow for the last 10 years.
    Rate of operating cash flow growth is 26.19 percent per year.
    The operating cash flow increased 26.19 percent per year over the last 10 years. This kind of growth is excellent.
    Result for this checklist item: **Pass**.

How Has the Business Performed in Previous Recessions?

Here are the net income numbers for Infosys for the last 10 years:

Year	Net Income
2001	$132
2002	$164
2003	$195

(Continued)

Year	Net Income
2004	$270
2005	$419
2006	$555
2007	$850
2008	$1,155
2009	$1,281
2010	$1,313

Numbers are in millions.

From 2001 to 2003, the U.S. economy was in a downturn, and it slipped into a recession again during 2008. Look at the net income numbers for Infosys; they never came down. The growth rate was reduced but did not generate a loss. Infosys performed very well during these recessions.

Result for this checklist item: **Pass**.

If a Particular Product's Success Attracted You to a Company, What Percentage of That Company's Sales Come from That Product?

There is no particular product success; Infosys is in IT and provides different IT services.

Result for this checklist item: **Not Applicable**.

Does the Company Have Client Concentration?

As of the second quarter report, which came out on September 30, 2010, no client individually accounted for more than 10 percent of Infosys's revenue.

Here is the content from the second quarter 6-K Form filed with the SEC:

2.20.3 significant clients[3]
No client individually accounted for more than 10 percent of the revenues for the three months and six months ended September 30, 2010 and September 30, 2009.

Result for this checklist item: **Pass**.

Does the Company Have Manageable Debt?

Infosys does not have any long-term debt, and finances its growth from existing company cash flow. That kind of financial condition is great.

Result for this checklist item: **Pass**.

Does the Company Have Manageable Short-Term Debt?

Infosys does not have any short-term debt as of September 30, 2010. That is great.

Result for this checklist item: **Pass**.

What Is the Company's Current Ratio?

The current ratio formula is:

Current assets ÷ current liabilities

As of September 30, 2010:

The current ratio is $5,211 ÷ $825 = 6.31 (numbers are in millions, except for the ratio)

The company's current ratio is excellent; you do not need to worry about the company's ability to pay the current liabilities.

Result for this checklist item: **Pass**.

What Is the Company's Long-Term Debt? Is It Manageable?

Infosys does not have any long-term debt, which is excellent.

Result for this checklist item: **Pass**.

Does the Company Pay Little or No Interest Expense?

There is no interest expense, which is great because Infosys can invest current earnings back into the company and those earnings will grow into the future. That will be a great advantage for the long-term shareholders.

Result for this checklist item: **Pass**.

Does the Company Have Preferred Stock?

Infosys does not have any preferred stock.

Result for this checklist item: **Pass**.

What Is the Company's ROE for the Last 10 Years? Does It Trend Upward?

Here is the return on equity (ROE) for Infosys for the last 10 years:

Year	% of Return on Equity
2001	51.8%
2002	43.6%
2003	36.5%
2004	34.2%
2005	38.0%
2006	35.9%
2007	37.3%
2008	34.9%
2009	33.3%
2010	28.7%

The average ROE is 37.42 percent

The average ROE is very high, which is great. Infosys is generating consistent ROE numbers. Even the low-end number, 28.7 percent, was very good.

Result for this checklist item: **Pass**.

Does the Company Have More Equity When Compared with Long-Term Debt?

Since there is no long-term debt, Infosys is in excellent financial condition.

Result for this checklist item: **Pass**.

What Is the Company's Net Profit Margin for the Last 10 Years? Does the Company Generate a Consistent Upward-Trend Profit Margin or at Least Maintain an Average Profit Margin?

Here is the net income profit margin for Infosys over the last 10 years:

Year	Net Income Profit Margin
2001	31.9%
2002	30.2%
2003	25.9%
2004	25.4%
2005	26.3%
2006	25.8%
2007	27.5%
2008	27.7%
2009	27.5%
2010	27.3%

The average net profit margin is 27.55 percent for the last 10 years.

This net profit margin number is excellent when compared with competitors, even in an IT outsourcing businesses.

Result for this checklist item: **Pass**.

What Is the Company's Gross Profit Margin for the Last 10 Years? Does It Consistently Grow or at Least Maintain an Average Rate?

Here is the formula to calculate the gross profit margin percentage:

Gross profit margin percentage = (Gross profit ÷ Revenue) × 100

Here are the gross profit margin percentages for Infosys for the last 10 years:

Year	Gross Profit	Revenue	Gross Profit Margin
2001	$197	$413	47.70%
2002	$252	$545	46.24%
2003	$337	$754	44.69%
2004	$460	$1,063	43.27%
2005	$688	$1,592	43.22%
2006	$908	$2,152	42.19%
2007	$1,313	$3,090	42.49%
2008	$1,723	$4,176	41.26%
2009	$1,964	$4,663	42.12%
2010	$2,055	$4,804	42.78%

Numbers are in millions.

Look at the consistent gross profit margin for the last 10 years. Average gross profit margin is 43.60 percent.

Result for this checklist item: **Pass**.

Does the Company Have a High Pretax Profit Margin?

If the company has high pretax profit margins, that is a good thing.

Here is the pretax profit margin information for Infosys over the last 10 years:

Year	Pretax Income	Revenue Pretax	Income/Revenue
2001	$147	$414	35.51%
2002	$192	$545	35.23%
2003	$237	$754	31.43%
2004	$321	$1,063	30.20%
2005	$491	$1,592	30.84%
2006	$630	$2,152	29.28%
2007	$936	$3,090	30.29%
2008	$1,326	$4,176	31.75%
2009	$1,475	$4,663	31.63%
2010	$1,669	$4,804	34.74%

Numbers are in millions.

The average pre-tax profit margin is 32.09 percent for the last 10 years.

Look at the consistent pre-tax income for the last 10 years and average pre-tax profit margin percentage, which is high.

Result for this checklist item: **Pass**.

What Is the Company's ROA for the Last 10 Years? Is It Growing Constantly or at Least Maintaining an Average ROA for the Last 10 Years?

Here is the return on assets for Infosys for the last 10 years:

Year	Return on Assets
2001	47.0%
2002	40.4%
2003	33.2%
2004	29.4%
2005	32.4%
2006	31.5%
2007	33.1%

Year	Return on Assets
2008	30.5%
2009	28.9%
2010	25.0%

The average ROA is 33.14 percent for the last 10 years. The average return on assets was very good. Infosys is generating consistent returns on asset numbers. Even the low-end number, 25 percent, was still very good.

Result for this checklist item: **Pass**.

Calculate the ROIC for the Last 10 Years. Does the Company Have Consistent ROIC Numbers?

We can get the return on invested capital (ROIC) numbers from the Quotes Research section, (Evaluator section). This way you will not need to calculate for each year.[1]

Average ROIC for Infosys is 32.20 percent for the last 10 years, which is a very good number and an excellent return.

Result for this checklist item: **Pass**.

Does the Company Need to Spend Large Amounts of Money as a Capital Expenditure to Stay Competitive?

Infosys needs to spend money to set up development centers, infrastructure, networks, and communication systems to provide service to their offshore clients. Here is their capital expenditure information as a percentage of pretax income:

Year	Capital Expenditure	Pretax Income	CapEx/Pretax Income
2001	$96.80	$147.00	65.85%
2002	$68.30	$192.00	35.57%
2003	$43.20	$237.00	18.22%
2004	$93.20	$321.00	29.03%
2005	$186.00	$491.00	37.88%
2006	$246.00	$630.00	39.04%
2007	$336.00	$936.00	35.89%
2008	$374.00	$1,326.00	28.20%
2009	$285.00	$1,475.00	19.32%
2010	$192.00	$1,669.00	11.50%

Numbers are in millions.

Average capital expenditure ÷ pretax income = 32.05 per.

Look at the capital expenditure as a percentage of pretax income; it trends downward and that is very good. Whenever business increases, the company needs to spend additional money on development centers in order to service the newly added customers.

Result for this checklist item: **Pass**.

What Is the Company's Investing Strategy? Is the Company Investing in Its Area of Expertise?

Infosys is expanding in the same field; they have acquired information-related companies in the past. They are reinvesting existing earnings only in other information technology fields. For the sake of growth they are not diversifying into other fields or paying high prices for the acquisitions.

As an example, let's look at a situation in which Infosys planned to acquire Axon Group plc, an SAP consulting company fromthe United Kingdom. Here is the announcement from Infosys:

Infosys Announces its Plans to Acquire Axon Group plc

Bangalore, India—August 25, 2008: Infosys Technologies Limited (Nasdaq: INFY) is pleased to announce that it has agreed to terms for a recommended cash offer for a leading UK-based SAP consulting company, Axon Group plc (LSE: AXO), in a deal valued at £407.1 million (INR33.1 billion[1]; US$753.1 million[2]). The transfer of ownership to Infosys is expected to be completed by November 2008, subject to the Scheme of Arrangement becoming effective.

Commenting on the transaction, Kris Gopalakrishnan, CEO of Infosys said, "We are excited about this acquisition. The strategic combination of our groups will accelerate the realization of our common aspiration—that of becoming the most respected provider of business transformational services in the global marketplace. We hold the management and employees of Axon in high regard and look forward to welcoming them to the Infosys Group."

Axon provides consultancy services to multinational organizations that have chosen SAP as their strategic enterprise platform and has about 2,000 employees. Specializing in the delivery of change through technology enabled transformation programs, Axon's consultants bring in-depth industry expertise alongside best practice functional knowledge to address the strategic, operational, information management and organization effectiveness challenges faced by organizations today. Founded in 1994, today Axon has offices in the United Kingdom, North America, Malaysia and Australia.

For the year ended 31 December 2007, Axon reported profit after taxation of £20.2 million (INR1.6 billion[1]; US$ 37.4 million[2]) on revenue of £204.5 million (INR16.6 billion[1]; US$378.3 million[2]).

[1] uses closing rate at 22 August 2008 of INR81.34/£

[2] uses closing rate at 22 August 2008 of US$1.85/£

Infosys believes that the Acquisition will accelerate the achievement of some of Infosys' current strategic corporate objectives including the continued expansion of Infosys' consulting capabilities that are required to engage with the large business transformation programs of Infosys' marquee clients

There will be a conference call for equity analysts with a Q&A session at 20:00 (Bangalore), 15:30 (London) and (10:30 New York). The conference call will be hosted by Infosys's CEO, Kris Gopalakrishnan, and CFO, V. Balakrishnan.

Axon Group subsequently received a competing offer from another company and Infosys decided that it would not increase the offer from 600 pence per share to beat the competing offer of 650 pence per share of Axon Group plc. This showed that Infosys has the discipline to handle shareholder money, and not pay the higher price for acquisitions.

Here is the announcement from Infosys regarding withdrawing its offer:

Statement re: Axon Group plc

October 10, 2008: On 25 August 2008, Infosys announced a recommended cash offer of 600 pence per share (including the Interim Dividend) for Axon Group plc. On 26 September 2008, the Axon Board informed us of a potential competing offer for Axon at 650 pence per share (including the Interim Dividend). Subsequently, the Axon Board announced the withdrawal of its recommendation of Infosys' offer and its intent to unanimously recommend the higher offer when made.

(Continued)

> After careful consideration, the Board of Infosys has concluded that it will not increase the price of its original offer dated 25 August 2008.
>
> Infosys has a fast-growing and profitable SAP—led business transformation practice. The company is confident that its decision will have no material impact on its strategic plans.
>
> Terms defined in the Infosys' announcement of 25 August 2008 have the same meaning in this announcement.

Result for this checklist item: **Pass**.

What Percentage of Revenue Is spent on Research and Development?

Since Infosys is in the information technology services field, it does not need to spend money on research and development activities. Infosys can use that money for expanding revenue or for acquisition.

Result for this checklist item: **Pass**.

What Is the Company's Growth Recently? What Plans Does Management Have to Grow the Business?

As per the EPS calculation, which we calculated in a previous checklist item, Infosys had EPS growth rate of 24.84 percent and an owner earnings growth rate of 36.28 percent for the last 10 years.

Here is the announcement from Infosys in a third quarter earnings presentation,

Revenue quarter over quarter (QoQ) growth was 12.1 percent; year over year (YoY) growth was 24.4 percent.

Net profit after tax, QoQ growth was 16.7 percent; YoY growth was 13.2 percent.

EPS QoQ growth was 16.7 percent; YoY growth was 13.0 percent.

For net profit after tax, you can consider this to be approximately equivalent to owner income because depreciation and amortization can cancel out capital expenditure. This means that the owner earnings growth rate was 13.2 percent compared with 36.28 percent for the last 10 years (this is much less).

EPS historically grew at 24.84 percent for the last 10 years, but, as per the latest earnings statement, YoY growth was 13 percent (this is also much less).

Infosys earns 65.8 percent of its revenue from U.S. customers. Because the U.S. entered into a recession in 2008 and was still in the early stages of recovery in 2010, the company's growth slowed recently. You need to look for improvement in the following years, depending upon the recovery.

Here is the management outlook for the fourth quarter of 2010:

- Quarter ending December 31, 2010
  - Revenues are expected to be in the range of YoY growth of 19.9 percent to 21.1 percent
  - Earnings per share (EPS) is expected to be in the range of YoY growth of 7.5 percent to 9.4 percent
- Fiscal year ending March 31, 2011
  - Revenues are expected to be in the range of YoY growth of 18.5 percent to 19.4 percent
  - Earnings per share (EPS) is expected to be in the range of YoY growth of 5.5 percent to 7.4 percent

The projection for a couple of quarters into the future is less than historical numbers. You need to take into account the recession and how the recovery plays a role in Infosys' revenue and earnings numbers into the coming quarters and years. When you are trying to project future earnings levels, you should use conservative numbers instead of historical numbers.

The company's size also matters. When a company is small, it can grow at a higher percentage every year. But, when a company's size reaches a certain level, like a large-cap company, the growth rate will be less than the previous year's growth rate.

Result for this checklist item: **Fail**.

Does the Company Have Related-Party Transactions with the Family Members or Relatives of the Senior Management or Board of Directors?

Infosys does not have any related-party transactions with outside companies in which Infosys insiders have ownership.

Result for this checklist item: **Pass**.

Are You Able to Understand the Footnotes of the Company's Financial Statements?

You need to study the annual and quarterly reports of recent years in order to understand the footnotes of financial statements. Infosys does not have many footnotes. A couple of footnotes are listed, but they are clearly written and easy to understand.

Result for this checklist item: **Pass**.

Is Management Candid in Its Performance Reporting?

Here are the comments from the CEO that were published in a press release from the second quarter 2010:

> "Though the economic environment continues to be challenging, we have leveraged our client relationships, solutions and investments to grow faster in this quarter," said S. Gopalakrishnan, CEO and Managing Director. "There are significant drivers for investment in Information Technology since any transformation program to build tomorrow's enterprises requires these investments to be made. We are partnering with our clients on these initiatives."

Here is another press release regarding the company's liquidity:

Liquidity

As of September 30, 2010, cash and cash equivalents, including investments in available-for-sale financial assets and certificates of deposits was $3.9 Bn (US $2.9 Bn as of September 30,2009).

"Our operating margins improved during the quarter while our liquidity position was further strengthened with cash and cash equivalents reaching US $3.9 billion," said V. Balakrishnan, Chief Financial Officer. "However, the continued global economic uncertainty, coupled with extreme currency volatility, is a concern for the industry."

Result for this checklist item: **Pass**.

Is Senior Management Success Oriented?

In 1981, seven people started Infosys with $250. Now, Infosys generates revenue of around $5.4 billion. One of the founders is the current CEO. So yes, the chairman, CEO and senior management are success-oriented.

Result for this checklist item: **Pass**.

Do the Financial Numbers on the Company's Earnings Release Match the Numbers on the Documents That Are Submitted to SEC (Especially Income Taxes Paid)?

As per second quarter earnings, which were released on September 30, 2010, Infosys paid around $246 million in income tax. The same number was reported on the 6-K form filed with the SEC.

Result for this checklist item: **Pass**.

Does Management Deliver What It Promises?

Infosys is always conservative in its projections. It does not make a habit of projecting above-average returns and missing expectations.

Result for this checklist item: **Pass**.

If You Are Buying the Stock for Dividend, Does the Company Pay the Dividend Without Interruption and Have a History of Raising Dividends?

Infosys has paid a dividend since 1999. Dividend information for the last 10 years is shown here.

Year	Dividend
2001	$0.01
2002	$0.05
2003	$0.06
2004	$0.07
2005	$0.07
2006	$0.36
2007	$0.14
2008	NA
2009	$0.80
2010	$0.46

Infosys did reject the dividend in 2008 and the dividend payouts varied every year.

Infosys is a growth company and retained earnings are increasing at better rates. As far as the dividends are concerned, Infosys failed this checklist item.

Result for this checklist item: **Fail**.

What Is the Percentage of Earnings Paid as a Dividend? Is It a Small Percentage of the Revenue?

Here is the payout ratio for the last 10 years:

Year	Payout Ratio
2001	1%
2002	17%
2003	16%
2004	14%
2005	9%
2006	36%
2007	9%
2008	
2009	36%
2010	20%

Average percentage of payout ratio is 18 percent. The dividend is safe.

Result for this checklist item: **Pass**.

Does the Company Have Any Hidden Assets That Have Been Overlooked by Wall Street?

The company has a couple of hidden assets:

- The established company brand name in IT and outsourcing companies from India.
- The company development centers are located in large cities in India. The land underneath those companies was bought in old dollars and India's real estate market has been in an

uptrend for many years. As of September 2010, the company claimed $1 billion in property, plants, and equipment. Equipment might cost less now, but property values should be more than the balance sheet number.

Result for this checklist item: **Pass**.

Does the Company Have a Low Percentage of Net Receivables?

A low percentage of receivables in terms of revenue indicates that the company can collect the receivables more quickly.

Here are receivables ÷ revenue for Infosys for the last 10 years:

Year	Receivables	Revenue	Receivables/Revenue
2001	$17	$413	4.12%
2002	$69	$545	12.66%
2003	$109	$754	14.46%
2004	$150	$1,063	14.11%
2005	$303	$1,592	19.03%
2006	$361	$2,152	16.78%
2007	$565	$3,090	18.28%
2008	$1,020	$4,176	24.43%
2009	$872	$4,663	18.70%
2010	$965	$4,804	20.09%

Average percent of receivables ÷ revenue = 16.26 percent

Infosys has just 16.26 percent average accounts receivable in terms of revenue, which is good.

Answer to this checklist item: **Pass**.

Does the Company Have More Pension Assets than Vested Benefits?

Infosys does not have any pension benefits. They contribute a certain percentage of employee salary to the provident fund, which is equal to a 401(k) plan in the U.S. Whenever an employee retires from Infosys, they get all the accumulated cash from their provident fund. After that, the company has no obligation to pay any post-retirement benefits.

Result for this checklist item: **Pass**.

If You Are Looking at Under-Valued Asset Plays, Are Any Large Shareholders or Raiders Working to Uncover the Value of the Company?

Infosys is not an asset play and no large shareholders or raiders are trying to do a proxy fight or take over the company.

Result for this checklist item: **Not applicable**.

What Is the Inventory Buildup?

Since Infosys is in the IT service business, there is no inventory buildup.

Result for this checklist item: **Not applicable**.

Are the Company's Total Outstanding Shares Decreasing over Time?

Infosys's total diluted outstanding shares have increased over the last four years. These dilutions happen because of management's stock options.

Year	Total Diluted Outstanding Shares
2006	566.1
2007	570.4
2008	570.6
2009	571.1

Share counts are in millions.

There is an average dilution of 0.22 percent every year. The dilution is not high, but the total number of outstanding shares is not being reduced.

Result for this checklist item: **Fail**.

Has the Company Bought Back Shares Recently?

Infosys did buy back shares recently, but in small quantities. Since the company is growth-oriented, it is investing in the future. Infosys's ROE and ROIC were very high during the last 10 years. Because of these high return possibilities, retained earnings should generate high future income.

Result for this checklist item: **Pass**.

Does the Company Have Any Treasury Stock on Its Balance Sheet?

Infosys has treasury shares of 2,833,600 as per its September 30, 2010, second quarter reported results.
    Result for this checklist item: **Pass**.

Does the Company Have a Retirement of Stock on Its Balance Sheet?

Infosys did not retire stock recently.
    Result for this checklist item: **Fail**.

Did an Insider Buy the Stock Recently?

There has been no insider stock purchase recently.
    Result for this checklist item: **Fail**.

Do the Insiders Own a High Percentage of the Company?

Insider ownership is around 16.99 percent. With the company market cap at around $42.53 billion as of December 2010, you cannot expect 50 percent insider ownership. When a company is this big, even 16.99 percent of insider ownership is a high percentage. The insiders' and shareholders' interests are aligned.
    Result for this checklist item: **Pass**.

Is the Company Not Followed Closely by Wall Street Analysts?

Infosys is not an unknown company. Eighteen analysts are covering this stock, including all the big brokerage houses from the United States.
    Result for this checklist item: **Fail**.

Does the Company Have a Small Percentage of Institutional Ownership?

Institutions and mutual fund ownership comprises around 17.72 percent of the outstanding shares, so Infosys is known by the institutional buyers, but not excessively owned by them.
    Result for this checklist item: **Pass**.

Is the Company Able to Raise the Price of the Product or Service According to Inflation?

Infosys signs contracts with customers to outsource software development and management projects. Once the contract is signed, it cannot raise the prices before that contract expires. When the contract is up for renewal, they can renegotiate the rates according to the inflation or employee expenditure. In India, the wages of software professionals increase yearly. If the company is not increasing the salary, it will be very difficult to retain the employees. For that purpose, whenever new contracts are signed, the company needs to increase the rate for the contract according to the employee cost. Competitors also need to do the same.

Result for this checklist item: **Pass**.

If You Are Looking at a Cyclical Stock, Do You Understand the Relationship of the Company's Revenue Cycle in Relation to Economic Cycles?

Infosys is operating somewhat in a cyclical industry. IT is an important function for any businesses, and a company can prioritize its IT needs and spend accordingly. It can postpone new projects or reduce the investments in existing projects as necessary.

Since Infosys operates in outsourcing fields, U.S. clients can save more during recessions. So, Infosys' business will not be affected much during recession periods. The advantage is that it can provide an information technology service that costs less than U.S.-based IT service providers.

Result for this checklist item: **Pass**.

If you Are Looking at a Turnaround Companies, Has the Company Taken the Necessary Steps to Turn the Business Around?

Infosys is not a turnaround company; it is a growth company.

Result for this checklist item: **Not applicable**.

Does the Company Trade at a P/E Ratio That Is Less than Its Growth Rate?

Infosys had an EPS growth rate of 24.84 percent for the last 10 years. In December 2010, the stock was trading at a price-to-earnings (P/E) ratio of 30.63, which meant the stock was selling for higher than the long-term growth rate of EPS. The company can manipulate the EPS numbers when they buy back the shares because the number of total diluted outstanding shares will be less.

For this reason, you need to look at the owner income growth rate. For Infosys, the owner income growth rate is 36.28 percent for the last 10 years. If you compare this growth rate with the P/E selling ratio of 30.63, the company is selling for less than the owner income growth rate.

Result for this checklist item: **Pass**.

Does the Stock Trade at a Discount to the Company's Intrinsic Value?

Refer to Chapter 23.

Result for this checklist item: **Fail**.

Does the Stock Trade at a Discount to Its Book Value?

Book value does not matter in software businesses. Book value for Infosys is $10.26 per share and the stock trades at $75.22 per share, which is 7.3 times the book value.

Result for this checklist item: **Pass**.

Does the Company Have Any Catalysts?

Infosys does not have any short-term catalysts.

Result for this checklist item: **Fail**.

23

Intrinsic Value

Question: Why does anyone buy any business?

Answer: To receive the future earnings of that company.

Question: How can you calculate the future earnings of a company?

Answer: You can get an approximate idea from the historical earnings of the company.

Question: How can you calculate the true worth (intrinsic value) of a company?

Answer: You can project future earnings of a company from the basis of historical earnings. The calculation of earnings that you wish to calculate is in the future, so you need to discount those future earnings to present value in order to get the true worth of the company. Here is the way Ben Graham puts it: "Any business is worth the sum of free cash flow from now, to eternity discounted to present value using a reasonable risk-free interest rate."

Calculating intrinsic value is not an exact science. You need to assume the earnings, discount rate, and share dilution of the company in the future. Because of this variation, you can get a range of intrinsic values for the business. When you incorporate those variables, you need to be as conservative as possible. Here are the explanations of those variables.

Future Earnings

We can define future earning as the earnings generated from the business in the future. Warren Buffett coined the term *owner income.*

He uses the owner income figure instead of the net income of a business. He also added the non-cash charges and subtracted the capital expenditure from the net income.

Depreciation and Amortization

When you buy a new machine, you need to spend money. You need to depreciate such expenses for multiple years, according to the life span of the specific machine. For example, if you spent $100,000 for a particular machine in 2010, you will not be able to deduct $100,000 from the company's 2010 tax return. If that machine has a 10-year life span, you can deduct $10,000 as a depreciation and amortization expense on your 2010 tax return and then deduct the same $10,000 on your 2011 company tax return too. You can continue these deductions until you depreciate the whole $100,000 investment.

Capital Expenditure

Companies need to spend money as a capital expenditure every year to stay competitive and to operate the businesses effectively, otherwise competitors will take away market share. This expense is necessary and it should come out of net income.

Owner income is the calculation of how much the owner earns from the businesses. Here is the formula for owner income from Warren Buffett:

Owner income = Net income + Depreciation and amortization − Capital expenditure

You can use the owner income figure instead of the net income numbers. The buyer needs to calculate the owner income growth rate for the last 10 years. From that previous year's detail, you can project the approximate owner income growth rate going forward.

For example, let's say that owner income has grown at 25 percent per year for the last 10 years. When calculating future owner income, you should not use the same 25 percent owner income growth rate into the future. You need to use a conservative calculation, for multiple reasons:

- The general economy might have been expanding for the last 10 years, which would have helped the company grow at 25 percent annually. But, the economy might slow or fall into a recession in the future. Therefore, you need to incorporate those risks to your owner income projections.

- Company size matters. As mentioned earlier, when a company is small, it can grow more quickly, because it is in a growth phase. But, once the company reaches a certain level, it will not be able to grow at the same rate as it grew before.
- A competitor might have introduced a competing product or service that may have slowed down the owner income growth of the business you are considering.
- The company you are considering may be operating in a cyclical industry. You need to have a clear idea of the company's revenue patterns and nature of its business.

The future is never clear. There may be many difficulties that come into the picture, so you need to consider all the risks and then project the owner income conservatively before calculating the intrinsic value of that business.

Discount Rate

The discount rate is the rate at which you are going to discount the future owner income of a business in order to calculate the present value of those future owner incomes. Warren Buffett suggests using the long-term Treasury rate as a discount rate.

If you choose not to buy the business, what rate will you earn from that money in an alternate investment? You can use that rate as a discount rate, and can add the risk premium to that discount rate. Risk premiums are used for incorporating the risk for certainty of the future owner income of that business. Some business future owner incomes are somewhat certain; for example, the owners of Coca-Cola and Procter & Gamble have some certainty. For those companies, you can add a smaller percentage of risk premiums to the discount rate. On the other hand, if the business operates in a high-technology field, owner income tends to vary a lot and you can add a higher risk premium to the discount rate. To put it in an approximation, the discount rate for a company like Coca-Cola is 15 percent and the discount rate for a high-tech business like Cisco is around 20 to 25 percent.

Share Dilution

When you are buying an entire business, you do not need to worry about share dilution. But when you are buying shares in a company, you need to consider share dilution. If the company is in need of capital, management can raise it through debt or equity offering. If management uses an equity offering to raise the capital for the business, existing shareholder ownership is going to decrease because of share dilution. The other way share dilution occurs is through the stock options that businesses use to reward management and employees. All companies have an employee stock option plan to attract and retain talented employees. Tech companies in particular provide high stock options to senior management and other executives.

As an investor, you need to identify what kind of share dilution has historically occurred in the particular company. Depending on that dilution rate, you can project what kind of share dilution will occur in the future.

As an example, let's incorporate the above-mentioned variables for the following event: You are living in a nice town and there is candy shop called "Joy Candies." You know about this candy shop because you have been purchasing candy there, and you love Joy Candies. One day you see a sign that says the candy shop is for sale. You have some cash and you think about buying it. You can run the candy shop or find an employee to run it for you. Before you buy into the business, you need to understand what the true worth of that business is. To calculate the true worth of that business, you need the following information.

Future Owner Income

First, you need to calculate how much you can earn after you buy into the business. The seller has been running the business for the last 10 years and has complete financial information. You need to find out the candy shop's revenue, expenses, and capital expenditures over the last 10 years. By seeing those numbers you can calculate the owner income growth for the last 10 years. The owner income was not in a nice uptrend for the last 10 years; the growth rate slowed during the last recession and started improving during the economic recovery period.

Let's say the average owner income growth rate was 10 percent for the last 10 years, the 2010 owner income was $50,000, and revenue was $500,000. The seller is asking $150,000 and the buyer needs to assume the existing $10,000 in bank debt. The business has no cash on hand.

Now you need to think about the owner income of that candy shop in the future. Here are some of the risks you need to incorporate in your future owner income projection.

- You saw a sign saying that there will be new candy shop opening next week on the same street. The new shop is preparing for its grand opening. Joy Candies has operated on the same street for the last 10 years. It is famous for selling quality candies and has a long list of loyal customers. Even so, some Joy Candies customers may be tempted to try the new shop, taste the candy, and test the selling price.
- The new candy shop owner might keep a smaller margin and sell candy at a lower price than you in order to take away your customers. There is the possibility of a price war between the two candy shops.
- The general economy is in an expansion mode right now and may be slowing down in the near future.

By considering the above possibilities, you need to be very conservative. You are projecting future owner income may increase around 7 percent for the next 3 years and 6 percent for another 2 years and then 5 percent for another 5 years. The future owner income earnings numbers for 10 years into the future follow.

Here is the formula for the future owner income calculations.

$$\text{Owner income (Final)} = \text{Owner income (Initial)}$$
$$+ (\text{Owner income (Initial)}$$
$$\times \text{Growth rate} \div 100)$$

Discount Rate   The candy business is not a highly volatile business like the technology business; it is stable and there is some certainty in the revenue. There is an additional benefit: There is a school near the Joy Candies shop. If kids want to go to the new candy shop, they have to walk another 10 minutes to reach it. That advantage gives

Year	Owner Income (Initial)	Growth Rate	Owner Income (Final)
2011	$50,000.00	7%	$53,500.00
2012	$53,500.00	7%	$57,245.00
2013	$57,245.00	7%	$61,252.15
2014	$61,252.15	6%	$64,927.28
2015	$64,927.28	6%	$68,822.92
2016	$68,822.92	5%	$72,264.06
2017	$72,264.06	5%	$75,877.26
2018	$75,877.26	5%	$79,671.13
2019	$79,671.13	5%	$83,654.68
2020	$83,654.68	5%	$87,837.42

some kind of certainty to Joy Candies. You can use a 15 percent discount rate for this kind of business certainty.

You can calculate the present value of the future owner earnings below.

Owner income = Owner income (Final) (from previous table)
Discount rate = 15%
First year = 1.5
Second year = $(1.5)^2$
Third year = $(1.5)^3$
It will continue to increase each successive year,
Tenth year = $(1.5)^{10}$
Present value = Owner income ÷ discount rate

Year	Owner Income	Discount Rate	Present Value
2011	$53,500.00	1.50	$35,666.67
2012	$57,245.00	2.25	$25,442.22
2013	$61,252.15	3.38	$18,148.79
2014	$64,927.28	5.06	$12,825.14
2015	$68,822.92	7.59	$9,063.10
2016	$72,264.06	11.39	$6,344.17
2017	$75,877.26	17.09	$4,440.92
2018	$79,671.13	25.63	$3,108.64
2019	$83,654.68	38.44	$2,176.05
2020	$87,837.42	57.67	$1,523.24

Dilution

You are going to buy the entire candy shop, so you do not need to worry about the dilution problem.

Bank Credit Line

Joy Candies has $10,000 worth of debt with various banks. The new owner needs to assume that debt.

Intrinsic Value Calculation

Now you can calculate the intrinsic value as explained here.

To calculate the sum of present discounted values, you need to add all the present discounted values from the previous table (last column).

Sum of present discounted values = $118,738.93

Now you need to calculate the residual value.

Owner income final at the end of 2020 = $87,837.42 (from the owner income table).

You can assume that owner income will increase 4 percent after the eleventh year.

At the end of 2021, owner income = $87,832.42 + ($87,832.42 × 0.04) = $91,345.72

You can use capitalization rate of 4 percent.

Residual value at the end of 2021 = $91,345.72 ÷ 0.04
= $2,283, 642.92

Present value of residual value = $2,283,642.92 ÷ $(1.5)^{11}$
= $26,401.24

Candy shop intrinsic value = Present value of residual value
+ Sum of present discounted value
+ Cash and cash equivalent − Debt

Candy shop intrinsic value = $26,401.24 + $118,738.93
+ $0 − $10,000 = **$135,140.17**

If you buy the candy shop at a 50 percent discount to calculated intrinsic value, that is excellent.

You need a minimum 25 percent discount to intrinsic value, so the maximum offer price is $101,355.13, but the asking price is $150,000.

Your maximum offer price should be **$101,355.13** and no more. You need to negotiate with the seller regarding the possible risks you may encounter in running the candy shop and mention the new competitor coming onto the same street. Also talk about the economy slowing. If the seller is firm on his $150,000 offer price, you have to walk away from the negotiation.

You did the intrinsic calculation for the simple candy shop in the previous example; now you can try to calculate with the actual stock for Infosys (INFY).[1] You can find all the required data in the stock research checklist chapter. You can use an Excel spreadsheet to calculate the intrinsic value, which will also be easy.

Infosys (INFY)—Owner Income Projection

As per the checklist items which we created for Infosys, here is the owner income detail for the last 10 years:

Year	Net Income	Depreciation and Amortization	CapEx	Owner Income
2001	$132.00	$24.50	$96.80	$59.70
2002	$164.00	$33.60	$68.30	$129.30
2003	$195.00	$39.40	$43.20	$191.20
2004	$270.00	$52.30	$93.20	$229.10
2005	$419.00	$66.00	$186.00	$299.00
2006	$555.00	$99.00	$246.00	$408.00
2007	$850.00	$118.00	$336.00	$632.00
2008	$1,155.00	$157.00	$374.00	$938.00
2009	$1,281.00	$165.00	$285.00	$1,161.00
2010	$1,313.00	$199.00	$192.00	$1,320.00

Owner income increase = 36.28 percent per year for last 10 years.

This excessive growth was possible because the company grew from owner income of $59 million to $1.32 billion in 10 years. You cannot assume the same rapid kind of owner income growth rate going forward.

What is the percentage of owner income increase from 2008 to 2010, when the United States was in a recession?

Year	Net Income	Depreciation and Amortization	CapEx	Owner Income
2008	$1,155.00	$157.00	$374.00	$938.00
2009	$1,281.00	$165.00	$285.00	$1,161.00
2010	$1,313.00	$199.00	$192.00	$1,320.00

Owner income increase is 18.62 percent per year for the last two years.

The U.S. economy was in a recession the last two years and it slowly started to recover at the end of 2010. Companies will continue to increase spending in the coming years. You can ignore that growth when you are projecting owner income. If that growth happens, it will be added to the margin of safety.

For conservative purposes, you can use a 17 percent owner income growth rate for another three years, a 12 percent increase in another two years, a 10 percent increase for another three years, and a 9 percent increase for another two years.

Year	Owner Income (Initial)	Growth Rate	Owner Income (Final)
2011	$1,320	17%	$1,544
2012	$1,544	17%	$1,807
2013	$1,807	17%	$2,114
2014	$2,114	12%	$2,368
2015	$2,368	12%	$2,652
2016	$2,652	10%	$2,917
2017	$2,917	10%	$3,209
2018	$3,209	10%	$3,530
2019	$3,530	9%	$3,847
2020	$3,847	9%	$4,194

Owner income numbers are in millions.

Discount Rate   Infosys is in the information technology service business and volatility will be there. For that risk, we can add a risk premium of 5 percent, so the discount rate will be 20 percent.

Year	Owner Income	Discount Rate	Present Value
2011	$1,544	1.20	$1,287
2012	$1,807	1.44	$1,255
2013	$2,114	1.73	$1,223
2014	$2,368	2.07	$1,142
2015	$2,652	2.49	$1,066
2016	$2,917	2.99	$977
2017	$3,209	3.58	$896
2018	$3,530	4.30	$821
2019	$3,847	5.16	$746
2020	$4,194	6.19	$677

Numbers are in millions (except year and discount rates).

Dilution

Share dilution for Infosys for the last four years is shown here.

Year	Total Diluted Outstanding Shares
2007	566.1
2008	570.4
2009	570.6
2010	571.1

Share counts are in millions.

There is an average dilution of 0.22 percent every year. For conservative purposes, we can use 0.5 percent dilution for projecting every year going forward, which means by 2020 total diluted outstanding shares will equal 600.30 million shares.

Infosys has zero long-term debt and had cash and cash equivalent of $3.42 billion dollars as of September 30, 2010.

Intrinsic Value Calculation

The sum of present discounted value is $10,089 million

Now we need to calculate the residual value.

Owner income final at the end of 2020 is $4,194 million (pulled from the owner income table).

You can assume that owner income will increase 4 percent after the eleventh year.

At the end of 2021 owner income is $4,361 million.

You can use a capitalization rate of 4 percent.

Therefore, residual value at the end of 2021 = $4,361 ÷ 0.04
= $109,037 million

Present value of residual value = $109,037 million ÷ $(1.20)^{11}$
= $14,675 million

Infosys intrinsic value = Present value of residual value + Sum of
(Market cap)   present discounted value + Cash and Cash
equivalent − Debt

Infosys intrinsic value (Market cap) = $14,675 + $10,089 + $3,420 − $0
= **$28,184 million**

Total outstanding shares with dilution is 600.30 million shares.

Per share intrinsic value for Infosys is $46.95 per share.

As of December 28, 2010, Infosys stock was trading at $75.01 per share with the market cap of $42.85 billion, which means the stock is 59.76 percent overvalued.

You can change the growth rate of the company and that will change the intrinsic value of the company. You used the conservative calculation and management also projected the same kind of growth rate in the future. You will not lose money if you are conservative in your calculation. Intrinsic value is not a fixed number; if the business picks up faster than you expected, you can increase the future growth rate and come up with a higher intrinsic value number, depending upon improving fundamentals in the underlying company. On the other hand, if the business fundamentals decrease, you need to adjust your growth projection and calculate the reduced intrinsic value of the business.

PART

III

INVESTMENT MANAGEMENT

Another main task of investor is to learn how to form and how to manage the portfolio. Managing a portfolio is part art and part science.

The following chapters explain each and every part of investment management, like where to find the stock prospects, how to manage the portfolio, when to sell the stocks, how to manage emotions to profit from stock investing., how to manage risk, and how to use options to enhance return.

Key Points

- You can search stock prospects in the Value Line investment survey, Magic Formula investing, *Wall Street Journal*, and company and shopping mall visits.
- Enough diversification is required to reduce the risk and volatility of the portfolio.
- Sell a stock after it reaches or is above the calculated intrinsic value of the company. Sell a stock only when the company fundamentals are deteriorating and there are no reasonable management actions to turn around the situation.
- Mr. Market and Fear and Greed should not command your buying and selling decisions. Be calm and make rational decisions as per your investment research and strategy.

- You can use 5 to 10 percent of the portfolio in Long-term Equity Anticipation Securities (LEAPS) to enhance return of your portfolio.
- You don't need to buy and sell all the time to generate great return all the time. Wait for the perfect pitch.
- Look for quality companies at bargain prices rather than cigar-butt companies.

CHAPTER

24

Margin of Safety

In previous chapters, you calculated the intrinsic value of businesses. When calculating the intrinsic value, you are using past owner earnings to try to project future owner earnings for the company for many years into the future. Future numbers are not going to be the same as those in the past. There may be multiple challenges in the future: The economy may slow down or go into a recession, a particular industry may fall into a temporary slump, or the company itself may develop problems and start to generate less revenue and earnings. You need to prepare for those kinds of variations; even if they happen, you should not lose money. This is where the margin of safety comes into play. You need to buy the stock at a discount to the calculated intrinsic value of the company.

For example, if you calculate the company's intrinsic value to be $30 per share and you buy the shares at $20 per share, that is a 33 percent discount to intrinsic value. If you buy shares at a 50 percent discount to the intrinsic value of the company, that is excellent. Your investment return will likely be higher when your discount to intrinsic value is higher.

Suppose you are buying the stock at a 50 percent discount to intrinsic value and you keep the stock until it reaches its intrinsic value; here is the return calculation:

Scenario 1: Buying at a 50 percent discount to intrinsic value.

Company X intrinsic value: $25 per share

Average buy price: $12.50 per share

Duration: 2 years to reach the intrinsic value

I = Compounded annual return

$I = ((25/12.5)^{1/2} - 1) \times 100$

Compound annual return: 41.42 percent.

Scenario 2: Buying at a 25 percent discount to intrinsic value.

Company X intrinsic value: $25 per share

Average buy price: $18.75 per share

Duration: 2 years to reach the intrinsic value

$I = ((25 \div 18.75)^{1/2} - 1) \times 100$

Compound annual return: 15.47 percent

Scenario 3: Buying at a 75 percent discount to intrinsic value.

Company X intrinsic value: $25 per share

Average buy price: $6.25 per share

Duration: 2 years to reach the intrinsic value

$I = ((25/6.25)^{1/2} - 1) \times 100$

Compound annual return: 100 percent

Look at the compound annual return variation, which depends upon the buy price (discount to intrinsic value). When the discount rate increases from 25 percent to 75 percent of the intrinsic value, the investment return increased 84.53 percent in compound annual return, which is an excellent difference. You need to try to find companies that offer deep discounts to the intrinsic value. You cannot get a deep discount to intrinsic value every time, but, when some negative economic event like a financial crisis or a market crash happens, you can often get a high percentage discount to intrinsic value. At those times, you need to bet a big percentage of your portfolio so that you can generate the highest possible return.

When you are searching for stocks, you can use a different kind of discount to intrinsic value in your calculation. For example, the company's earnings are mostly predictable and the earnings are growing at a decent rate, which is more than 15 percent for the last 10 years. Your buy price should be around a 25 percent discount to intrinsic value of the business. You may think this is a smaller discount to intrinsic value, but think about the growth in earnings many years into the future.

Here is an example of Buffett's investment in Coca-Cola:

"We like the stocks that generate high returns on invested capital where there is a strong likelihood that it will continue to do so. For example, the last time we bought Coca-Cola, it was selling at about 23 times earnings. Using our purchase price and today's earnings that makes it about 5 times earnings. It's really the interaction of capital employed, the return on that capital, and future capital generated versus the purchase price today."[1]

How was that possible? The answer is growth in earnings. If Buffett avoided Coca-Cola stock during 1988 because he was looking for a higher discount to intrinsic value, he might have missed excellent earnings on the Coca-Cola company for the last 22 years. For companies like Coca-Cola, waiting to buy at more than a 25 percent discount to intrinsic value will be difficult. You may never get that kind of opportunity.

You can increase the discount to intrinsic value when you are dealing in highly volatile businesses like tech businesses. This is because of the earnings variation, competitive pressure, and short-term product life cycle. Take Intel, for example; it introduced microprocessors with speeds that doubled every 18 months. If Intel lagged behind any new product innovation, its earnings would have been affected very quickly. In these kinds of companies, you need to seek a higher discount to intrinsic value. When there is a sudden drop in the earnings of a company, obviously the market price of the stock drops significantly. If you bought the stock at a high discount to intrinsic value before the drop, you can still generate respectable returns instead of posting losses.

If you buy at a discount to intrinsic value, it does not mean that you will not see a loss in your portfolio. Market prices change irrationally during the short term for various reasons apart from underlying company fundamentals. But, if you are confident that you calculated intrinsic value based on valid reasons, you can buy more when the prices are depressed.

Entry price is very important to investment success. Never buy any stock without at least a 25 percent discount to intrinsic value. This rule should never be forgotten. If you buy at the wrong price, you likely will not make money on your purchase, even if the underlying business is successful. If you buy at a bargain price, which has a higher discount to intrinsic value, even moderate business success will give you an excellent return on your investment.

Suppose you are buying an asset-rich or troubled company and you buy the stock at a price that is discounted to the underlying assets of the company. Even if the company goes into the liquidation process, you can still make a profit from your purchase.

Before purchasing any stock and before considering possible upside potential, calculate the potential downside. Ask yourself what the probability of losing that investment is. If you buy the stock with a high enough discount to intrinsic value, you can make a great return on that investment.

Here is the example from my investment in RCM Technologies (RCMT), which is a relatively unknown information technology (IT) company. I started buying RCMT at around $1 per share to $1.50 per share during the fourth quarter of 2008 and the first quarter of 2009. RCMT has three different divisions:

1. The information technology division, which provides IT solutions and consulting services to S&P 500 companies in the United States.
2. The engineering segment, which offers engineering and design professionals and also construction management.
3. The commercial division, which provides staffing of health-care professionals.

When I was analyzing the business, the market cap of the company was around $13 million. The economy was in a recession. During recessionary periods, staffing businesses are also depressed. When the economy started to recover, RCM also started to recover. I analyzed the business as per the stock research checklist items and calculated the intrinsic value to be around $3 per share. The stock was trading at around $1 to $1.50 per share, which is a 66 percent to 50 percent discount to intrinsic value. I was totally confident that the stock was trading at a discount to the intrinsic value of the business.

Apart from the discount to intrinsic value calculation, the liquidation value also gave me the confidence to invest 20 percent of my portfolio in one single stock. The liquidation value calculation is explained below. At the end of 2008, the company had $62 million in accounts receivable, cash around $0.85 million, and other current assets totaling $3 million. Therefore, its total current assets were $66.7 million at the time.

Total current liabilities: $23.4 million, and there was no long-term debt.

You can take 75 percent of the accounts receivable as *collectable*: $46.5 million

Cash = $0.85 million

You can eliminate the other assets.

Conservative assets: $ 47.35 million

Total current liabilities: $23.4 million

Liquidation value of the company: $23.95 million

The company had 13.19 million shares outstanding.

All of this means that the per share liquidation value was $1.81 per share. I used conservative values in the above calculation. Normally, companies can collect more than 90 percent of their accounts receivable, excluding some doubtful accounts. I used only 75 percent of the accounts receivables, which is a very conservative calculation. In March 2009, when the company released its 2008 numbers, the stock was trading as low as $0.90 per share and as high as $1.22 per

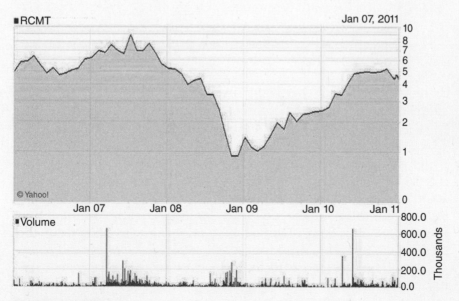

Figure 24.1   RCMT Chart

share, which is 45 percent and 32.5 percent discounts to conservative liquidation value. The intrinsic value and liquidation value calculations convinced me to buy into the stock at an average price of around $1.15 per share.

See Figure 24.1 for RCMT's prices.

In June 2010, CDI Corporation tried to acquire RCMT at $5.20 per share, but the board rejected the deal, saying that the offer was too low. The stock bounced around $4.5-to-$5 per share. I sold the position at between $4.50 and $5 per share. The average sale price was around $4.75 per share, which is a 360 percent return within one and a half years. That is a 134.8 percent compounded annual return.

Even if you like a stock that passes all the items in the stock research checklist very easily, never buy the stock if it trades at a price near or over the intrinsic value. You must be disciplined and wait until the stock trades at least at a 25 percent discount to intrinsic value of the company. If that particular stock does not fall to that level for some time, put it on a monitor list and try to find another under-valued stock; this way you can avoid permanent capital loss.

Where to Search for Stock Prospects

You learned about the stock research process in previous chapters, but before you start researching stocks, you need to identify stock prospects. There are many places you can find stock prospects and those places are explained in this chapter.

Value Line

Value Line (www.valueline.com) is one of the best places to search for stock prospects. Warren Buffett regularly uses Value Line to identify valuable stocks, as do I. When you get a subscription to Value Line, you are able to search for stock prospects where Warren Buffett is searching; both of you are on the same playing field. I suggest you subscribe to the following editions:

- Value investment survey—Standard edition
- Value investment survey—Small and mid-cap edition

The standard edition costs $538 and the small and mid-cap edition costs $255 annually. The total cost for both is $763 for a yearlong subscription. This money is well spent because you can find many great companies from these reports. You can get either paper or electronic versions, depending upon your preference. I subscribed to an online version so that I do not need to worry about keeping the old Value Line reports. Warren Buffett uses the paper version because he prefers not to use the computer for investment purposes. (The only thing he uses the computer for is to play bridge online with his buddies.)

Now we can delve into these reports that allow you to find great stocks.

Value Line Investment Survey—Standard Edition

Every week, Value Line issues a new report; to see it, go to the Summary & Index (S&I) report. Here are the areas to start analyzing:

1. Stocks with the highest three-to-five-year price potential
2. Biggest "Free Flow" cash generators
3. Best-performing stocks over the past 13 weeks
4. Worst-performing stocks over the past 13 weeks
5. Widest discounts from book value
6. Stocks with the lowest price-to-earnings (P/E) ratios
7. Stocks with the highest annual total returns
8. High returns earned on total capital
9. Bargain basement stocks
10. Highest growth stocks

There are hundreds of companies that will be listed under each heading. You do not need to do in-depth research on each one of the companies under these headings because that will take a lot of time and nothing will get done. You need to define the perimeter for your circle of competence. That means the industries in which you understand the business very well. How are the companies within that industry generating profits? How do the business cycles work?

As Warren Buffett puts it:

I would take one industry at a time and develop some expertise in half a dozen. I would not take the conventional wisdom now about any industries as meaning a damn thing. I would try to think it through.

If I were looking at an insurance company or a paper company, I would put myself in the frame of mind that I had just inherited that company and it was the only asset my family was ever going to own. What would I do with it? What am I thinking about? What am I worried about? Who are my

competitors? Who are my customers? Go out and talk to them,
Find out the strengths and weakness of this particular company
versus other ones. If you have done that, you may understand
the business better than the management.[1]

Stocks with Highest Three-to-Five-Year Price Potential

Here you see the list of stocks with three-to-five-year potential in
descending order. Do not blindly believe that the indicated return
will happen and try to buy the stocks that offer the maximum
returns. Look at the warning information they use:

> Some of the stocks tabulated below are very risky and apprecia-
> tion potentialities are tentative. Please read the full-page reports
> in Ratings & Reports to gain an understanding of the risks
> entailed. Some of these stocks may not be timely investment
> commitments. (See the Performance Ranks below.)[2]

Here you should eliminate the stocks that do not fit in your circle
of competence, and note the stocks that do reside in your circle of
competence. Create a Value Line folder on your computer and add
those selections to a "Value Line Research" document and date it.
The reason to date the document is that when you are creating a
new Value Line research document for each week and going over
those selections after a month, you can see that some stocks repeat
many times and new ones are added. You can continue to research
those repeated names, but do not limit yourself to the higher return
names; go over the whole list.

Biggest "Free Flow" Cash Generators

These companies earned more "cash flow" in the last five years than
required for capital expenditure and to pay dividends. Cash flow is
the lifeblood of any business. If the company is generating more
cash flow, this means the company balance sheet will be healthy. The
company can use the excessive cash flow to expand the business,
acquire other businesses, or buy back shares. You can see the ratio
of cash flow to cash out. Select the names of the companies in your

circle of competence and add the names to your "Value Line Research" document.

Best-Performing Stocks Last 13 Weeks

Here you find the list of stocks that performed the best for the last 13 weeks, measured by the stock price change. Just because they performed better over the last 13 weeks does not mean they will continue to outperform over the next 13 weeks. You need to select the stocks that reside within your circle of competence and add them to your research document. You need to find out why those stocks have outperformed in the last 13 weeks. Was there fundamental improvement in those companies? Do your research as per the stock research checklist. Some of the stocks that appear under this headline might be trading at a 52-week high.

Worst-Performing Stocks Last 13 Weeks

This list contains stocks that lost most of their price over the last 13 weeks. You might see that most of the stocks are trading at or near a 52-week low. For the stocks on this list, you need to concentrate and do your research diligently. Here you can find turnaround stocks that are on the way to bankruptcy. You need to find out why these stocks lost most of their value over the last 13 weeks. Maybe they missed their earnings marks, experienced fundamental deterioration of the business, experienced a lawsuit, had an industry downturn, or took on a heavy debt load. I found most of my winners from this list and found the best return investment of my investment career: Select Comfort (SCSS). This stock came from this list and produced a 2,000 percent return in less than two years. I also found the ATP Oil and Gas (ATPG) stock from this list. The stock was trading around $8.20 per share; it was in a 52-week low after trading at around $18 per share in April 2010. In two months, it had lost around 54.4 percent. When I found that stock, I wanted to know why its price had dropped so much within two months.

On April 23, 2010, ATPG announced that it had entered into $1.5 billion of senior second lien notes. On May 6, 2010, the company announced its first quarter 2010 results, which posted a loss. The reason behind the drop was debt concern. I did the research and found out that the company would be able to handle the debt load and not end up in bankruptcy. I got into the position at around $10 per share and bought and sold multiple times to earn a profit from that drop. The last entry price was around $14 per share and I was still holding in December 2010 when the stock was trading around 16.69 per share. The chart is shown in Figure 25.1.

Look at the return. If you got into the position when the company reached a 52-week low at $8.16 per share in June 2010 and held until December 31, 2010 at $16.69 per share, the return would be around 104 percent in six months time. This type of great return could be found in this list.

Widest Discounts from Book Value

This list contains stocks that are trading at less than book value of the company. The column "Percent price to book value" shows what the percentage of price is in terms of the book value. You should not automatically buy the lowest percentage companies from this list. Book value may not represent the true worth of the company. For example, with a capital-intensive business like an industrial company, book value is always higher. But, if the company goes into

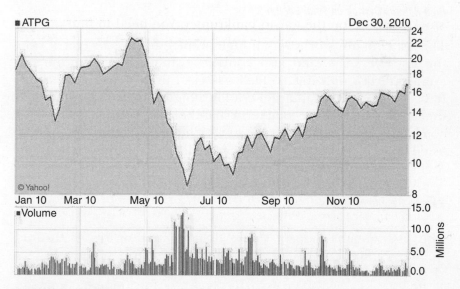

Figure 25.1   ATPG Chart

Reproduced with permission of Yahoo! Inc. ©2011 Yahoo! Inc. YAHOO! and the YAHOO! logo are registered trademarks of Yahoo! Inc. Reproduced with permission of CSI ©2009. Data Source: CSI www.csidata.com/

liquidation, its machines will sell for a fraction of their worth. You need to select the companies from this list and add them into your Value Line stock selection list. From here, you can work to discover the bargain opportunities.

Stocks with Lowest P/Es

This is a list of stocks that are trading at the lowest P/Es and is useful in finding bargain stocks. Select the stocks that are in your circle of competence and add them to your list.

Stocks with Highest Annual Total Returns

This list contains bargain securities. You see the estimated total return column, which contains the estimated compound annual stock appreciation and annual dividend income. Most of the companies overlap when it comes to those with the highest three-to-five-year price potential and those with the worst-performing stocks over the last 13 weeks. Select the stocks that are in your circle of competence and add them to your list for further research.

High Returns Earned on Total Capital

This list contains stocks with a high average of capital returns over the last five years, and also contains columns that indicate the average return on capital. Quality stocks can be found on this list. If a company is constantly generating a high return on capital, then that is very good for the long-term shareholders. You can find quality companies like Colgate-Palmolive (CL) and GlaxoSmithKline (GSK) listed here. Whatever stocks reside in your circle of competence, add them to your list for further research.

Bargain Basement Stocks

This list contains bargain stocks that are trading below the net working capital.

Net working capital = Current assets − All liabilities including long-term debt and preferred

Most of this list overlaps with the lists of stocks with the highest three-to-five-year price potential, stocks with the highest annual total returns, and worst-performing stocks over the last 13 weeks. When you buy stocks that are undervalued, you can make a lot of money when the companies turn around.

Highest Growth Stocks

This list shows the growth rate for the last 10 years and estimated growth for two to five years in the future. You can see high-flier stocks listed here, like Apple (AAPL) and Decker's Outdoor (DECK). Most of the stocks on this list trade at a high multiple. You need to search for stocks that operate in your circle of competence and add them to your list for further research. If those stocks pass the checklist items, put them on your monitor list. Whenever there is a market sell-off, as during the financial crisis of 2008, these stock prices drop significantly. These kinds of opportunities are only open for a short time; you need to act fast and buy a meaningful number of shares and hold them for the long term for a maximum return. Again, the entry price is very important.

Value Line—Small and Mid-Cap Edition

Now you can explore the *Value Line—Small and mid-cap edition*. Go to the small and mid-cap S&I report:

1. Biggest "Free-Flow" Cash Generators
2. Widest Discounts from Book Value
3. Highest Percentage Earned on Capital
4. Bargain Basement Stocks
5. Best-Performing Stocks (Last 13 weeks)
6. Worst-Performing Stocks (Last 13 weeks)

Repeat the same processes you performed for the standard edition and add the selections to your "Value Line Selection List" document and start researching the stocks as per the stock research checklist.

Magic Formula

The book *The Little Book that Beats the Market*[3] was written by Joel Greenblatt, who created the magic formula to find the highest quality stocks selling at bargain prices and set up the web site www.magicformulainvesting.com.[4] Go to this web site and register yourself for free. Login to the web site, then go to "Magic Formula Investing Stock Screener." Select a minimum market cap of $50 million (you can change this depending on your requirements), select a number of stocks (up to 50), and click "Get Stocks." This will generate a list of stocks in alphabetical order. Select the stocks that are in your circle of competence and add them to a new document you name "Magic Formula List." You can change the minimum market cap to $100 million and keep on increasing it up to $500 million. Most of the stocks will be repeated, but a couple of stocks will be added for each market cap change; add those selections to your list.

The web site advises that you invest methodically, but you do not need to do that. Do your research against the stock research checklist and calculate the intrinsic value of the businesses. Never invest methodically; you need to understand the true worth of a business and you should have a thorough understanding of that business and how that business' cycle behaves, how that business makes money, and how it performs against competitors. You will then be able to hold the stocks until the business realizes its intrinsic value. Sometimes market-related events decrease the price of stocks dramatically. If you do not know the true worth of a business, you will probably panic and sell at the lowest price point. Never buy a stock without researching against the checklist items.

The Wall Street Journal

You should read the *Wall Street Journal*[5] every day, but do not automatically react to the news. The following sections will be useful to get stock ideas from the *Wall Street Journal*.

Insider Trading Spotlight

Every week, the Saturday edition of the *Wall Street Journal* publishes a list of the biggest weekly insider individual trades that happened within that week. This list shows the biggest buying and selling activities by insiders. Do not worry about the selling; the insider selling may not be a bad sign. They may need money for personal reasons apart from factors affecting the company. If the insider is buying, that means he or she thinks the present price is undervalued compared with the true intrinsic value of the business, or that the insider thinks the future of the business is going to improve. You can select the stocks in your circle of competence and create a list called "Insider List." Do in-depth research against the checklist items and calculate the intrinsic value.

There are multiple web sites created to follow insider trading. You can usually get the data faster online than through the newspaper, but, you have to subscribe for that information. In truth, you do not need them, because as soon as the insider buying is reported, a lot of people will try to buy those stocks, and the sudden spike of buying activity will immediately increase the price of the stock, especially if that company is a small-cap company. After that initial spike, in couple of weeks, traders will likely cash in their immediate gains. There will be pull-back and then you can get in at a reasonable price.

Market Data

Market data are published every day in the *Wall Street Journal*. Take a look at the percentage of gainers, percentage of losers, and volume movers. You can find the highest percentage moves in either direction or a sudden volume increase in stocks. There should be a reason for those moves. Select the stocks that are in your circle of competence and find out why the moves happened. You can get that information from http://finance.yahoo.com under the particular stock's headline options or go to the company's web site and look at the press releases.

For positive price movements, there may be an earnings surprise, a large order, or a management change; *something* will be there. If you like what you see, create a "*Wall Street Journal* List" and do the research against your stock research checklist. Do not overreact to the positive news and buy the stock immediately. You have to complete your stock research and that will take time. Even if you like the stock after doing your research, just leave it for a couple of weeks. You will see the pull-back as soon as the positive news fades and then you can buy the stock for a slightly cheaper price.

For negative price movement, there may be negative events that have happened in the company. These may include an earnings miss, a lawsuit against the company, a sudden departure of senior management, or the loss of a huge order. Select the stocks in your circle of competence and do research to discover the reason for the price drop. If you feel the reason for the price drop is temporary and the market is overreacting, that means you can get a great company at a bargain price. Immediately start the research process and calculate the intrinsic value. You need to act fast to make use of the buying opportunity, but do not buy any stock without doing in-depth research against the stock research checklist.

A positive or negative event within the company may be the reason for a volume increase list, so complete the research process, and add the selected stocks to your *Wall Street Journal* list for further research.

Company Visits

After you have researched a company against the stock research checklist and calculated its intrinsic value, try to visit the company and meet with senior management. If you are dealing with a small company, you can probably meet the CEO. If the company is mid-size, you can probably meet the CFO, COO, chief sales officer, vice president of sales, or vice president of investor relations. If you tell them that you are planning to buy 100,000 shares, they will give you an appointment. After researching the company, you should have a pretty good idea about the business and its revenue trend, net income trend, profit margin trend, financial condition, and management revenue projection. Before the appointment, read the competitor's annual reports so you will have a pretty good idea of how the company is doing when compared to competitors. When you are visiting with management, make sure to have prepared questions. Find out the company's plan for the next 5 to 10 years. How is management planning to grow the businesses? What steps are they taking to increase profit margin and reduce expenses? What is the plan to reduce debt or use cash holdings efficiently? At the end of the interview, ask them who the competitor is that they admire most and why. Normally, you get an honest answer and you can start researching that company too. Most of the time, that information will be very beneficial to you. Create a list called

"Company Visits" and add any companies you find through company visits.

Magazines

By subscribing to *Fortune, Forbes, Business Week,* and *Barron's,* you can get information about many companies. You can use this information as a starting point for your research, but never make buy-and-sell decisions solely based on the articles. You have to complete your usual research process before making any decision. Create a document called "Magazine Lists" and add any companies you find through magazine research.

Shopping Mall Visits

Again, I got this tip from Peter Lynch. Make a regular habit of visiting different retail malls and while walking around, look at the crowded and new stores. Check out the products and casually ask other shoppers why they like the store. Research whether the company is publicly traded and start the research process. I found many of my big winners this way.

Buffett performed credit card research at a Ross's Steak House in Omaha, Nebraska. He checked how many people were using American Express charge cards to find out the brand loyalty of American Express before his big investment during American Express's salad oil scandal.

If you have children and a spouse, examine their shopping habits; their interests may constantly be changing to different products manufactured by different companies. Pay attention to whether they recently started buying new products. If you have teenaged children, you can get easily learn about a new fashion-products company.

If you are traveling, pay attention to any new chain stores or restaurants you see. You may be spotting the next McDonald's or Home Depot. Create a document titled "Mall Visits" And add any companies you find through mass visits.

Now you will have created seven lists:

1. Value Line Selection List
2. Magic Formula List

3. Insider List
4. *Wall Street Journal* List
5. Company Visits
6. Magazine Lists
7. Mall Visits

Now you need to start researching these lists for companies that pass each item in your stock research checklist. Read annual and quarterly reports and listen to conference calls. Read the companies' competitors' annual and quarterly reports and listen to their conference calls. Short-list the companies that pass most of the checklist items and then calculate the intrinsic value for those companies. Create a spreadsheet for those companies and include the calculated intrinsic value. Calculate the current price relative to the intrinsic value; is it overvalued or undervalued? If the stock price is less than the intrinsic value, calculate the percentage discount to intrinsic value. If the stock price is trading above the intrinsic value, calculate the percentage that it is overvalued. You can name this spreadsheet "Intrinsic Value Monitor List." You can create the portfolio in finance.yahoo.com and label it as a monitor list.

If you find that any of the stocks are trading at a 25 percent discount to intrinsic value, those stocks are eligible for purchase. First select the maximum discount to the intrinsic value companies, and then move to lesser discount-to-intrinsic-value companies. Start purchasing incrementally. Now, you need to adopt the portfolio rules as explained in Chapter 26.

CHAPTER 26

Portfolio Management

Portfolio management is another very important task for an investor. In this chapter, we will split the portfolio management into three parts:

1. Portfolio creation: Diversification, number stocks in the portfolio, and position sizing.
2. Managing the portfolio: How to add new positions and trim existing positions.
3. Consider different countries.

Diversification

You probably already know that you should not invest all of your money in a single industry or related industry. If your portfolio is diversified and any one particular industry is down, you should not experience a loss.

For example, when the 2008 financial crisis struck, the real estate industry was hit the hardest. Real estate started booming in 2004 and banks started lending recklessly to sub prime borrowers. If you invested all of your money in home-building companies and/or banks that lent the money to sub prime borrowers, you might have lost 50 to 70 percent of your portfolio assets when the financial crisis hit. With diversification, your main task is to not invest most of your money in a single industry or related industries.

You should diversify your portfolio with at least 7 to 10 companies in different industries that are not related to one another so that one industry downturn does not affect your portfolio in a negative way. This does not mean investors should try to spread out their investment dollars between 50 or 100 companies, ranging across 20 different industries. That behavior would likely yield mediocre results.

In order to diversify, try to define a perimeter of industries in which you are going to allocate your money. You should have expert knowledge in those industries and you should know how to analyze the businesses within it. You should start with the industry in which you are working. For example, if you are working in the banking industry, you know the industry very well. You can concentrate on identifying the best and most undervalued companies in that industry and allocate at least 10 percent to 20 percent of your portfolio assets to them. Your expertise should allow you to identify an industry turn well before Wall Street acknowledges it so that you can buy stocks at bargain prices.

For our example, let us consider an investor who is working in the banking industry. He might have noticed in 2004 that his bank was making residential and commercial mortgage loans to only worthy borrowers. Banking was in good condition, generating usual revenue and net income. Then, real estate prices started going up and banks started loosening their lending standards, reducing loan-to-value (LTV) limits and accepting stated income. Banks started lending to subprime borrowers. As a banking executive, this investor should realize that banks were making more risky loans, reducing their lending standards. These behaviors would eventually lead to more loss. If his bank was making bad loans, other banks were probably also doing the same.

Please note: I am not advising you to invest by using insider information that is unknown to the public. That is illegal. Insiders have specific rules for trading their company's shares and you should always follow Securities and Exchange Commission (SEC) rules.

Here is another example from my own experience. I am a basically a software engineer. I graduated from a college in India and came to the United States as a software consultant and then started my own software business. I know how to analyze this industry and have knowledge about the best companies and upcoming companies in this industry. Here I will explain one of my investments in the iGATE Corporation (IGTE).

iGATE Corporation is a software-development company offering both onshore and offshore development services. It is headquartered in the United States, and has development centers in India. From a small consulting business, iGATE's founders built the business into a larger consulting company, adding some software development, and listed it on Nasdaq in 1996. The founders own more than 50 percent of the company, but the performance and growth of the company were not great for many years; revenue and earnings numbers were erratic. At the time of their initial listing I was not interested in iGATE, but I knew that I should watch its progress. Then in 2008 came an important event that turned out to be great for the company: the hiring of a new Chief Executive Officer (CEO), Phaneesh Murthy, who transformed the consulting business into a software-development company. He had previously worked with Infosys and increased revenue from $2 million to $2 billion in 15 years. When iGATE hired him as the new CEO, I was confident that the company would soon be in a significant growth mode. Sure enough, he transformed the business, and revenue and net income increased from that year forward.

I calculated the company's intrinsic value to be around $12 per share and got into the position at around $9 per share. That is a 25 percent discount to intrinsic value. I thought the new CEO would add more value to the company, which is the industry knowledge that gave me an edge compared to other people. When the financial crisis happened, the stock dropped to around $3.25 per share. At that time, iGATE had around $2 per share in cash, no long-term debt, and it generated $200 million revenue and $32 million net income. Their market cap was around $150 million, out of which $75 million was cash or cash equivalents. So, the whole company was selling at around $75 million, which was just 2.5 times the net income, and very cheap. I started adding more positions in the company. Prices started moving up from April 2009 and in November 2010 the stock was trading at around $22.90 per share. It was around a 604 percent return in 18 months. Take a look at the impressive chart shown in Figure 26.1.

I did not enjoy the whole ride, though. In June 2010, stock price went up to around $15.25 per share and started coming down. To protect the profit, I sold around $14.83 per share in June 2010, and

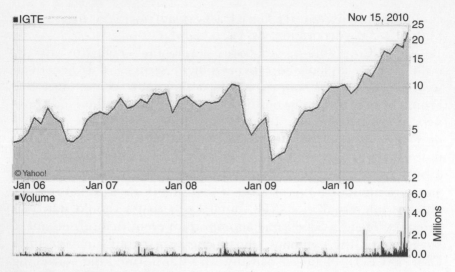

Figure 26.1   IGTE Long-Term Chart

Reproduced with permission of Yahoo! Inc. ©2011 Yahoo! Inc. YAHOO! and the YAHOO! logo are registered trademarks of Yahoo! Inc. Reproduced with permission of CSI ©2009. Data Source: CSI www.csidata.com/

thought about buying back low. But, the opposite happened; as soon as I sold the position, it started going up. The company was doing great because U.S. corporations were increasingly starting to use offshore solution providers during the recession. The projects that they postponed during 2008 and 2009 were implemented in 2010, and the company increased revenue more than 35 percent in 2010. I bought into the position again at around $16.50 per share in August 2010 and still hold the investment. As per Warren Buffett's principle, if the company grows at a reasonable growth rate into the foreseeable future, the holding period is forever. My industry knowledge gave me an opportunity to profit when the market presented a great business at bargain prices.

The above example proves that if you invest within your circle of competence, you can generate great returns. If you look at Buffett's investment career, he learned about GEICO at an early age and continued to make investments in the insurance industry. After Berkshire Hathaway, he bought the National Indemnity Company and other insurance companies were folded into Berkshire Hathaway.

In 1967, Berkshire Hathaway's insurance float was $16 million. At the end of 2009, that float was around $62 billion. But Buffett did not invest 100 percent of his assets in the insurance industry alone; he merely invested a larger percentage of his assets in the insurance industry where he possessed excellent knowledge and experience. He has always tried to improve his circle of competence one industry at a time.

Because Buffett was attracted to sustainable competitive companies like Coca-Cola, Gillette, Procter & Gamble (P&G), and Wells Fargo, he invested a major portion of his investable assets in those companies and held those shares for a long time. He understood those businesses very well and slowly started increasing his circle of competence. When the technology stocks peaked in the late 1990s, he was asked at Berkshire Hathaway's annual meeting: *Why are you not investing in tech stocks when other hedge funds and money managers are making a killing?*[1] He responded to the question saying that,

> Our principles are valid when applied to technology stocks, but we don't know how to do it. If we are going to lose your money, we want to be able to get up here next year and explain how we did it. I'm sure Bill Gates would apply the same principles. He understands technology the way I understand Coca-Cola or Gillette. I'm sure he looks for a margin of safety. I'm sure he would approach it like he owned a business and not just a stock. So our principles can work for any technology. We just aren't the ones to do it. If we can't find things within our circle of competence, we won't expand the circle. We will wait.[2]

But in the real world, an investor who is working as a doctor or drug researcher tries to invest in semiconductors or Internet companies. An investor working in the tech sector tries to invest in a drug company. Investors always think that the grass in other industries is greener than in their industry. It just does not make any sense. Investors' biggest risk is when they try to invest in companies that they do not have enough knowledge of or experience in. As Buffett puts it, *"Investing must be rational; if you can't understand it, don't do it."*[3]

Buffett always works to increase his circle of competence one industry at a time. Berkshire Hathaway's subsidiary MidAmerican

Energy invested in BYD Company Ltd. (BYDDF.PK) because of the influence of Charlie Munger. They invested around $230 million in September 2008 and that investment grew to $2.3 billion at the peak of BYD's stock price in October 2009. Electric cars are not a technically complex business; it is easy to understand the business. Buffett told a CNBC interviewer that he was planning to keep those shares for the coming decade and even longer.

You have to construct your portfolio with companies that are available in the industries as per the following priorities:

- Start with the industry in which you are working.
- Identity the industries in which you can understand the business dynamics and trends very well.
- Select the industries where the changes will be limited in the future. This does not mean you should not select the tech industry. If you are working in the tech industry and you can spot industry trends and know the businesses very well, you can invest in those industries.
- Form a portfolio with 5 to 10 different non-correlated industries so that one particular industry downturn does not affect your portfolio in a big way.

Number of Stocks in the Portfolio

Too much diversification will reduce a portfolio's performance. Too little diversification means the portfolio contains too much risk. A properly sized portfolio is the best way to achieve maximum returns, but what is the proper size? How many stocks should you own? These answers depend on your industry knowledge and the amount of available capital you have to invest. A well-selected concentrated portfolio will yield great returns.

Warren Buffett tries to run a concentrated portfolio to generate great returns. He does not believe in too much diversification consisting of 50 or 100 or 200 stocks in the portfolio. When he ran his investment partnership, he invested around 40 percent of the fund's assets ($13 million) in American Express when it was involved in the Salad Oil Scandal and made a $20 million profit in two years. That return helped his partnership post a great compounded return. In 2010, he managed a $100 billion portfolio that consisted of just 25 names.

I have heard that Peter Lynch, the great investment manager, generated a compounded annual return of more than 28 percent in the 13 years that he ran Fidelity's Magellan mutual fund. If he used to hold more than 1,000 stocks in his portfolio, then how did he generate such a great compound annual return? The answer is because even if he held 1,000 stocks in his portfolio, his top 10 positions were comprised the major percentage of the portfolio; other positions were very small percentages of the portfolio. Whenever he was interested in a company and wanted to monitor that company's progress, he used to invest a small amount of money in them. His concentrated portfolio allowed him to generate maximum possible returns.

The fund I run, GJ Funds, generated a great cumulative return from 30 months using a concentrated portfolio. The SEC does not allow GJ Funds to put the return numbers up for view by non-accredited investors. I try to hold 10 to 20 names in the portfolio and the top 10 positions make up the major part of the portfolio.

Warren Buffett and Ben Graham differ in their stances on diversification. Ben Graham likes to diversify the portfolio with a higher number of stocks since his method is one of buying securities that are trading at bargain prices less than networking capital. Some of these companies will end up in bankruptcy, but one company loss should not affect the portfolio's returns. Warren Buffett, on the other hand, believes in running a concentrated portfolio of great companies that are bought at cheaper prices. So, the conclusion is running a concentrated portfolio with 10 to 20 names will give you the best return possible.

Position Sizing

After considering the number of stocks in the portfolio, the next objective in portfolio management is position sizing. What percentage of the portfolio will be allocated to each security in order to generate the maximum possible return? This depends upon the number of securities that are available at that particular time. If you have decided to go with a 15-stock portfolio when you are selecting the stocks for investment, assign numbers for those selections, with number 1 being the best selection and number 15 the stock with the least potential. You should allocate around 35 to 55 percent of the portfolio to the top five selections, 20 to 30 percent of the portfolio for the next five positions, and the remainder to the last five positions. This will be the optimum level of position sizing and will be better than having an equal amount of position sizing for each stock.

If you take Berkshire Hathaway's current portfolio, the top 10 positions occupy the major part of the investment portfolio. Buffett's best ideas—like Coca-Cola, P&G, American Express, Wells Fargo, and Kraft Foods—occupy the major part of the portfolio. See the chart that follows.

Berkshire Hathaway common stock investments that at year end had a market value of more than $1 billion as of 12/31/09.

S.No	Company Name	Cost*	Percent of Portfolio	Market Value
1	American Express	$1,287	3.71	$6,143
2	BYD Auto	$232	0.67	$1,986
3	Coca-Cola	$1,299	3.75	$11,400
4	ConocoPhillips	$2,741	7.91	$1,926
5	Johnson & Johnson	$1,724	4.98	$1,838
6	Kraft Foods	$4,330	12.50	$3,541
7	POSCO	$768	2.22	$2,092
8	Procter & Gamble	$533	1.54	$5,040
9	Sanofi	$2,027	5.85	$1,979
10	Tesco	$1,367	3.95	$1,620
11	U.S .Bancorp	$2,371	6.84	$1,725
12	Wal-Mart	$1,893	5.46	$2,087
13	Wells Fargo	$7,394	21.34	$9,021
14	Others	$6,680	19.28	$8,636
		$34,646	100.00	$59,034

*Numbers in millions.

This is our actual purchase price and also our tax basis; GAAP "cost" differs in a few cases because of write-ups or write-downs that have been required. In addition, we own positions in non-traded securities of Dow Chemical, General Electric, Goldman Sachs, Swiss Re, and Wrigley with an aggregate cost of $21.1 billion and a carrying value of $26.0 billion. We purchased these five positions in the last 18 months. Setting aside the significant equity potential they provide us, these holdings deliver us an aggregate of $2.1 billion annually in dividends and interest. Finally, we owned 76,777,029 shares (22.5%) of BNSF at yearend, which we then carried at $85.78 per share, but which have subsequently been melded into our purchase of the entire company."[4]

I added the percentage of the portfolio as a cost basis. Look at the portfolio sizing of the top five investments:

Wells Fargo: 21.34%
Kraft Foods: 12.50%
ConocoPhillips: 7.91%
U.S. Bancorp: 6.84%
Sanofi-Aventis: 5.85%

These top five positions occupied 54.44 percent of the $34.6 billion portfolio. This kind of position sizing yields great performance.

Managing the Portfolio

Ongoing administration of the portfolio is the next objective in portfolio management. Once the portfolio is formed, try to hold it for at least two years. When you are making changes to the portfolio, you have to trim the existing positions as explained in the next chapter. If you add or replace one or two positions in a quarter, that should be acceptable. If you are investing in undervalued securities or companies in turnaround situations, you need to allow sufficient time for the company's management to work through the company's problems and start posting the positive earnings.

A relevant example of a turnaround situation comes from when I was following Select Comfort (SCSS) around 2005, when they were rapidly growing, as shown in Figure 26.2.

I liked the company, but I did not like it enough because of the stock price and the company's debt position. I bought about 100 shares at around $18 per share and kept them in a watch list. The price reached around $25 in early 2006 and trading was around $20 to $25 for a couple of years. In 2008, a recession started, company revenue started coming down, and the company posted less revenue and earnings.

I continued to follow the company; its debt load increased and its revenue decreased. It was going to violate the bank covenants, and was looking to raise capital from private investors or existing institutional investors. It was in the process of decreasing expenses and reducing its number of stores. Select Comfort was closing

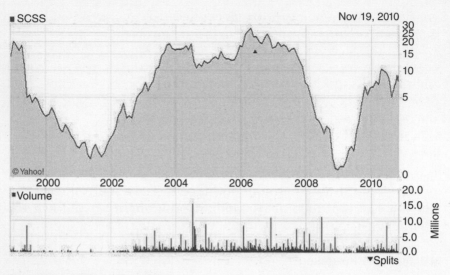

Figure 26.2   SCSS Long-Term Chart

Reproduced with permission of Yahoo! Inc. ©2011 Yahoo! Inc. YAHOO! and the YAHOO! logo are registered trademarks of Yahoo! Inc. Reproduced with permission of CSI ©2009. Data Source: CSI www.csidata.com/

non-performing stores, removing its dealership relationships, and concentrating on company-owned stores.

Management started lowering management salaries and spent less on marketing initiatives. By listening to the conference calls and reading quarterly and annual reports, I got a feeling that the actions to fight the downturn were appropriate. Stocks started trading at around $0.20 per share. The company announced the signing of an agreement with Sterling Partners for an infusion of $35 million in equity capital scheduled for July 2010, pending shareholder approval. I became confident that the company would survive. I started a hedge fund in November 2008 and started building up the position. Between the last quarter of 2008 and the first quarter of 2009, I invested 20 percent of the portfolio in SCSS at around $0.45 per share.

Select Comfort started recovering and its cost-cutting initiatives were almost finished. Terminating the dealership relationships and closing down non-performing company stores were helping to improve the business. Select Comfort started increasing revenue numbers and reducing loss in the second and third quarters of 2010. They started paying down the bank debt and satisfied the bank covenants from the cash flow generated from the business. Since management no longer needed the equity capital, shareholders rejected the Sterling Capital deal. The stock kept increasing. I sold it at around $9 per share and made 20 times the initial investment within 16 months of purchase. The company paid down the debt completely and cash flow continued to increase. Even after I sold the stock, I followed the company's fundamentals, which were improving. When the European debt crisis and double-dip recession surfaced, the stock came down to around $4.75 per share. I thought I would wait for an even lower price to start buying, but it quickly rebounded. I invested around 10 percent of the portfolio at $6.45 per share in the third quarter of 2010. In November 2010, it was trading at $8.45 per share and the fund was still holding the shares. This investment helped me to generate great returns to the fund, which is why position sizing is very important. Whenever odds of success are increasing, you need to invest a sufficient amount of your portfolio in that particular opportunity so that you can increase returns.

In this example, we see that another lesson is patience. When you are confident that a company's fundamentals are improving, you should patiently hold the stock for the maximum possible return. I might have sold SCSS shares at $0.90 per share as soon as they doubled and made a quick profit within a couple of months. It might have made me happy thinking that I did well, but, I also might have lost another 1,900 percent return from that investment.

Diversification with Different Countries

Because the economies of different countries grow at different rates, it is beneficial to diversify your portfolio with foreign stocks. The U.S. market is growing slowly at about 2 percent to 3 percent of its gross domestic product (GDP) and is expected to continue growing at the same rate in the near future. European growth is expected to slow until European countries reduce their deficits. Emerging markets like China, India, Brazil, and Latin America, though, are growing at about 7 percent of their GDP.

When you have limited capital, you do not need to go directly to foreign exchanges for foreign stocks. Foreign stocks are traded on U.S. exchanges as American Depository Receipts (ADRs). You can buy these shares to avoid currency risk.

In a balanced portfolio, about 30 to 40 percent is invested in emerging markets such as China, India, Brazil, and Latin America. You can divide the position sizing depending on the available opportunities in those countries.

Buying ADRs requires thorough research. You need to research management profiles thoroughly and try to get the backgrounds of the management professionals. Search the management professionals through Google and try to read all of the applicable links. Determine if the management professionals are linked with any frauds or lawsuits related to ethical standards. If so, you should obviously avoid those companies.

Many Chinese small-cap stocks are caught up in accounting frauds and have lost investors a lot of money. In India, Satyam software committed accounting fraud, showing $1 billion of fictitious money on its balance sheet. Mahindra took over the company and is now rebuilding it. Extensive research is necessary to avoid a total loss of your investment. If you doubt the ethical standards of a company, then just skip that company and move forward.

You need to read the company's annual and quarterly reports carefully to identify warning signs, which include:

- Footnotes in quarterly and annual reports—If you do not understand them, skip that company and move forward to identify another company.
- Related-party transaction—If you find many related-party transactions, skip the company.
- Management background—Research management's background carefully. Find out which companies its members have worked for before. Read about those companies. If you discover any accounting fraud, reject the present company.
- Scuttlebutt approach—Try to speak to the company's suppliers, agents, customers, and competitors. If you uncover any unpleasant information, skip the company.

Selling Strategy

Up to this point, we have discussed the strategies for *buying* securities, but selling is also a crucial part of successful investing. Selling takes discipline so that you can achieve maximum possible returns from your investments. As Warren Buffett often says, "My favorite timeframe for holding a stock is forever." However, that does not mean that he will not sell the stocks in his portfolio. He used that statement in the context of forever holdings like Coca-Cola and American Express.

Here are the situations in which you should think about selling a position:

- You should hold the stock until it reaches your calculated intrinsic value of the business. If the price movement of the stock is very good, you can hold the stock even after the stock price crosses your calculated intrinsic value. For example, imagine you calculated the intrinsic value of the company at around $20 per share and bought the stock for $10 per share. In a couple of years the price of the security reaches $20 per share. Growth companies keep growing every year. You can calculate the current intrinsic value of the company using the current owner income. If there is no fundamental improvement in the company commanding more than $20 per share intrinsic value, you can start selling the security at $20 per share and above. Suppose the company is in a growing mode and the company is increasing revenue and net income at around 20 percent annually; try to calculate the new intrinsic value at that time. If you come up with a new intrinsic value at around $30 per share, do not sell, try to hold the stock until the price reaches around $30 per share.

- When you decide to sell, you have to make up your mind about the minimum price at which you can sell the stock. In this example, say the minimum is $20 per share. When your stock reaches $20 per share, unload 5 to 10 percent of your position. After the first sell action, if your stock reaches $19.90 per share and lower, do not sell any more shares. Patiently hold the stock until it again reaches your minimum sell price at more than $20 per share. This time, after couple of weeks, if the stock reaches $22 per share, unload another 5 to 10 percent of the position. This way you can sell at the maximum possible price.

- You can sell a current position to buy other undervalued stocks. Consider the following example:

Company A

Buy price is $10 per share, purchase date is January 1, 2009. The number of shares is 100, so the invested amount is $1,000.

Your calculated intrinsic value of the business is $20 per share.

You hold this position for 18 months, so the date is now July 1, 2010.

The stock is trading at $18 per share.

Now your position is valued at $1,800.

There is a 20 percent upside available in this investment. If it takes another six months to reach $20 per share, that means you can earn another $200 if you keep the investment.

Suppose that you have another opportunity, Company B, which is trading at around a 50 percent discount to intrinsic value.

You can sell Company A shares and have cash available to invest of $1,800.

Company B

Company B's share price is $10 per share, so you can buy 180 shares on July 1, 2010.

The stock of Company B appreciates the same 20 percent and on December 31, 2010, the company share price is $12 per share.

The stock's value on December 31, 2010, is $2,160, so the profit made from this investment is $2,160 − $1,800 = $360.

Because you bought another undervalued stock, you earned an additional $160, which is 8.88 percent more than if you kept the Company A shares.

This example shows the velocity of money. Here, the rule is if you have an opportunity to buy another undervalued stock, you will sell the existing position and buy the undervalued stock. If you repeat the same process for many years, you can compound the money faster.

- Suppose you bought the stock because of faulty research with incorrect assumptions or a certain outside event changed the dynamics of a particular industry; then you can sell the stock. For example, after the 9/11 terrorist attacks, the airline industry went south and revenues plummeted. In those situations, cut your losses and use the proceeds to buy another undervalued stock to try to recover the losses.

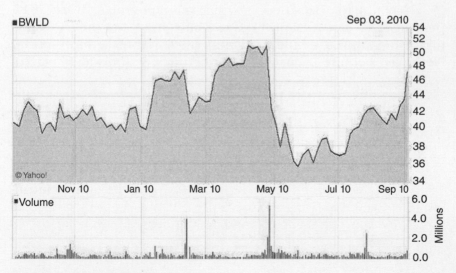

Figure 27.1   BWLD Long term Chart

- The market is ruled by fear and greed, and can therefore go down for many reasons. Bad economic news sends stocks lower without any underlying changes in the company's fundamentals. In those situations, do not panic and sell, because the market will turn and your sold position will go higher immediately. You might not get a chance to reenter. In those situations, if you know more about the company and its intrinsic value, you should buy more so that the average purchase price will be less.

Figure 27.1 shows a trading example.

In July 2010, Buffalo Wild Wings (BWLD) was trading at around $38 per share; it went to $42 per share in a month, which was around a 10.5 percent gain. Bad economic reports came out and the market started to sell off. BWLD share price was coming down. My stock profit was also coming down. I did not want to lose the profit, so I sold at around $39.51, taking a 3.91 percent profit. My thought process was that I would take a profit and use that money to buy more BWLD at the lower price. It would have been a good idea if I could have timed the market, but reality was different. After I sold my position, BWLD slowly began turning around. One day BWLD closed at $40.53. Within one week, it was trading at around $47.41 per share. Because of my market-timing plan, I lost 20.85 percent of the potential profit. If you have an idea of the true value of a company, you should hold your stock and make more profit. Never sell because of macroeconomic news or short-term market variation.

CHAPTER

28

Mr. Market and Investor Psychology

In order to generate maximum returns possible in the investing business, it is important to understand investor psychology and market psychology. As Ben Graham explained in his famous Mr. Market analogy, you and Mr. Market are partners in business. Mr. Market has a peculiar character; sometimes Mr. Market tries to sell you his portion of the interest or tries to buy your interest in the business. Mr. Market comes up with a quote every day. Sometimes, Mr. Market sees only a rosy outlook for the business, so he quotes you a very high price for his share of the business. Sometimes, he is depressed, so he tries to quote bargain prices for his shares. You can ignore the quote or try to take advantage of his bargain prices. If you fall under his influence, then you will lose your investment capital.

This understanding of the market is one of the secrets to Warren Buffett's success, but 98 percent of the people do the opposite. They react as per the market price of their stocks. The market is dominated by two conditions, fear and greed. Sometimes, there will be fear in the market; people feel that the world is coming to an end so securities are priced at bargain levels. Another feeling is when greed pumps up the price of stock beyond the true intrinsic value of the business it represents. In those situations, asset bubbles form and eventually burst. Because of this process, most of the investors lose money and get out of the market at the same time. We need to spend more time analyzing fear and greed with examples to help you control these feelings to your advantage.

Fear

When the market is in fear, there will be bargains everywhere and that is the best time to invest. Most of the great investors earn large amounts of money investing during times of fear. You should analyze the situation logically and then make a decision; you should not act emotionally. There are many examples for fear in the market. We can look at recent examples and think them through logically.

Take for example the 2008 financial crisis. Because of subprime lending and the real estate bubble bursting, Lehman Brothers filed for bankruptcy and other large banks were hit hard. The Federal Reserve intervened and injected capital into the largest banks. The market reaction is shown in the S&P 500 chart in Figure 28.1.

The S&P 500 declined from a September 2008 high of 1,303 to a March 2009 low of 666, a 48.8 percent decline because of the financial crisis. This decline was due to fear in the market. Whoever sold the stocks during the downturn did it because of fear, not logical reasoning. They thought the world was going to come to an end. When they turned on CNBC, market gurus predicted the end of the stock market and newspaper headlines predicted the stock

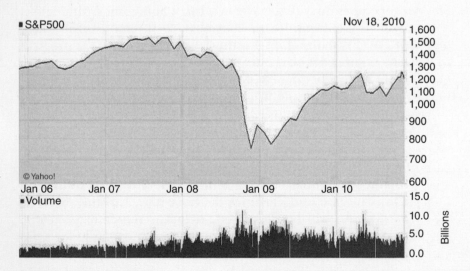

Figure 28.1   S&P 500 Index

market crash. When investors reacted to the news, they sold their shares for a big loss out of fear of losing their money. If they had thought logically, they would have held or even bought more at bargain prices.

Whoever sold shares might have bought securities before the financial crisis and bought the securities below the intrinsic value. After the financial crisis, discount to the intrinsic value should be higher because there was less downside risk. Investors could have added more shares to their portfolio thinking that the future return would be higher. This is the time when I added iGATE and Select Comfort stocks as explained previously. Those purchases generated an excellent return in 12 to 24 months.

I can explain the previously mentioned market action with a fictitious example: An investor might have bought Company X shares at $7.50 per share in January 2008. The investor calculated reasonable intrinsic value of the company to be around $10 per share and bought at $7.50 per share, which is a 25 percent discount to intrinsic value. After the financial crisis, a recession was expected and there would be a revenue decline in that company and, in turn, earnings would decrease.

In this situation, the investor needs to consider the following questions:

- If the recession continues for two or more years, how will the company survive? Does it have enough cash and cash equivalents on its balance sheet?
- How much debt does the company have? Does it have enough money to pay the debt interest or cash flow to support the debt interest payments?
- Is there any debt coming due in those two years? If yes, how is the company going to handle the situation?
- Is the company cutting costs fast enough to handle a lower revenue-generating environment to deal with the downturn?
- When revenue and earnings decrease, the intrinsic value of the business will be decreased. If that is the case, what will be the new, reduced intrinsic value? For our example, let's say the reduced intrinsic value comes to around $6 per share.

The previous buy price of $7.50 per share is higher than the $6 per share intrinsic value. Because of the financial crisis and fear in the market, Company X's stock price is reduced to $3 per share. You are getting a 50 percent discount to intrinsic value. If you were in a panic, you might have sold the shares at $3 per share, which is a 60 percent loss.

If you are certain about the $6 per share intrinsic value, you can buy the undervalued stock at $3 per share. Now your average price will be $4.50 per share; you are still at a loss, but if you hold the shares for couple of years, it could reach $7.50 to $10 per share, which is a 66.66 percent to 122.22 percent return in two years.

This is exactly what happened during the 2008 crisis. The market reached pre-crisis levels in November 2010, which was exactly two years and two months later. As per the previous example, if you made sell decisions because of fear, you might have lost 60 percent of your money. If you bought Company X shares at bargain prices, you might have gained 66 percent to 122 percent in a couple of years. This is the importance of thinking logically and controlling emotions.

Greed

Another aspect of the market is greed. When the market is in an upswing, investors are willing to pay higher prices for the stock and they do not think about the intrinsic value of businesses. Greed takes hold of the market. Everyone feels that if they do not buy, they are not part of the party.

There are multiple scenarios where greed will take over an investor's mind. These scenarios include:

Concept companies: The company is in the processes of developing a new product or service that is a revolutionary concept. It is going to change the world and generate a great deal of money in the process. A talented entrepreneur who formed the company gave an excellent revenue projection. The leading investment bank underwrites the initial public offering (IPO) and there will be hype about the company in the marketplace. The higher valuation is priced into the IPO price. As soon as the business comes to the market, on the first day of trading even, the IPO price doubles. This is what happened in the Internet boom years of 2000.

Internet companies' management were touting that they were going to change the way business had been done for years. There were a lot of dot-com companies coming to the IPO market with lofty valuations and no underlying revenue to support them. Those investments were the main cause of the bubble market. The secondary offering from the same companies was an even higher priced stock offering. Still, there was no revenue, only promises. Greed ruled the market. Investors were boosting the price for the stocks, thinking that those companies were going to generate tremendous amounts of money in the future. Bubbles started forming in the stock market. When investors realized that there was not going to be a revenue explosion from those companies, reality came into play. Everyone wanted to dump stock at the same time and market crashed.

There were thousands of Internet companies that went out of business. Those that had revenue survived. Some of the survivors were Amazon, Priceline, Yahoo!, eBay, and Netflix. Here, we can examine at least one example in detail.

Amazon (AMZN) (see Figure 28.2) came in at a split-adjusted price of $1.50 per share in May 1997. It reached $91 per share in January 2000. In two years and seven months, the total return was 6,000 percent, which is 60 times the initial investment. Did the company generate 60 times the initial revenue within three years of the IPO? No. Did the company support such a high valuation? No, but there was underlying revenue there.

Why did this happen? The answer is greed. The bubble burst in 2000 when reality set in. The AMZN stock price reduced to $5.50 in October 2001. Think about the investor who bought the stock around $90 per share because of greed; he might have lost 93 percent of his invested money in 21 months. You should not buy stock because of greed; there should be a logical reason to buy the security.

For example, consider Amazon when its stock was trading around a 52-week low value in 2001. At that time Amazon generated $3.1 billion of revenue, but lost $551 million. There was no reason to buy into that stock because the company was not generating positive net income. That would be a stock to put on the monitoring list. Amazon generated $5.2 billion of revenue and generated $35 million of net

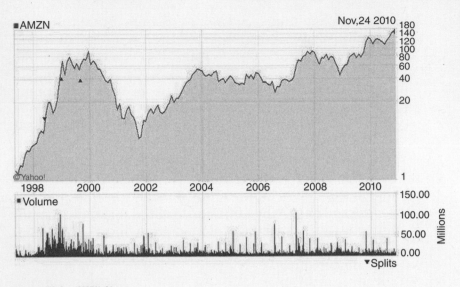

Figure 28.2　AMZN Chart

Reproduced with permission of Yahoo! Inc. ©2011 Yahoo! Inc. YAHOO! and the YAHOO! logo are registered trademarks of Yahoo! Inc. Reproduced with permission of CSI ©2009. Data Source: CSI www.csidata.com/

income in 2003. In 2003, the stock was trading between $18.55 and $61; we can say the average buy price was around $30. In November 2010, the stock was trading at around $177 per share, which is a 590 percent return in seven years and a 28.86 percent compound annual return.

As Warren Buffett says, "The dumbest reason in the stock market is buying the stock because it is going up."[1] You should not make a buy or sell decision because fear or greed is an emotional influence. The buy and sell decision should have logical reasoning behind it.

Emotionless Investing

The biggest enemy investors have is themselves. When they buy into a security and the price goes up within a couple of weeks or months, they feel great. They want to enjoy that feeling, so they sell that position and take the profit. They feel that no one goes broke by taking a profit. After they sell the position, the stock keeps going up. At that point in time, they kick themselves because they sold too early and lost the upside return.

When investors buy into a position and the stock price goes down, they feel depressed. They sell the position and take a loss. Maybe after a couple of months, the stock might have turned the corner and started to move up, crossing the buy price and continuing up. They kick themselves again for taking the loss. This is what happens when investors make decisions based in emotions.

A way to correct this cycle is to remove the emotions from investing. The decision to buy and sell should not depend on price alone. There should be a fundamental and logical reason for buy and sell decisions. If you follow this emotionless path, you can be very successful in investing.

Warren Buffett's success came from removing emotions from his investing decisions. This carries over to his personal life, in which he is also very good at removing emotions from his actions.

In his *The Making of an American Capitalist*[2] Buffett describes a time when his daughter took his car and got into an accident. She was standing there in front of her father, crying. Buffett asked if anyone was hurt and she said "no." She stood and waited, but Buffett did not say anything, and actually continued his reading. After waiting there for some time, she left the room. A couple of hours later, he told his daughter there are many crooks in the road and not to worry about it. Compare this situation with others who might have overreacted, maybe scolded their daughter, checked out the car, and made a big scene. Buffett did not do all of this. He was concerned if anyone had gotten hurt, and that was the extent of it. His concern was addressed and he did not do anything rash. This characteristic is one of the important attributes that have made him a greatest investor.

Compare that personal situation to investing. Bad news will continue to surface in the world. The stock market will continue to react to bad news. If you try to react to all the bad news, I promise you will lose money in investing. Removing emotion from investing is very important.

On the other hand, there will always be good news about a particular stock or industry. You should not buy as soon as good news appears. If you do that, you will pay a higher price for that stock. You can wait for a couple of days and buy the stock after some pull back.

The process of buying and selling depends on the fundamental change in a company, not on the market price. You should give sufficient time for a stock to appreciate, at least a couple of years. Do not make a buy-or-sell decision during the short term.

For example, when Warren Buffett started buying *Washington Post* stock, the market cap of the company was around $80 million. The analysts were valuing the company at $400 million, but the stock kept on dropping. During the short term, Buffett lost 23 percent from the initial purchase. He kept buying the stock, investing around $10 million in the 1960s. In 2008, that investment was worth more than $357 million, more than 35 times the initial investment, and with no capital gain taxes paid to the IRS. As mentioned before, that is one major advantage of long-term investing.

During Buffett's lifetime, his Berkshire Hathaway stock price was cut in half three times. What did he do at those times? Did he sell? No. He knew Berkshire Hathaway's holding companies were going to generate higher income in the future.

The Berkshire Hathaway stock chart during the 2008 financial crisis is shown in Figure 28.3.

In September 2008, Berkshire Hathaway's A stock (BRK-A) traded for around $147,000. During the 2008 panic sell off it reached

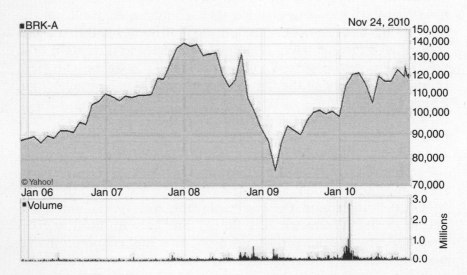

Figure 28.3   BRK Chart

Reproduced with permission of Yahoo! Inc. ©2011 Yahoo! Inc. YAHOO! and the YAHOO! logo are registered trademarks of Yahoo! Inc. Reproduced with permission of CSI ©2009. Data Source: CSI www.csidata.com/

$70,050 in March 2009, which is a 52.34 percent loss. Did he sell his shares during the panic? No. During the recession, the earnings of Berkshire's operating companies were reduced. He believed that in the coming years, once the economy started to recover, his operating companies would earn more. The stock recovered from a low of $70,050 to $120,500 in November of 2010. Berkshire operating companies were in the recovery stage and set to earn more income into the future. He did not sell the holdings at the wrong time.

Investing takes willpower to withstand stock price reductions of as much as 50 percent from the initial purchase price. At any point in time, it can happen because of market variation that has nothing to do with the company's fundamentals. You can check the 52-week low and 52-week high price of any security and there will be at least a 50 percent variation. Did the company's revenue or earnings go down or increase 50 percent within one year? Absolutely not. The market variation created that kind of price difference. When the market gives you an opportunity to invest at bargain prices, you should take that opportunity.

Media

All of us are overloaded with a ton of information all the time by different media. Every day in newspapers, television shows, magazines, ezines, financial web sites, and radio programs, experts try to predict what the market will do months or even years into the future. No one can predict the future accurately, but a tremendous amount of time is wasted trying to predict the market. Beware, and never act on expert advice alone. As Warren Buffett puts it, "Forecasts usually tell us more of the forecaster than of the future."[3]

The person who appears on a TV show as an expert is sharing his or her opinion about the market and what he or she would like the market to do. If a hedge fund manager or large mutual fund manager appears on TV and is 100 percent long, he or she wants the market to go up; that manager will be bullish on the market. If another market commentator is 70 percent short on his portfolio, he will predict the market will go down a lot and pinpoint all the negatives. This commentator has compelling reasons as to why the market is going to go down. You should not act on commentator advice. In reality, none of the predictions are going to happen because unexpected events happen anytime and all the time. Take for example the 9/11 terrorist attacks; they changed the whole market environment in a couple of days. Do not act on the advice given by market commentators who appear in the media.

Perfect Environment

Some investors look for the perfect world in which to invest. Some investors always look at the negatives that are happening at any given time. They want to wait until those negatives get resolved and then they will invest. Before those negatives get resolved or after they are resolved, new negatives will occur. Again, they want to wait. Negatives will always be there and new ones can emerge at any time. If investors are worried about each and every negative event, they will never invest.

In 2010, the U.S. economy started to recover, but then came the European debt crisis. Greece came into the spotlight and got a bailout, and then fear of a double-dip recession started. Those fears abated as soon as the Federal Reserve announced a second round of quantitative easing (QE2), and then the Ireland bailout happened. During November 2010, there was fear about Portugal and Spain. Will you stay out of the market because of those fears? No. You need to concentrate on the position you hold. If any of the companies that you hold have exposure to those nations, then you need to research what percentage of company revenue and earnings are coming from those nations. Depending on those revenue expectations, calculate what kind of hit the company may face in the coming quarters or couple of years. Recalculate the reduced intrinsic value of the company. If company shares are trading at least at a 25 percent discount to intrinsic value, then you can add more shares. Suppose the market price of the stock is more than the calculated intrinsic value and the stock price comes down a lot because of the negative news. Wait a couple of more days until the bad news subsides and the stock price will increase; the market has a short memory. You can sell the position and take the profit. Here you used your logical reason to sell the position, not because of fear. You did not make the decision emotionally. Instead you researched logical reasoning behind your selling decision.

You should not be out of the market every time bad news is reported.

Market Timing

Most investors and traders think that they can time the market in order to generate maximum possible returns. Because of that hope, they try to buy and sell numerous times and spend excessive time trying to predict the market. Based on their stock price movement prediction, they try to buy and sell. This is not a good practice. Supply and demand patterns determine the price of a particular stock. There is different news released every day that may affect the market movements and affect the price of the stock. Fear and greed always rule the market during the short term.

Investors and traders always think that they can sell at a profit and try to buy at a lower price and make a profit again. For example, an investor buys Company X stock at $10 per share and it reaches $13 per share in a couple of weeks. They think that the 30 percent return in a couple of weeks is great. They feel good about their purchase. When the stock comes down to $12.75 per share the next day, they fear that they are losing the accumulated profit and because of that fear they start selling at $12.75 per share. A 27.5 percent profit is all well and good, but after a month, the same stock is trading at $15 per share. Now they feel that they sold the stock too soon so they kick themselves and buy again. A 50 percent increase in a couple of months is substantial. Other investors holding the stock try to take the profit and start selling large amounts of stock. Because of the mass sale, stock prices are reduced to less than $12 per share. Now they think that they made a mistake buying again at $15 per share and then take the loss.

Think about the outcomes of this situation. We can assume a $1,000 initial investment into this transaction.

The buy price for 100 shares at $10 per share plus a $10 commission is $1,010.

The sell price of $12.75 per share is $1275 minus a $10 commission is $1,265.

Therefore, gross profit is $255.

Since this is a short-term profit, it will be taxed at a personal level, say at a 30 percent tax rate.

Taxes on capital gains that need to be paid while filing taxes next year is $76.50.

The net profit after capital gains tax is paid is $178.50.

Now the investor has $1,265 for the next transaction.

Since $10 will go for commission on that transaction, the remainder is $1,255.

$1,255 ÷ $15 = $83.66, so this investor can buy 83 shares of Company X stock at $15 per share.

He sold those shares at $12, so the proceeds will be 83 × $12 = $996 − $10 commission = $986.

With a loss in the second trade = $1,255 − $986 = −$269, the investor can claim this loss against the previous gain and the net result is loss for the whole transaction.

Total loss of this company trade is 1000 − $986 = −$14.

If the investor kept quiet and did not do anything, the $12 per share market price might have given $200 of unrealized gain.

This is due to the excessive trading and trying to time the market. Here is the emotional journey:

1. When the stock increased to $13 per share, the investor felt good. Happy mood.
2. Stock decreased to $12.75 per share, the investor kicked himself for not selling at $13, feeling he missed $0.25 per share. Depressed mood.
3. To protect the profit, he sold the shares at $12.75 per share, happy that at least he took the profit, and did not miss it all. Happy mood, but not *that* happy.
4. When the stock reached $15 per share in a month, investor is depressed again and kicking himself for selling too soon. Depressed mood.
5. Bought at $15 per share so as to not miss the further upside. Happy mood.
6. Stock price reduced to $12 per share, the shares are sold, and the investor took the loss. Depressed mood.

Think about the mental pressure the investor might have gone through within a couple of months for this particular stock. During those months there were six different emotional states.

Multiply these mental feelings for 20 positions in a particular portfolio and you will go insane: 20 × 6 = 120 different mental states in a couple of months. These feelings affect the investor's sleep patterns, health, and personal life. Even after going through all this emotional pressure, the investor still experiences a loss.

Compare these feelings with the person sitting calmly, not trading excessively. He or she is calm and as for our example still made an unrealized gain of $200 and did not have to pay any taxes or commissions to the broker.

Charlie Munger always says that Warren Buffett is one of the happiest people he knows. He does not worry about much. Buffett said one time, "I never attempt to make money on the stock market. I buy on the assumption that they could close the market the next day and not reopen it for five years."[4] Warren Buffett also said that, "When I go to the office every morning, I feel like I am going to the Sistine Chapel to paint."[5]

How did he attain that happiness? His holdings experience constant ups and downs. Is he depressed when his portfolio goes down and happy when his portfolio goes up? No. Buffett does not worry about the daily market prices; he thinks long term and determines the progress of his holdings as per the business progress, not the market quotation. He knows that in the long term his holdings are going to do fine, and that thinking gives him peace of mind.

Charlie Munger once told an interviewer that he could not recall Buffett ever getting angry: "Even when I took him fishing in Minnesota and upset the boat and we had to swim to shore, he didn't scream at me."[6]

That kind of mental calmness will help you to generate great returns over the long term.

This chapter isn't meant to suggest that you should totally ignore market movements and macroeconomics; you should have a general perception about market values. For example, during the bubble times you cannot find enough bargains in which to invest. At those times, you can have less money invested in the market or be totally out of the market. When the market appears as it did in late 2008, bargains will be everywhere; you can invest most of your available money. Warren Buffett did the same thing in 1973 when stocks were overvalued: "I felt like an oversexed guy on a desert island. I didn't find anything to buy."[7] In 1974, he found bargain opportunities everywhere: "I feel like an oversexed guy in a harem. This is the time to start investing."[8]

The simple solution, when you feel the market is in a bubble state like early 2000, is to be completely out of the market. When a 20 percent growth company is trading at around 35 to 40 times its earnings, it shows that the market is in a bubble state and it can burst at any time. That kind of optimism and inflated stock price will eventually come back to reality; the market will readjust. During bubble times, you can be out of the market fully or have a portion of your money invested in even greener stocks such as Procter & Gamble (PG), Kellogg's (W), and General Electric (GE). After a bubble bursts, investors and traders become afraid of losing their money and try to sell all their holdings at the same time, which will create bargains everywhere. At that time, you can invest all of your money at bargain prices.

Investing is simple when related to market psychology. Invest all of your money when there are available bargains everywhere and reduce your portfolio, or be completely out of the market when a bubble forms. Other times, spend the time and energy to find bargain opportunities and do not make frequent trades.

CHAPTER

29

Risk Management

Before investing in stocks, you need to reduce the risk as much as possible. There are two types of risks, which are:

1. Systematic risk
2. Unsystematic risk

Systematic Risk

Systematic risk means risk that affects the entire stock market. The recession, interest rates, wars, the 2008 financial crisis, and terrorist attacks are examples of events that affect all stocks. To mitigate this risk, your position needs to be hedged. You can buy *puts* to mitigate downside risks. This is like buying insurance with a finite duration; after the expiration date, you need to buy again. Buying puts is an expensive process because you cannot predict when systematic risk events will happen.

Unsystematic Risk

This is company-specific or industry-specific risk. You can avoid unsystematic risk by diversifying your portfolio. There is no way you can reduce systematic risk because it is related to outside events. However, you can minimize common investor mistakes and thereby minimize your portfolio risk. The following tips can minimize port-folio risks and increase investment return:

1. Don't use margin accounts.
2. Maintain sufficient diversification.
3. Stay away from the herd mentality.
4. Avoid day trading.
5. Use a research-based investment approach.

No Margin

Margin means borrowing money from a broker to buy shares. For example, if you have $100,000 in your account, you can borrow up to another $100,000 from a broker and then buy shares worth up to $200,000. Different stocks have different margin requirements and vary with each brokerage house. Normally you can borrow up to the amount of cash available in your account. Brokers charge you inter-est for the money you use on margin.

Margin is great in a bull market because you are making higher returns on your cash investment. As in the previous example, let's say that $100,000 is your cash investment and you generate a 25 percent return in that year. Your account has $125,000 at the end of the year. If you used 100 percent margin, your 25 percent return for $200,000 would be $50,000. Your account has $150,000 at the year's end. That means you generated a 50 percent return that year. Wow, that is great. You doubled your return because you used a margin account. This kind of appeal makes normal people use the margin in their account. This is just the positive side of margin usage. But there is a negative side: if the price falls, you are in trouble.

When the stock price falls below the margin requirement, you have to put up more money to comply with the margin requirement or the broker will sell your holdings to raise cash. For example, you bought a certain company's shares at $20 per share and you are 100 percent leveraged with a 50 percent margin requirement. When the stock price falls to $10 per share, your equity is already gone. If the price falls below $10 per share, you are losing the broker's margin money. You are thinking that selling at this price is an idiotic idea and you would like to keep the stock because the worth of the company is far more than the market price of the stock. Suppose the stock falls to $8 per share; you have to put up $2 per share to comply with the margin requirement. If the stock falls to $2 per share, you need to put up whatever the difference is to comply with margin. If you do not have the money or are not willing to fund the account, the broker automatically sells your holdings, even if you do not want to sell.

Even if you did all the research explained by this book, you can still be sideswiped by the unpredictable. You calculated a conservative intrinsic value of the company at $30 per share, bought the shares at $20 per share—which is a 33 percent discount to intrinsic value—thought you found a great company, and bought at a large discount to intrinsic value. You can make a killing, you, think, if you use the margin. You used 100 percent margin to buy as many shares as possible and the company is doing great. But then the market crashes (like what happened in September 2008). Your stock loses 60 percent and is trading at $8 per share because of the market sell-off. There is no fundamental change in the business. You are thinking this is a steal, a lifetime bargain opportunity, because if you calculate $8 per share trading price with $30 per share intrinsic value, that is a 73 percent discount to intrinsic value. But you already violated the margin requirement. If you do not have money to fund the account, the broker will automatically sell your shares. Even if the market gave you a chance you consider to be an once-in-a-lifetime opportunity, you may not be able to take advantage of it because you used margin. Instead of buying, you are forced to sell at bargain prices. If you do not use margin, you can stay in the market until your stock reaches the business's intrinsic value.

If you are a fund manager, then using margin is very difficult. Whenever the market crashes, the following situations can happen:

- When the stock price falls, margin accounts start to violate margin requirements; brokers start selling the shares to satisfy the margin requirement.
- When there is more fear in the market, investors put a redemption request in to their mutual funds and hedge funds to withdraw their money. Fund managers have no choice because they need to sell the holdings at bargain prices to meet the redemption.
- Because they are selling and pulling cash out to pay the investors (and the market is still crashing), the account equity is coming down, again violating the margin requirement and brokers will sell.

The same process continues until all of the funds and the investing public de-leverage their portfolios. This is what happened during the 2008 financial crisis; the market continued to fall until March 2009. Even though margin has its upside, the lesson here is to never use margin accounts.

Enough Diversification

Diversify your portfolio. Never invest everything in stocks in one industry because if there is a downturn in that particular industry, it will affect your portfolio substantially. Keep at least a minimum of five stocks in your portfolio from different industries that are not related to one another. As mentioned earlier, you can diversify the country risk too. Nowadays, emerging markets are growing faster than the United States and Europe. You can invest a certain percentage of the portfolio there too.

No Herd Mentality

As an investor, never act with a herd mentality. You have to think for yourself. Whenever the market crashes because of systematic events, you have to analyze that particular market event, and decide how much it is going to affect the earnings of the particular company you are holding or planning to buy. Recalculate the intrinsic value of the company and act accordingly. Just because everyone is selling, it does not mean you have to sell. Investing is a rationality game.

Avoid Day Trading

Never be involved in day-trading activities. There is no way you can predict what the price of the stock will do on any given day. If you are trying to predict stock and market movements, you are definitely going to lose. The reasons for this include:

- Any news event in a particular day changes the direction of the market immediately. You cannot control the news flow.
- When you are involved in day trading, you are competing against computer software that is placing trades using an algorithm that is much faster than you can enter the trade.

- Even if you are successful in day trading, the trading cost, taxes, and occasional losses will eat up all of your profits.

Use a Research-Based Investment Approach

Never buy any stock without doing in-depth research about the company using the stock-research checklist and calculating the intrinsic value. Buy only when there is a sufficient discount to the intrinsic value. Never act on your hunches, charts, guru's suggestions, or media tips.

30

Options

Options are not part ownership of a company. Buying options means you are betting on which direction the price of a stock will move in the short term or long term. We are not going too deep into the option techniques. But the following option basics are enough to enhance return.

Here are the basics of options.

Calls

The buyer of the call gets the right, not the obligation, to buy the stock before a specified time by paying a small fee. The small fee is called a premium. The specified time period means there is an expiration date, which is traditionally the third Friday of the month. Calls are used to bet that the stock price will increase above the strike price, which is the specified price.

Puts

Puts give the buyer the right, not the obligation, to sell an underlying asset before a specified time period at a set price by paying a small fee. The buyer of the put expects the underlying stock price to go lower than the strike price before the expiration date. This depends upon the relationship between the stock price and the excise price. Three kinds of options are:

1. In the money
2. At the money
3. Out of the money

In the Money

For a call option, the strike price is below the market price of the underlying stock. For this kind of *in-the-money* option, the premium will be higher than the other two options. For a put option, the strike price is above the market price of the stock. Even if the stock price goes down, you can sell the stock at a higher strike price if you choose to exercise the put. This kind of put option costs you more money than the other two option types.

At the Money

Here the strike price of the option equals the market price of the stock. This is applicable to call or put options.

Out of the Money

For call options, the strike price is above the current stock market price. For a put option, the strike price is below the current price of the stock. These kinds of options cost you a smaller premium compared with the other two option types.

This concept is explained in the following example of Terex (TEX) stock option that expired in February 2011. Stocks were trading at $28.84 per share on January 7, 2011, and the option expired at close on Friday, February 18, 2011.

Strike	Symbol	Last	Chg	Bid	Ask	Vol	Open Int
24.00	TEX110219C00024000	6.18	0.00	5.20	5.30	1	1

In this example, $24 is the strike price. Stock was trading at $28.84 per share in the money option.

Last: $6.18 Premium per share

Bid: Premium bid price is $5.20

Ask: Premium sell price is $5.30

Open interest: 1 means 100 options

If you buy at the sell price, you have to pay the premium of $530.

The expiration date is February 18, 2011.

If the stock price goes to, for example, $35 per share before February 18, 2011, you can exercise the option or sell the call option, depending on your wish.

If you excise option, it means you buy at $24 × 100 = $2,400

Premium already paid: $530

Total price: $2,930 + option commission of $10 = $2,940.

You can sell the 100 shares of TEX at the market $35 per share × 100 shares = $3,500 − $10 commission = $3,490

Your profit is $550.

Initially you paid the price of $530 for controlling 100 shares upside potential from $24 per share until the option expiration date. The rate of return is a 103.7 percent return. Since you took the exercise option, you bought the shares at $24 per share, and immediately sold at $35 per share. Because of that, I did not include that money as investment money.

If you do not want to excise the option, you can sell the call option before February 18, 2011, for an increased profit. Depending on your selling price you can calculate the profit.

If the stock price falls down below $24 per share before February 18, 2011, your call option expires and becomes worthless. The maximum loss for you is your initial investment of $530 plus the commission of $10.

LEAPS

LEAPS are *long-term equity anticipation securities.* These options have expiration dates but have more time before the expiration date. The premium will be high compared to the short-term expiration dates. You analyzed the company and it passed the stock-research checklist. You calculated the intrinsic value of the company and it is higher than the current price. You feel that the stock price will reach the intrinsic value maybe within two years. You do not have enough capital to buy enough shares at the time, so you buy LEAPS to control the upside potential of the stock before that expiration date. This will increase your portfolio returns.

You can use is strategy to increase the return for your portfolio: Use up to 10 percent of the portfolio in LEAPS and buy up to five different securities in the money options. This strategy allowed me to generate higher returns for my portfolio. Warren Buffett used options strategies to enhance his return for his personal portfolio for many years.

CHAPTER

31

Cigar-Butt

Warren Buffett started as a "cigar-butt" investor, learning from Benjamin Graham, and progressed to buying quality companies on sale as influenced by Phil Fisher and Charlie Munger. His later approach gave him the better investment success than the cigar-butt approach did.

Warren Buffett says that, "You find these well-smoked, down-to-the-nub cigars, but they're free. You pick them up and get one free puff out of them."[1] He learned the hard way that his cigar-butt approach was a fault in an early investment decision in Berkshire Hathaway.

In 1967, Buffett bought National Indemnity Co. for Berkshire Hathaway from Jack Ringwalt.[2] Berkshire Hathaway had $20 million net worth in the textile operation and was losing money every year. Buffett continued to invest money in the textile business for 20 years, hoping to turn it around, but finally shut down the textile business. If he had bought an insurance business and liquidated the textile business immediately, those actions might have added another $200 billion net worth for Berkshire Hathaway's shareholders over the years. Buffett once said, "Our conclusion is that, with few exceptions, when management with a reputation for brilliance tackles a business with a reputation for poor fundamental economics, it is the reputation of the business that remains intact."[3]

He started buying quality companies like National Indemnity and See's Candies, and they were quite profitable for him. Those businesses generated high income over many years. Nowadays, See's Candies net income per year is more than he initially paid for the whole company.

As an investor, you need to look for a quality company that is surrounded by temporary problems that offer you a bargain opportunity to buy in.

CHAPTER

32

No Shortcut Approach

There is no shortcut approach for finding investment success. If you want to replicate at least 25 percent of Warren Buffett's stock market success, you need to work hard and spend time identifying great companies at bargain prices. After making a purchase, think like a business owner to deal with market volatility and act accordingly.

When he started his partnership, Buffett read *Moody's* manual page by page, twice. If you want to find bargain opportunities, you have to work hard; no one is just going to tell you about them. There are always bargain opportunities available to you. If you research 10 companies, you can find one. If you want to have 10 stocks in your portfolio, you need to research around 100 companies every year. In five years, you will know about 500 companies. When you know about 500 companies, you are a stock market guru; you do not need to listen to any market pundits on CNBC.

Here are the tasks you need to complete to improve your investment success.

1. Identify the stocks
2. Research the stocks
3. Calculate intrinsic value
4. Manage the portfolio
5. Monitor the company's portfolio
6. Make sell decisions

Identify the Stocks

Chapter 25, Where to Search for Stock Prospects, gives you the details about where you can look to identify the stock characteristics such as Value Line, magicformulainvesting.com, the *Wall Street Journal*, and noted points like insider purchases, daily stock pops and drops, and magazine reading lists.

Research Stocks

Any stock needs to be researched through the stock-research checklist as explained. You need to read at least recent annual reports, but get the numbers from the last 10 years of data. Listen to at least two years of quarterly and annual conference calls. Read competitors' annual reports and listen to their conference calls so that you can do a comparative analysis. You need to find all of the data for each one of the stock-research checkpoints and hold each company to each checklist item to see if they receive a *pass* or a *fail*. You are not going to find a stock that passes all the checklist items.

For example, high insider ownership is nice to have. A stock may pass most of the checklist items and not pass the high insider ownership checkpoint, but you should not reject that company. On the other hand, if the company has a huge debt and they do not generate enough cash to service the debt, then you have to reject that company. You have to make a decision yourself after you analyze a company against the checklist items.

Calculate Intrinsic Value

Calculate the intrinsic value of the stock as explained in Chapter 23, Intrinsic Value. This is a dynamic concept; when the company is performing better than your calculation, you can adjust the intrinsic value calculation upward. When the company fundamentals are deteriorating, you have to adjust the intrinsic value downward to reflect the true operating numbers. You can update your monitor list accordingly.

Manage the Portfolio

You can manage your portfolio as explained in Chapter 26, Portfolio Management.

Monitor the Company's Portfolio

Every quarter you need to listen to conference calls and read the quarterly reports. Find out how the company is doing against your assumption. If one-quarter's revenue and earnings are down, you do not need to adjust your intrinsic value calculation; doing so annually is a reasonable timeframe.

After the company releases its annual report, update your research checklist items and recalculate the intrinsic value calculation. If the company presents at any investor conferences, those presentations should be available on the investor section of its web site. Read those presentations. Read the Securities and Exchange Commission (SEC) filing every quarter. You can meet with the management and talk to them and learn as much as possible about the company.

Make Sell Decisions

Sell as explained in Chapter 27, Selling Strategy.

CHAPTER

33

Perfect Pitch

To make money in stock investing, you need to wait for the perfect pitch to buy into securities. After you buy into a stock, you can trust the management to do their job and monitor the progress of the business' performance. Stock price will take care of itself.

Even if you like the company very much, if the company does not trade for at least a 25 percent discount to intrinsic value, do not buy that stock. After extensive research you can create a spreadsheet with the list of stocks that are passing the majority of the checklist items. You can calculate the intrinsic value of the companies and add that information to the spreadsheet. You can add another column in the spreadsheet for buy price. You can increase the discount-to-intrinsic value depending on the earning patterns of the particular company. You can also create a portfolio on http:// finance.yahoo.com and monitor the stocks, but always wait for the perfect pitch.

Whenever the monitored stock price goes below your purchase level, you can buy into those stocks. At other times, you can ignore the market prices. You should not violate this rule at all. If you violate it, you will end up paying more for the stock and encounter a loss in that investment. When you find bargain opportunities you can invest a higher percentage of the portfolio. You need to adjust your investment size as explained in Chapter 26, Portfolio Management.

Warren Buffett follows the same kind of process. He follows the company for a very long time and whenever a company's stock price goes to a bargain level, he invests a large portion of the portfolio.

Warren Buffett has an analogy involving Ted Williams. Williams swung only when the ball reached his comfortable point. He did not swing the bat any other time. In baseball there are three strikes, but in investing you do not have to take a single strike. You can patiently wait for the perfect pitch. If the market price is not in your buy range, simply ignore the quote. The next day, the market comes back with a new quote. If you like the price of it, swing; otherwise ignore it. If the market makes you act, then you will end up losing money. You need to be a decision maker; do not let the market price influence you to act. The simple rule to follow is to buy the stocks that are trading at or below your buy price. You should not violate this rule at any time.

If you are not buying and selling all the time, it does not mean that you are not making progress. Just wait for the perfect pitch and when it comes, swing big. At other times, just monitor the progress of the company. When the stock reaches a price substantially above the intrinsic value of the business, sell the holding and buy other undervalued securities.

Notes

PART I: Warren Buffett Principles

Chapter 1: Replicating Warren Buffett's Investment Success

1. Warren Buffett interview with Charles Brandes, May 1993.
2. Buffett Partnership Ltd. letter, May 29, 1969.

Chapter 2: Business-Like Investing

1. "Buffett Listed by Fortune with Wall Street Winners," *Omaha World-Herald*, July 31, 1983. Quoting from *Fortune* magazine, August 8, 1983.
2. Horsehead holdings corp., News, www.horsehead.net.
3. Janet Lowe. *Warren Buffett Speaks—Wit and Wisdom from the World's Greatest Investor*. New York: John Wiley & Sons, 1997, p. 150.
4. Janet Lowe. *Warren Buffett Speaks—Wit and Wisdom from the World's Greatest Investor*. New York: John Wiley & Sons, 1997, pp. 94–95.
5. Ibid, Page 150.
6. Sam Thorson "Warren Buffett, Omaha in search of social challenges," Lincoln, Nebraska. *Journal and Star*, March 18,1973, p. 6F.
7. Robert Dorr. "Newspaper Holdings Kind to Omaha Investor Buffett." *Omaha World-Herald*, April 16, 1978, p. 6J.

Chapter 3: Long-Term Investing

1. Roger Lowenstein. *Buffett: The Making of an American Capitalist*. New York: Random House, 1995, p. 152.
2. "Warren Buffett Talks Business", The University of North Carolina, Center for Public Television, Chapel Hill, 1995.
3. Berkshire Hathaway annual meeting, Omaha, 1996.
4. "Warren Buffett Talks Business", The University of North Carolina, Center for Public Television, Chapel Hill, 1995.

5. Andrew Kilpatrick, *Of Permanent Value: The story of Warren Buffett*, (Birmingham: AKPE, 1994) p. 568, Quoting from *Forbes*, August 6, 1990.

Chapter 4: Permanent Loss of Capital

1. "The Forbes Four Hundred Billionaires," *Forbes* 400, October 27, 1986.

PART II: Stock Research Checklist

Chapter 5: Stock Research Checklist—Business Characteristics

1. "The Forbes Four Hundred Billionaires," *Forbes* 400, October 27, 1986.
2. Berkshire Hathaway Annual report, 2009.

Chapter 6: Stock Research Checklist—Earnings

1. Coca-Cola (KO) annual and quarterly reports, SEC filings, news releases, and content from www.coca-cola.com.
2. Janet Lowe. *Warren Buffett Speaks—Wit and Wisdom from the World's Greatest Investor*. Hoboken: John Wiley & Sons, 1997, pp. 94–95.
3. Goodyear Tires (GT) annual and quarterly reports, SEC filings, news releases, and content from www.goodyear.com.
4. Berkshire Hathaway Annual report, 2009.
5. Sharp Compliance Corp (SMED) annual and quarterly reports, SEC filings, presentation, news releases, and contents from www.sharpsinc.com.
6. Pinnacle Airlines (PNCL), annual and quarterly reports, SEC filings, presentations, and press release from, www.pncl.com.

Chapter 10: Stock Research Checklist—Capital Investment

1. Roger Lowenstein. *Buffett: The Making of an American Capitalist*. New York: Random House, 1995, p. 200.

Chapter 11: Stock Research Checklist—Management

1. "Warren Buffett talks business", The University of North Carolina, Center for Public Television, Chapel Hill, 1995.
2. Robert Dorr. "Investor Warren Buffett Views Making money as 'Big Game.'" *Omaha World-Herald*, March 24, 1985, p. 11.

Chapter 13: Stock Research Checklist—Assets

1. Courier-Express v. Evening News, testimony of Warren Buffett, pp. 50–52.

Chapter 16: Stock Research Checklist—Insiders

1. iGATE, annual and quarterly, SEC filings, and news items and contents from www.igatecorp.com.
2. finance.yahoo.com, iGATE insider information.

Chapter 18: Stock Research Checklist—Inflation

1. Warren E. Buffett. "How Inflation Swindles the Investor", *Fortune*, May 5, 1977, p. 250.

Chapter 20: Stock Research Checklist—Turnaround

1. Select Comfort Annual report, 2008.
2. Select Comfort annual and Quarterly reports, SEC filings, news release, and content from www.selectcomfort.com.

Chapter 21: Stock Research Checklist—Stock Price

1. Warren E. Buffett. "The security I like best", *The commercial and financial Chronicle*, December 6, 1951.

Chapter 22: Stock Research Checklist—Infosys

1. Infosys annual and quarterly reports, SEC filings, news releases, and content from www.infosys.com.

Chapter 23: Intrinsic Value

1. Infosys annual and quarterly reports, SEC filings, news releases, and content from www.infosys.com.

PART III: Investment Management

Chapter 24: Margin of Safety

1. Berkshire Hathaway Annual Meeting, Omaha, May 1, 1995.

Chapter 25: Where to Search for Stock Prospects

1. Jim Rasmussen. "Billionaire talks Strategy with Students." *Omaha World-Herald*, January 2, 1994, p. 17S.
2. Valueline Investment Survey, www.valueline.com.
3. Joel Greenblatt. *The Little Book that Beats the* Market. Hoboken: John Wiley & Sons, 2010.

4. Magic Formula Investing, www.magicformulainvesting.com.
5. *Wall Street Journal.*

Chapter 26: Portfolio Management

1. Berkshire Hathaway Annual Letter, 2009.
2. Berkshire Hathaway annual meeting, Omaha, May 1, 1995.
3. "Warren Edward Buffett" *Forbes* 400, October 21, 1991, p. 151.
4. Berkshire Hathaway annual report, 2009.

Chapter 28: Mr.Market and Investor Psychology

1. Warren Buffett, 1984 Graham and Dodd seminar.
2. Roger Lowenstien. *Buffett: The Making of an American Capitalist.* New York: Random House: 1995.
3. Warren E. Buffett, "How Inflation Swindles the Equity Investor," *Fortune,* May 5, 1977, p. 250.
4. "Buffett listed By Fortune with Wall street Winners," *Omaha World-Herald,* July 31,1983. Quoting from *Fortune* magazine, August 8, 1983.
5. "Eye," *Women's Wear Daily,* October 10, 1985, p. 10.
6. Robert Dorr. "Buffett's Right-hand man," *Omaha World-Herald,* August 10, 1986, p. 1.
7. Robert Lenzner. "Warren Buffett's Idea of Heaven: I don't have to work with people I don't like," *Forbes* 400, October 18, 1993, p. 40.
8. L.J. Davis. "Buffett Takes Stock," *The New York Times Magazines,* April 1, 1990, p. 16.

Chapter 31: Cigar-Butt

1. Warren Buffett and Walter Schloss, discussion, New York Society of Security Analysts, December 6, 1994.
2. Roger Lowenstein. *Buffett: The Making of an American Capitalist.* New York: Random House: 1995. p. 133.
3. Robert Lenzner, "Warren Buffett's Idea of Heaven: I don't have to work with people I don't like," *Forbes* 400, October 18, 1993, p. 40.

Bibliography

1. Roger Lowenstein. *Buffett: The Making of an American Capitalist.* New York: Random House: 1995.
2. Janet Lowe. *Warren Buffett Speaks—Wit and Wisdom from the World's Greatest Investor.* New York: John Wiley & Sons, 1997.
3. Robert G. Hagstrom. *The Essential Buffett, Timeless Principles for the New Economy.* New York: John Wiley & Sons, 2001.

4. Peter Lynch & John Rothchild. *One up on Wall Street: How to Use what you Already Know to Make Money in the Market.* New York: Simon & Schuster, 1989.
5. Peter Lynch & John Rothchild. *Beating the Street.* New York: Simon & Schuster, 1994.
6. Robert G. Hagstrom. *The Warren Buffett Way.* Hoboken, NJ: John Wiley & Sons, 2005.
7. Robert G. Hagstrom. *The Warren Buffett Portfolio: Mastering the Power of Focus Investment Strategy.* New York, 1999 John Wiley & Sonc Inc.
8. Mary Buffett and David Clark. *Warren Buffett and Interpretation of Financial Statements: The Search for the Company with a Durable Competitive Advantage.* New York: Simon & Schuster, 2008.
9. Mary Buffett and David Clark. *The New Buffettology: ThePproven Techniques for Investing Successfully in Changing Markets that have made the Warren Buffett the World's Most Famous Investor.* New York: Simon & Schuster, 2002.

About the Author

Jeeva Ramaswamy is a managing partner of GJ Investment Funds, an investment fund modeled after the original 1950's Buffett partnership. Since its inception in November 2008, GJ Investment Funds delivered compounded annual return of more than 72 percent (net to investors). He has been favorably profiled in *International Alternative Investment Review* and *Hedge Fund Exchange.* Prior to GJ Investment Fund, he was CEO for Miracle Software Inc., an information technology and solutions company. He holds a bachelor's degree in Electrical Engineering from the Coimbatore Institute of Technology and is a member of the Indus Entrepreneurs (TiE) Association. He strongly believes in a balanced life between work, family, and personal time. He enjoys spending time with his wife and child. He loves reading and analyzing business investment opportunities.

Index